THE SECULARIZATION OF THE EUROPEAN MIND IN THE NINETEENTH CENTURY

Canto is a new imprint offering a range of titles, classic and more recent, across a broad spectrum of subject areas and interests. History, literature, biography, archaeology, politics, religion, psychology, philosophy and science are all represented in Canto's specially selected list of titles, which now offers some of the best and most accessible of Cambridge publishing to a wider readership.

THE SECULARIZATION
OF THE
EUROPEAN MIND
IN THE
NINETEENTH CENTURY

OWEN CHADWICK

Published by the Press Syndicate of the University of Cambridge
The Pitt Building, Trumpington Street, Cambridge CB2 1RP
40 West 20th Street, New York, NY 10011–4211, USA
10 Stamford Road, Oakleigh, Melbourne 3166, Australia

© Cambridge University Press 1975

Library of Congress catalogue card number: 75–16870

First published 1975
Reprinted 1977
First paperback edition 1985
Canto edition 1990
Reprinted 1993, 1995

Printed in Great Britain
at the University Press, Cambridge

ISBN 0 521 39829 0 paperback

CONTENTS

I

INTRODUCTION

I

I want to write a historical preface to the treatment of a theme much talked of in our contemporary faculties of sociology and history. The theme is not philosophical, in the common tradition of this Gifford foundation. Its matter concerns students of human society; especially students of society in the relatively recent past. The historian starts to feel scruple when confronted by the will of Lord Gifford. For Lord Gifford wanted to know what was true, or wanted men to confirm what he already believed to be true. The historians of the last hundred years have eschewed, or have looked as though they eschewed, any attempt to answer questions on whether a belief is true, and have devoted their endeavour to questions appropriate to their discipline, why belief arose, how it was believed, how its axioms affected society, and in what manner it faded away. Lord Gifford preferred lecturers who prove that witches are powerless. Historians refrained from any such bold assertion, and asked themselves only how men came to think witches powerless when their power looked obvious. And therefore the historian, confronted by Lord Gifford's will, suffers a twinge of scruple.

A student of this theme, however, may console himself that he is nearer to Lord Gifford than the fringe of some subsidiary enquiry which can be relegated to a trivial appendix in a future system of philosophy. Lord Gifford wanted his men to diffuse the study of natural theology 'in the widest sense of that term, in other words the knowledge of God', and 'of the foundation of ethics'. Historical study is not knowledge of God but part of it is knowledge about knowledge of God. It looks at first sight as though Gifford wanted us to deal in metaphysics whereas the historian is bound to deal in human beings. But, religion being what it is, the relation between a society and the systems of metaphysics professed within it may easily bear upon the nature of those metaphysics. Though religious doctrines reach upward towards a realm conceived (usually) as beyond the material world, they are also doctrines about human beings; at least imply doctrines about human beings. History can affect

1

divinity, by discovering new documents like scrolls from the desert. It can affect divinity, also, in more indirect ways. If it were proved by historians, for example, that whole societies spent untold centuries believing in a god or gods and then within a hundred years suffered such an intellectual *bouleversement* that they no longer believed in any such person or things, it would have momentous consequences for those whose business is not history but a study of the nature of religious experience.

So far, then, by way of dismissing the tiny scruple that comes like a shadow cast over the lecturer's desk by the grateful memory of Lord Gifford and his generosity.

The next people whom I must dispose of, if I can, are those who say that the subject which I propose to you does not exist. They say that secularization only exists in the minds of those who wish it to occur and who are puzzled that it does not occur; in short that it is merely a word of propaganda; and that we shall therefore do better not to use it. Their excuse lies in the perception that a goodly number of those who write about secularization write out of dogma and not out of open-minded enquiry. The dogma has been caricatured by David Martin as 'God is dead. Therefore secularization must be occurring. Therefore secularization is a coherent notion.' 'The whole concept appears as a tool of counter-religious ideologies which identify the "real" element in religion for polemical purposes and then arbitrarily relate it to the notion of a unitary and irreversible process.' The word, says this sociologist, 'should be erased from the sociological dictionary'.[1]

Without subscribing to any of these hard sayings I think the warning is salutary. This is a subject infested by the doctrinaire.

But what of a dictionary which concerns us more intimately, that of the historian? The historian often has to use words to describe large processes. He finds it handy to write of the Renaissance. Driven by his enquiries or by ruthless critics, he finds it hard to say precisely what the Renaissance was: a mysterious movement of ideas in men and society incapable, by its nature, of statistical definition and frequently failing to conform to the expectations of romantic historians of culture or philosophy or politics. From these difficulties of definition it does not follow that the umbrella-word is misused. It is often easier to be sure that a process is happening than to define precisely what the process contains and how it happens. It is easier to be sure that there was a Renaissance in the fifteenth century than to explain what you mean when you say that there was a

Renaissance in the fifteenth century. In this respect secularization, as a large idea used by historians, is no different from other such large ideas. By the nature of historical science, vagueness, blurred edges, recognition of the unchartable mystery in human motives and attitudes and decisions, are no necessary obstacle to an authentic though broad judgment in history. At least they offer scope for that humility of heart and openness of mind which are proverbially said to be indispensable to historical understanding.

Descriptions of historical process often suffer from one concealed assumption, and none more than the theme before us: the assumption that all was well, or at least was plain and coherent, at the point where the process is believed to start; the historiographical sin known as *Decline and Fall* history; where the writer knows that he is setting out, for example, to describe a steady decline in civilization until he reaches the point which he thinks of as 'the triumph of barbarism and religion', and consequently, like Edward Gibbon with the Antonines, must start with an idyllic picture of the hill-top from which men began to slide. Like Kenelm Digby or the romantic historians of the Middle Ages a century and a half ago, they imagined an age of faith, where bishops were prime ministers, religion the only source of physics or astronomy or morality, kings deposable by popes, all art inspired by gospel narratives, and theology queen of sciences. From this paradise or this hell, according to the point of view, all that followed was decline or progress. Then any change in constitutions or in society since the thirteenth century can be labelled secularization.[2] A man enquires into a process and understands the process so far as the evidence allows him, and then postulates an imaginary picture of society before he starts his enquiry in order to make the process easier for him to understand, not just as one thing after another, but as process.

Paradise or hell. Two can play at this game and we need to be on the watch for both of them. 'The nineteenth century', say you, 'is the age par excellence of secularization.' You are imagining a religious society before the nineteenth century which never existed. Look how respectable in French upper-class society was atheism before the end of the reign of Louis XIV. Look at the statistics of illegitimate births in Toulouse: 1668–75: 1/59; 1676–99: 1/36; 1700–19: 1/17; 1720–31: 1/10.6; 1732–43: 1/8.4; 1751: 1/7.2; 1788: 1/4. From figures like these you might ask yourself, as a brilliant enquirer has asked, what would be left of the French Church of the eighteenth century if you removed from it:

all mere formality
all mere rejection of the world, with no religious motive
all magic
all Manichaeanism
all religion of fear

What, he asks, would remain? 'Have we not too long called by the name of Christianity a jumble of practices and doctrines which had only a remote connexion with the gospel message – and, if so, have we to talk of *dechristianisation*?'[3]

The point is taken. We cannot begin our quest for secularization by postulating a dream-society that once upon a time was not secular. The world drank barrels of sack and fornicated though Zeal-of-the-land Busy stalked through Bartholomew Fair crying of enormity. Yet still we have the uneasy feeling that a question is somewhere begged. Remove from Christianity all mere conformity – when is conformity mere? Remove from Christianity all religion of fear – is it certain that religion may not be religion of fear and still authentic? You can be aware that there was never a world that was not secular. And yet you need to beware of defining your religion in narrow terms with the object of enabling yourself thereafter to plead that 'true' religion never declined, and so to make the quest for secularization into a quest for a misnomer. When describing a historical process, you may as easily place your unproven axiom at the end of the process as at the beginning.

If you place your historical axiom at the beginning, you say that there was never a merry world since fairies left off dancing and priests could take wives. If you place your historical axiom at the end, you assume that religion as seen round us is 'true' religion and everything not part of that is not true religion. Therefore anything jettisoned over the last two centuries, like belief in witches or belief in devils or belief in Noah's flood, was the dropping of the irrelevant, or of noxious clutter, and has not touched the gold of religious faith and practice.

Of course I do not deny that such stripping has been in part the banishment of clutter. At the moment I only want to speak a warning against treating the axiom as a basis for a view of a historical process which ought to be judged, not from any axiom whatever, but from evidence.

I next need to defend the plan to talk more about the nineteenth century than the eighteenth.

This subject, though not quite in this form, was invented by students of the European mind in the eighteenth century. Here, in the years between 1650 and 1750, the age of Sir Isaac Newton and Leibniz, of Fontenelle and Spinoza, of John Locke and David Hume, and finally of Diderot and Voltaire, were the seminal years of modern intellectual history. In these years the Middle Ages ended at last. Here men could study the distant origins of modern science, the beginnings of the idea of progress, the first historical criticism of the Biblical records, the discoveries of the true nature of other great religions and cultures of the world. If you want to know about this theme, it may be said, you must ask questions about the Enlightenment, and its revolution in men's thinking. Old-fashioned histories of this subject dealt in the Enlightenment, usually in nothing but the Enlightenment.

No one denies that that age was seminal in the European mind. The distant origins of modern science, the idea of progress, the first true investigation of the Bible, these were all momentous. Why then do I call these histories – Lecky on rationalism or on morals, Bury on the law of progress, Robertson on the history of Free Thought – *old-fashioned*? Because, by the progress of enquiry, the subject as we now have it is not quite the same subject.

As we meet the theme today, it was invented by the faculties of social science, not by the faculties of history. The founders of modern sociology could hardly conceive of any branch of enquiry more pressing than this.

Durkheim was the nearest claimant to the proud title of founder of the modern social sciences. Looking back to Auguste Comte as his master, he accepted Comte's axiom that religion was one of the foundations of social and moral life. As a positivist by education and early conviction, he was bound rather to observe and criticize religion than to practise it. But he had no doubt that social life hung as firm upon religion as religion upon social life, and the more experienced he became the more prominent became this aspect of his thinking. In order to isolate the problem he selected a small and closely-knit society with limited evidence, the aborigines of Australia and their totemism, and wrote: *Les formes élémentaires de la vie religieuse*. In this study he believed that he proved how a society, to cohere at all, shares principles or axioms, the beliefs which are necessary if it is to remain a society; and how religion is a part of these shared principles. He always saw religion in the context of a social pattern of order, of the self-preservation of society as society.

5

Making his ultimate distinctions between sacred and secular, beliefs and rituals, he brought out as no one before him brought out, the non-rational, sub-conscious inarticulate elements in a society, its moral axioms and its attitudes to the world. The analysis became afterwards, and has remained, controversial. But it was an analysis of such power and penetration that it changed men's ideas over the place of religion in society. Henceforth no one could any more write the history of modern religion in the terms which Lecky and Bury thought sensible. You proved that Noah's flood did not cover the whole earth, and so you weakened the authority of the Bible, and in this way reason started to drive religion out of men's minds – these well-trodden paths of intellectual history suddenly looked as though they stopped short of entering the forest which they were formerly supposed to open to the explorer. Instead of solving the riddle, they were superficial. They talked more about symptoms than causes. Durkheim, whose attention was fixed upon modern society and not at all upon history, changed the conditions of a momentous historical enquiry.

The Victorian father goes to church. The Edwardian son stays at home. Is 'reason' the cause? Did 'reason' prove or suggest that the activity was unprofitable, or meaningless, or even harmful? Did 'reason' suggest that the origins of religious awe lay in fear of earthquake or wind, uncontrollable terrors of nature, and now that we are afraid no longer we can do without awe? After Durkheim, no one who thought about the matter could answer these questions so easily and cheerfully.

Going to church is ritual. Do men believe something about the world and then make a ritual to express their belief? If so, when their belief about the world is shaken or disturbed, their practice of the ritual will weaken or fade away. But, perhaps, men sometimes make ritual, and then the ritual needs explanation. Sometimes prayer comes before creed instead of after. Perhaps the disturbance to ritual is what matters, some half-conscious distaste for its underlying symbolism, and disturbance to belief is but secondary. Durkheim showed that a society held certain things sacred, but to assert the cause of the sacredness of this or that object easily ran beyond evidence that anyone could get. The sacredness of an object was not caused by rational thinking. Therefore the end of that sacredness could not be caused only by rational thinking.

Durkheim showed how the religious ideas of a society were related to their ultimate social values. Changes in religious ideas were bound to mean changes in ultimate values – or, rather, changes in ultimate values were bound to mean changes of religious ideas. The positivists, and every adherent of a scientific theory of society, began with the axiom, *religion is a social phenomenon*. But Durkheim, it is said by one of his expositors, accepts the axiom and yet comes near to inverting it into another axiom, *society is a religious phenomenon*.[4]

The student of reason and religion among aboriginal tribes might be presumed to be in error if he made from his observations too dogmatic inferences about reason and religion in western Europe. But without convincing the world of all his argument, Durkheim shattered the theories of intellectual advance which passed for orthodoxy among Whig intellectual historians of western Europe. *If* religion declined in western Europe, orthodoxy supposed that it declined because men got knowledge and education and so rid themselves of irrationality. Durkheim shattered the axiom that men could, or had, rid themselves of irrationality.

Therefore the new school of sociology, stemming ultimately from Auguste Comte, but with Durkheim as its real founder, focussed attention upon the relation between societies and their religion; that is, among other things, the place of religion in contemporary society. They began to approach the problem of secular and sacred with fresh insight. Thereby they cut obliquely across the mental habits of historians of intellectual Europe. The problem of 'enlightenment' began to turn into the new problem of 'secularization'.

This interest of sociology in religions was fostered by the second of its founder-giants. Max Weber is known to English readers of history as the author of the thesis on *religion and the rise of capitalism*. And as this thesis is regarded by most historians as fallacious, they are inclined to undervalue Weber. But the famous title of Tawney's book on that theme represents an important truth about Weber. Convinced like Durkheim that religion was creative in forms of social life and organization, he looked to find examples from an unusual range of historical sources in the sixteenth century; in order to show how not merely moral consensus but social and economic structure were conditioned by the nature of religion in society. Whether or not the particular evidence stood up to the weight which Weber thrust upon it, all his system of enquiry went to show how religion was immensely more powerful in intangible or hardly to be discovered ways, than in the upper intellectual assertions, that is, formulas in which it was taught or understood. When he argued that Calvinist ethic led insensibly towards the spirit of mind which lay beneath a capitalist economy, he was not so crude as to argue that this happened only by the pronouncements of religious leaders, or suppose that capitalism owed its origins merely to an open mind about credit and rates of interest among Reformers. The Reformation made all secular life into a vocation of God. It was like a baptism of the secular world. It refused any longer to regard the specially religious calling of priest or monk as higher in moral scale than the calling of cobbler or of prince. Christian energy was turned away from the still and the contemplative towards action. The man who would leave the world turned into the man who would change it. Religion centred upon ritual veered towards religion centred upon ethic. Supreme good which once was Being now began to be Doing. Once they waited for the New Jerusalem which should descend from heaven, now they resolved not to cease from strife till they had built it in this green and pleasant land.

The historical right and wrong of Weber's famous theory hardly concerns us here (though there is an element in it which touches us later). What concerns us now is the cutting of new social theory into the traditions of intellectual enquiry pursued in schools of history. Like Durkheim, though in a way very different from Durkheim, Weber thrust before the public the power of ethical attitudes, related to religion, within a relatively advanced society. Weber's thesis caused controversy for more than one reason. It was controverted partly because it was wrong – that is, what Weber said about the Reformation had truth but its link with the origins of capitalist economies was more tenuous than he supposed. It was controverted also because it was unfamiliar to the habits of mind prevailing in schools of history. The intellectual historian of that age thought that a man had a new idea and this new idea was slowly accepted in a society until the attitude of the society changed. Calvin was not rigid against lending money at interest, and so the willingness of Christians to accept interest became ever more common. Some of those who assailed Weber assailed him because they supposed that this was all that he was saying.

The study of the history of ideas moved into a new phase. You could no longer explain the movement of minds by seizing only upon what was expressed in formal propositions, articulately. These could be due to movements of men's minds which ran deeper, of which men's outward teachings were more result than cause. Simultaneously, historical study moved away from élites, a history of kings and prime ministers and patriarchs, to seek out feelings and ways of life among ordinary men and women; a history not of the visible few but of the invisible many.

That is why the problem of secularization is not the same as the problem of enlightenment. Enlightenment was of the few. Secularization is of the many.

Naturally, this made the historical problem far more difficult. That is why it has produced dogmas more frequently than evidence. To track the course of one man is hard enough for the historian. A single mind is mystery enough; what shall we say of the 'mind' of Britain or even the 'mind' of Europe? But the social question, of course, is the more important question. Leslie Stephen became a clergyman and then suffered conversion and became an agnostic. Why this happened is an interesting study. But of itself it tells us little enough about the social and intellectual condition of the age which made it possible.

Paul Hazard wrote a justly famous book, called in a literal translation *The Crisis of the European Conscience*. Here was a study of an intellectual shattering of Christian foundations at the end of the seventeenth century, the background of the European Enlightenment. That shattering was an intellectual crux in the appearance of habits of mind that concern our enquiry. The book reported the arguments of an intellectual élite. The social historians have been little interested in intellectual élites until their conclusions are seized upon by a society which is ready to seize upon them.

Father Mersenne provided a celebrated statistic: that the Paris of 1623 housed no fewer than 50,000 atheists. That is a statistic useful if we want to confute men who imagine so religious a world of their dreams. Here men are complaining of men's irreligion now and they can console themselves that Paris in 1623 had 50,000 atheists.

This phalanx of 50,000 atheists has marched into all the books of reference. I do not like its smell. By what Gallup poll or mass observation did Father Mersenne discover the opinions of 50,000 men or women, and of all the other men or women who did not share the opinion of the 50,000? This statistic is no statistic. It is on a par with the pious severity of the Princess Palatine, when nearly a hundred years later she refused to believe that 'in all Paris, clerical or lay, there are more than a hundred people who have the true faith and even who believe in our Lord'. We shall not take Father Mersenne too literally. Just at the same time that he counted his

9

heads, another observer reckoned that Paris held five atheists and three of those were Italians.[5]

Even if we could rely on information like this, it concerns élites: academic debate, aristocrats speculating over their soirées, bluestockings in French salons, middle-class merchants arguing in cafés. Voltaire refused to let men talk atheism in front of the maids. 'I want my lawyer, tailor, valets, even my wife, to believe in God; I think that if they do I shall be robbed less and cheated less.' So long as the argument kept out of the kitchen, it does not quite meet our needs. The attitude went on into the nineteenth century, if not beyond. Mérimée said to Cousin at dinner, 'Yes, you go to mass, but you are only a hypocrite, and you don't believe any more than I do.' Cousin said 'Sh! Look out for the servants. You can be cynical in front of the important but not in front of the unimportant. . .Do you believe that I could make the governess and the cook understand the morality of my philosophy? It is easier if I appear to accept the form of their faith; because at bottom I believe as they do, though in another form; in their faith they find the virtue to serve me honestly and devotedly.'[6] The middle class of the nineteenth century still refrained, for the most part, from being atheists in front of the maids. But after a time this was not much use, because the maids could read these things for themselves.

Here we enter one of the difficult and inconclusively debated problems of contemporary historical writing: the nature of intellectual history. At first sight a study of secularization examines how men's minds work; whether by new knowledge, or better logic, or prophetic insight. Therefore this is a proper subject of intellectual history; which would start with Descartes and move through Bayle and the new science into the Enlightenment and pass via the Encyclopaedists into Kant or the Utilitarians and the new philosophers of the nineteenth century. Half a century ago this, and nothing but this, would have formed the substance of this course of lectures. A man gets an idea, or proves a proposition. He advocates it. Slowly, because it fits the available evidence, it commends itself to other minds. The pebble is thrown into the pond and ripples move outwards. A hundred years later the idea becomes axiom of a whole society, accepted by a mass of people who do not understand the reasons behind it. Intellectual history moves like the advance of a scientific theory, say the force of gravity or the structure of the solar system. Of course the proposition need not be true to work in this way. To say nothing of erroneous theories at one time believed by the people, like ether, we cannot forget a proposition of Rousseau which is still potent though everyone knows it to be false: *Men are born free but everywhere they are in chains.* Many shelves of reputable books used to assert that Rousseau's ideas were 'the cause' of the French Revolution.

Modern social science made too sharp an impact upon the study of history to make that traditional theory of intellectual history either pleasing or credible. The theory of historical truth in Karl Marx is easy to caricature; but it unexpectedly proved to be one of the most influential ideas in the inheritance which he left for western Europe. Man's material advance controls the nature of his society and the nature of the society begets the ideas which enable that society both to be stable and to advance. Then the social scientists came in to look for the social origins of social ideas. Men did not need Rousseau to tell them that they were hungry. If you are hungry it is impossible not to know it. Because they were hungry they started to listen to Rousseau. And when men like Durkheim came into the debate, they brought with them knowledge that a society has a 'collective consciousness', consisting of a body of feelings and beliefs which are shared by the average majority of the society; together with the insight that this body of feelings and beliefs is not the same as the sum total of all the individual beliefs of the separate members of the society, but has a life of its own, a development independent, in some manner, of the individual opinions in the mass. Durkheim found this easy to see in primitive peoples. He began to apply it by analogy, and fruitfully, to modern Europe. Society threw up the idea of God because it needed him. Now it needs him no longer, and he will die.

The phrase, *the secularization of the European mind,* is a phrase of Heinrich Hermelink.[7] He meant, the intellectual processes of intellectual history. But if the social historians are right we ought to be asking a different and more fundamental question: what changes in economic or social order lay under the willingness of a society to jettison notions which hitherto were conceived as necessary to its very existence?

We still find both approaches. It seems to depend a little upon the standpoint from which a man starts. Vernon Pratt[8] has no doubt that the cause of all is change in intellectual ideas and better logic; that clever men thought cleverly and unclever slowly followed. To the contrary, Alasdair MacIntyre[9] has no doubt that the social process caused the intellectual process, that ordinary men and women experienced new forms of social life, and then clever men were clever in suiting their mental gymnastics to the new forms. 'It is not the case', he wrote (p. 54), 'that men first stopped believing in God and in the authority of the Church, and then started behaving differently. It seems clear that men first of all lost any overall social agreement as to the right ways to live together, and so ceased to be able to make sense of any claims to moral authority.' Putting this question in an antique form, as the early Victorians in their troubled time might have put it: does Doubt produce Sin, or does Sin produce Doubt? Vernon Pratt, the intellectual theorist, is sure that Doubt begets Sin though he would not call it Sin. Alasdair MacIntyre, who though a philosopher is also a social theorist, restates in a fascinating modern form the old conviction that Sin begets Doubt.

The philosopher certainly (because concepts can be precise) and the social theorist possibly (because social classes, especially theoretical social classes, behave less variably than people) can deal in tidier worlds than the historian. Early social scientists were often trained in a school derived from French positivism. And though the association between social sciences and a narrow positivist background has long been broken as the subject broadened its base and deepened its enquiries, we still find a certain attitude, sometimes, which dismisses the intellectual aspect of this double problem as unworthy of further consideration. Nothing has more easily caused the unwarranted assertion of dogmas.

Social history or intellectual history? Orthodox Christianity was proved untrue because miracles became improbable, and Genesis was proved to be myth by science, and philosophical axioms were transformed by intellectual processes derived from the Enlightenment, and the intellectual revolution passed from universities to newspaper, and newspaper to drawing-room, and drawing-room to housekeeper's parlour, and newspaper to working-men's clubs – are *ideas* what move the souls of men? Or did the working-man, thrust by economic development into a new and more impersonal class-structure, develop a consciousness of his class, and distrust or hatred of the middle class, and find the churches middle-class institutions, and start to beat them with whatever sticks lay to hand, and found the weapons of atheist pamphleteers and potted handbooks of evolutionary science? Did men's minds move because educated men told them their axioms about God needed changing, or did they move because they felt a need to be 'free' from their fellow-men and that seemed to mean being 'free' from God? Was the process the result of new knowledge, or the result of a new development of society?

The problem is easier – easier for the historian, I mean – if the Marxist historians were right. To see why German radicals of the 1840s hated churches is simpler to chronicle by external signs and events, than to see how some men changed from believing in God to believing in no God. Everyone knows how impossible the autobiographer finds it to describe, intelligibly to others, what moved his mind at its deepest well. St Augustine beautifully if misleadingly explained the course of his mental and devotional history until the moment of conversion. In that moment we have only beauty and no more explanation. Newman eloquently justified his past against Kingsley's attack and left the decision to become a Roman Catholic almost as intellectually mysterious as when he began. C. S. Lewis wrote an autobiography with personal and devotional insights on (if we exclude one repellent chapter) most of his pages. Yet readers find his change from philosophical theism to Christianity the least convincing paragraphs of the book. These inward movements are too profound for those who experience them to articulate successfully. They can give hints and suggestions and poetic phrases. Biographer or historian can hardly pass beyond such little lights.

But when you have interrogated Rousseau, or Karl Marx, or Bakunin, or Proudhon, on the why of their mental intricacies, you have scarcely begun. The word God is not a word which could be replaced by the phrase 'that opinion', or 'that philosophy'. We could not say that some Victorian radical or dissenter, a Clough or a Francis Newman, changed from being Christian to not Christian as a man ceased to follow Plato and followed Aristotle. We have to probe what difference is made, not merely what different language was used. Whatever Christianity is, it contains a way of life. The question before us, so far as it concerns individuals, is not just a question about opinion. Power lies hidden within what we seek; power over the individual and his future on one side, over society on the other. Among the numerous insights of Karl Marx, this was an insight which historians took to their hearts as true. Men do not fathom intellectual history if they ask about nothing but the intellect.

The evidence so far collected supports the social historian. It is easier to collect evidence that tithe mattered than evidence that utilitarian philosophy mattered. What is not clear is whether this weighting in favour of social rather than intellectual issues is due to the nature of historical enquiry. Is the evidence about tithe more plentiful solely because measuring tithe is easier for the historian than measuring the inside of John Stuart Mill?

I think – and believe this judgment to be derived from inspection of history and not from desire in my soul – that without the intellectual enquiry the social enquiry is fated to crash; as fated as was the intellectual enquiry when historians asked no questions about the nature of the society in which ideas were propagated or repudiated.

The subject, treated historically (at least in this new form, as thrust upon us by the social sciences), is not far from its beginnings. It will eventually depend in part, though never totally, upon a mass of localized statistical investigations which have only begun in recent years and which will take many men and many years before they can be synthesized. My aim in these lectures is the modest one of offering some considerations near the beginning of a relatively new branch of research. No one will think that what I adduce will be thought by its author to be more than prolegomena to an enquiry.

2

I need to say what I take secularization *not* to be. It is not a change in fashion or custom.

In 1905 the prime minister of Great Britain, Mr Balfour, was observed to play golf on a Sunday. He was also a Scotsman. His appearance on a golf course was publicly regretted by various critics. Was this a mark of a new neglect of the Lord's day and therefore a symptom of a society always more neglectful of the traditional ordinances of religion? Then we remember how, in the early 1840s, the grandfathers of the same critics publicly lamented when young Queen Victoria drove through London to a theatre in Lent. What we are chronicling is not specially to do with religion but changes in custom and social acceptability, like the new fashion in length of hair on men's faces after the Crimean war. All men do not adjust at once to new fashion and occasionally attribute moral obliquity to innovation. In the same year, 1905, Dean Wace of Canterbury illustrated a decline in the moral fibre of the nation by citing the new provisions to enable boys in boarding schools to stand under a shower after football.[10]

Not that custom is irrelevant to our theme. Custom is part of the unspoken axioms which make up consensus in society. Changes in custom can have consequences beyond custom. Part of the reason for a decline in churchgoing, during the last decade and more of the nineteenth century, was nothing to do with Christian doctrine or enmity towards the churches, but change in habits and in men's ideas of behaviour which was acceptable. We want to know why habits altered, how notions of socially acceptable behaviour slid (or climbed) insensibly. What we must not do is, to confuse mere changes in habit with something called 'secularization': or we shall find ourselves in paradoxical postures of the intellect like those of Dean Wace of Canterbury on shower-baths.

The next thing that European secularization is not, is a change in Christian doctrine. To believe that the universe started in 4004 B.C. in one year and next year to believe that it is many millions of years older than that, might be seen as a step to making man more secular in his intelligence; for in the former year he derived his physics and geology from a religious book and in the latter year he derived them from newspapers reporting what scientists said. More properly it should be seen as better knowledge, irrelevant to faith. When in the fifteenth century Laurentius Valla proved the Donation of Constantine to be a forgery and forced less obscurantist apologists to drop it from the papal armoury, he provided new knowledge which contributed a mite to the shattering of papal power. But faith adjusted to this new knowledge without more than a hesitation and a backward glance of regret. Despite Galileo's tears, churches easily adjusted to the Copernican universe. Churches are institutions concerned with truth; not concerned with truth only, but still, concerned with truth. When a theory could be shown to be well-founded, they hesitated and cast regretful glances backward, but they accepted it because it was true and soon were again serene. Let us not confuse secularization with the perpetual task of adjusting religious understanding of the world to new knowledge about the world.

Older historians of the European intellect, like Lecky or J. B. Bury, doubted what I have just said. To them the progress of truth consisted in the light of science invading dark chambers inhabited by mysticism, until at last no darkness should be left. What I have called religious restatement they saw as a shrinking of religion into an ever smaller corner of the intellectual world. I doubt that way of stating the matter.

But the underlying point – namely, that secularization and Christian restatement are connected – cannot be denied. I will put it thus: were there some ideas or doctrines which could neither change nor develop without Christianity ceasing to be Christianity? without the churches ceasing to propagate 'their' gospel and becoming instruments for propagating some other kind of ethical message? Was secularization a process only concerned with religion in its broad sense? – for example the loss by politicians of a feeling that they owed an ethical duty to something or someone sacred, or the loss by artists of a feeling that they painted to the glory of God, or the loss by historians of the feeling that they recorded the acts of God? Or was it a process inseparable from an actual *reduction* of Christianity? Could Christianity slowly turn into Islam without the world becoming in the least 'secularized' in the process, as once, two thousand years ago, Judaism begat Christianity? Or if, as observers like Raymond Aron have thought, Communism is a modern form of religion, could Christianity slowly change into Communism without any 'secularization' on its way thither? Perhaps the taking of the Church of the Virgin in Leningrad and turning it into an anti-God museum was just as much a change from one religion to another as the taking of the Parthenon and turning it into a Christian cathedral, or the taking of St Sophia and turning it into a mosque.

To state the paradox in this extreme form is to thrust the mind back upon the foundations of religious faith and practice; upon what the second generation of the Reformation began to call 'fundamental articles'; upon the *articuli stantis aut cadentis ecclesiae*. If miracles, which had been thought to be supernatural interruptions of the course of nature, ceased to be regarded as possible, or began to be regarded as so improbable that rational men would assume them (despite any evidence) not to have happened, was that only a change in Christian doctrine like the change from belief in a universal flood within Mesopotamia, or was it touching some vital root-canal of religious power over men's minds and hearts? Some men, both Christians and non-Christians, a Henry Sidgwick as well as a Charles Gore, thought that to be a Christian a man must believe that the body of Jesus rose from the dead. And other men, both Christians and non-Christians, thought that the historical question over Jesus' body was no more to do with faith than other historical questions of lesser moment like uncertainty over the years of his birth or crucifixion.

In selecting this belief in miracle (in the sense of supernatural intervention with the course of nature) we touch a matter of weight in our study. It might be true that a Christian is no less of a Christian if he takes it as an axiom that *miracles do not happen*. Nevertheless, we shall hardly be able then to say that changes in Christian doctrine are wholly separable and distinct from a process of secularization.

For this very axiom, *miracles do not happen*, comes near the heart of that elusive shift in the European mind which we seek.

Distinguish, then, the process of secularization from the process of change in Christian doctrine. But, in distinguishing, we are aware that one touches the other at many points. Part of the development of Christian doctrine was forced upon the churches by advances in knowledge which in other directions made men's minds more 'secular'. And part of the development of Christian doctrine, during the nineteenth century, contributed to the growing 'secularity' of men's minds. If I say that secularization is not the same as an alteration in ideas about religion, I do not assert that one had no effect upon the other.

3

Ought a man, embarking on this theme, to define what he means by religion? If 'secularization' is supposed to mean, a growing tendency in mankind to do without religion, or to try to do without religion, presumably we need to know just what it is which he is supposed to be doing without.

That would be a logical proceeding, but not a historical. When we talk of the Renaissance we deal in a mass of illustrative evidence of every variety of new knowledge and new attitudes, and yet of deep-running continuity of thought and culture. The historian does better not to attempt the impossible task of defining an alleged state of culture from which the European mind began to be reborn. He can handle the novelty of knowledge more easily than he can handle ignorance or 'obscurantism'. He does better to seek to illustrate a movement of minds without making the crass error that minds were at any time not in motion, and the still crasser error that all individual minds started from the same axioms or the same relation between those axioms and workaday living. We are not trying to chronicle a loss of conviction about (let us say) justification by faith, or transcendentalism, or witches, or demons, or the age of the world, or miracles. We are not trying to estimate whether monks, or clergymen, or preachers, or sermons were more or less highly regarded by public opinion. We ask, first, whether statistics show a decline in attendance at churches, or in the giving of money to churches; and secondly, whether (if the statistics so point) that means something momentous about the development of the human mind; whether we could chart an increase in the numbers of people refusing to say *I believe in God*, and whether (if we could so chart) that would mean something momentous about man's religious attitudes; whether we could find an increasing number of people who think religion to be unimportant to society; or bad for society; whether we could find a growing body of attitudes which deny a link between religion and moral behaviour; and whether (assuming that we could find some or all of these things), we could judge the nature of the social development which they might record.

In this vast subject a man may easily get lost amid the decades, and wallow in tendencies, trends, movements, processes, and similar ways of avoiding clarity and definition. I limit it in space and time:

In *space*, by drawing your minds into modern Europe. Towards the end of the century Friedrich Engels looked back and contrasted 'the religious bigotry and stupidity of the English respectable middle class' with its more civilized state forty years later. He attributed this to the end of English insularity. England became 'gradually internationalized'. The introduction of salad oil, he wrote, 'has been accompanied by a fatal spread of continental scepticism in matters religious'.[11] Without needing to accept this Marxist sacramentalism of the relation between matter and spirit, we can see that Western Europe – that is, old Western Christendom – moved in interdependence.

In *time*, I seek evidence mainly from the second half of the nineteenth century; from the publication of the *Origin of Species* in 1859 until the downward turn in French, German and English churchgoing statistics during the 1880s, or in part until 1914. This start and end are arbitrary. They bear small relation to each other. The start is an intellectual fact and the end a social fact. They symbolize, however, an age admitted by every historical observer to be central to any consideration of the theme. And these forty years have the first merit, that during them the word *secularization* came to mean what we now mean when we use it. If we know what we mean when we use it.

PART I:

THE SOCIAL PROBLEM

2

ON LIBERALISM

From the moment that European opinion decided for toleration, it decided for an eventual free market in opinion. A toleration of a minority is not the same as equality before the law between opinions. But in the circumstances of European history the one must lead into the other. This happened at different speeds among the states of western Europe. Speed depended upon the division of the state into religious denominations, where a minority could not be repressed, and must first be tolerated and then conceded equality before the law. Russia or Spain never reached equality, or only fitfully attained it, and have not quite attained it yet. But when the country divided on religion, minorities successfully gained the right to differ. Although politicians tried for a time to restrict this right to those who were near to the approved orthodoxy of the state, and refuse it to those far from that orthodoxy, it came to be found that the distinction was untenable. Once concede equality to a distinctive group, you could not confine it to that group. You could not confine it to Protestants; nor, later, to Christians; nor, at last, to believers in God. A free market in some opinions became a free market in all opinions.

The first word we must consider is the word *liberal*. Confused, vague, contradictory, the idea of liberalism dominated the nineteenth century, more a motto than a word, more a programme of what might be than a description of what was; a protean word, which some claimed to rest upon coherent philosophies and economic theory and others saw as the destruction of the stable structure of a reasonable society.

The question is whether a 'liberal state' is of necessity a 'secular state' if it is to be truly 'liberal'; and, arising, whether a 'liberal-minded' society must be, in a manner, a 'secular' society.

In origin the word simply meant free; that is, free from restraint. It might mean, too free. In the age of the later Reformation it was often used to mean such freedom as led to immorality, or to illegality. It meant licentious, or anarchic; tending, anyway, towards licence and anarchy. And men of the nineteenth century, especially religious men, sometimes continued to use the words *liberal* and *liberalism* in this sense of evil. A liberal was one who wanted more liberty, that is, more freedom from restraint; whether the restraint was exercised by police, or by law, or by social pressure, or by an orthodoxy of opinion which men assailed at their peril. Everyone agreed that unlimited freedom was antisocial, that freedom needed to be tempered by law and custom. The liberal thought that men needed far more room to act and think than they were allowed by established laws and conventions in European society. And some religious men thought that liberals wanted too many freedoms and that too many freedoms ended in liberty for wickedness and therefore the end of freedom to live a secure and good life.

'Religion', said the preacher Edward Irving in one of the earliest uses of the term liberalism, 'is the very name of obligation, and liberalism is the very name for the want of obligation.' 'The more serious thinkers among us', wrote John Henry Newman in 1841, 'are used. . .to regard the spirit of liberalism as the characteristic of the destined Antichrist.' Twenty-three years later the Pope condemned the proposition that 'The Pope can and ought to reconcile himself to. . .liberalism.'[1] We need to try to explain this antagonism. To limit the powers of government, or to weaken the conventions of society if they are seen to be obsolete, is not at first sight an irreligious plan. At various times of Christian history the churches had spent endeavour or money or blood to limit the powers of government and were not backward in upsetting conventions which they found to be corrupt. Even in the nineteenth century religious men and liberal men often stood close. They agreed in refusing to see the state as naked force. One of the anathemas of the most illiberal of Popes – condemning the proposition *authority is nothing but people with guns*[2] – would have been music to the ears of every liberal if they were not deaf to any sound from the mouth of that Pope.

Odd men in society were always liable to penalty, either from the law or from public dislike. Men were accustomed to walk in the ways of their fathers, and treated deviation as sin or as crime. Society was built upon a willing acceptance of conformity; a recognition of duties as sacred; a suspicion that men who turned off the tried and good paths would damage the framework of law; a belief in the fragility of social order, in the precious and yet precarious nature of peace, in the vile tensions which could rise among men to destroy justice and prosperity. Part of the true ways of the past – a main part – was the public attitude to God, acts of respect and worship offered by the community, moral attitudes which those acts of worship fostered and consecrated.

The Reformation, in dividing Europe by religion, asked for a toleration which hardly anyone at first thought right. Men believed that society could not cohere if it permitted difference in religion. Everyone saw how Catholic subjects were disloyal to Protestant sovereigns, Protestant subjects disloyal to Catholic sovereigns. Separate religions seemed to mean civil war or separate states. Little by little they discovered how the world had changed. In old conditions the state must be intolerant to survive, now it must tolerate or be destroyed. The experience of Germany and France and Britain forced the state and then society to recognize, first reluctantly and later freely, the 'right' of the individual to profess the faith which he found to be true. Christianity had never been content merely to enforce an external performance of public ceremonies. Always it sought for religion of the heart, and confessed from its founder that religion of the heart transcended due celebration of rites. But religion of the heart was not a recess which state or society could penetrate. That reverence for individual conscience, which Christianity nurtured in mankind, weakened the desire for conformity to public rites. The legendary saying of Luther *Here stand I, I can do no other* represented so Christ-like a Christian attitude that, though its consequences were not yet seen, the attitude must in time destroy the ideal of conformity to rites or to faith by social pressure or by law.

Christian conscience was the force which began to make Europe 'secular'; that is, to allow many religions or no religion in a state, and repudiate any kind of pressure upon the man who rejected the accepted and inherited axioms of society. My conscience is my own. It is private. Though it is formed and guided by inherited wisdom and by public attitudes and even by circumstances which surround me, no man may intrude upon it. It is the most important part of a man, that which forms the roots of his character and personality. How I may be true to it, whether I may be true to it, whether allegiance to it is compatible with comfort or with happiness, these decisions are for me and no one else. It shows me that I cannot trample upon other people's consciences, provided they are true to them, provided they do not seek to trample upon mine, and provided they will work with me to ensure that our differing consciences do not undermine by their differences the social order and at last the state. This last proviso reaches far. But it reaches not so far as the earlier doctrine that all men must conform in faith to that which society approves.

But suppose the state itself were to undermine the social order, for example, by tyranny to annihilate justice, by wild spending to destroy prosperity, by aggressive war to force men to fight for what they think wicked, by failure to maintain order and so inability to protect the weak. This inner freedom of the individual man is no doctrine of acceptance. It could be conformist and ultra-conservative as it sought to preserve the social city against real or imaginary enemies at the gate. But it could also be radical, even revolutionary. *I can do no other* was a doctrine of resistance, passive resistance at first, profession of willingness to suffer. But passive resistance and rebellion are near neighbours. A man who disobeys government in conscience can seldom limit the issue to private crucifixion.

The right of resistance was and is the anxious problem of liberal theory. Law and order are precious, are the making of society. Without law, freedom is not. To resist governments in the name of freedom is in one aspect to resist men believed to tyrannize over freedom. Simultaneously it is to weaken or wipe out law which is the ground of freedom.

Revolutionaries have never found it easy to give power to the people when revolution is accomplished. Liberals were not always democrats. The power of the people is not invariably exercised to make men more free. On the contrary, it was an insight of ancient Greek experience that the power of the people often begets despots. Masses of men, especially masses of men in trouble, often prefer tyrants. Plebiscites are the typical device of dictators. Demagogues are seldom democrats. An individual is safe in a family, a clan, a community, a nation, but not safe in a crowd. The liberal of the nineteenth century put freedom above the logic of liberal constitutions. But liberal theory led logically to democracy. The respect for the right of each citizen to go his own way where he harmed no one, and the desire to make this right available to more and more people, continually pressed towards equality before the law, in rights political and social and at last economic. Deep in the liberal consciousness was the right to believe as you like, think as you like, argue, discuss, express, publish, campaign. And these rights are hardly compatible with the power of the state unless by some constitutional device government is representative and therefore democratic. Only in this way could liberals seek to solve their difficulty in reconciling law with the right of resistance. If government were representative and democratic it might be changed by argument and law would still be respected. If government was unrepresentative it could be changed only by force, and the use of force risked the destruction of liberal ideals.

The ultimate freedom was liberty to worship God as the conscience called. Modern ideas of freedom, as they stemmed from John Locke in the later seventeenth century, were founded in religious toleration. Locke's intention, after the age of intolerance and party conflict which he experienced as a young man, was to justify religious toleration. He based his argument, not upon policy – such as, we cannot hold England together as a state unless we allow Protestant dissenters to worship God as they please – but upon the principle of a natural right. Man has a natural right to freedom of conscience, and no government has a right to tamper. But this right carries other rights, freedom of opinion, freedom to meet, freedom to express. Of course Locke depended on a long tradition of political thought in Europe. But his statement of it founded liberal convictions in the form in which they conquered the Europe of the nineteenth century. The expression of them was widened, adjusted, expanded to new circumstances. But this way of thinking about freedom and the power of government ran henceforth in a continuous tradition.

For the first time in history freedom was seen from the standpoint of the individual man. Men had talked of a free people, or freedom of Protestants to say their prayers, or freedom from censorship of the press. They had talked since the later Greek age of a natural law or law of reason which established justice between the peoples or cities or states. But in the age of Locke they moved from talk of natural law to talk of natural right. Law and right stand together as ideas. In some languages the same word is used to mean both ideas. But they are not the same idea. The notion of inalienable rights belonging to the human individual, which no government assailed without tyranny, was new in European thinking.

These freedoms, except for religious freedom, were not clear. Perhaps they could not, and cannot, be made precise. Some theorists have seen them only as a useful myth, like the idea of a contract between a people and its rulers, a contract which never happened in history but was a notice to politicians that they must govern for the sake of the people or go.

The doctrine of human rights arose partly out of religious war and partly out of the rise of the modern centralized states. The state became more powerful; its bureaucratic fingers reached into every corner, its system of taxation could not be evaded, its new police force patrolled the streets. The king might not be more powerful, because he could no longer rule without the aid of many others, and the others often gained the authority which men once attributed to the king. But the state was more sovereign. And as it reached out to the furthest frontiers of the land, it trampled over the local customs and local rights on which men once relied for their freedom in a community. In destroying local authorities – in finally ending the feudal world – the modern state was a liberator; freeing, for example, the peasant from the age-long rule of his lords, or the economic supremacy of rich landowners. But in destroying local rights it also threatened the kinds of freedom which custom brought. To protect themselves against the new power of a sovereign men needed rights that were wider than the rights of the old community where they lived. They seemed to need rights as wide as the world; natural rights.

The liberal faith thus owed something to religious division, something to fear of modern power in the state. But it acquired a third source, or was fostered by a new habit of mind. Europe developed a new society of trade and industry. In this new world a man need no longer follow the habits or vocation of his father and grandfather. He could move away from his village, make his fortune by enterprise, climb the social ladder, occupy a different niche in society from the niche of his father and mother. For him the structure of the state could be a tool. Custom or law which hampered progress could be changed. This mentality, afterwards condemned as 'bourgeois' by realistic thinkers like Karl Marx, saw the laws and customs of the state as there to be manipulated. These structures were a human edifice; manufactured by man, alterable by men. They should be reorganized for the sake of prosperity, or happiness, or enterprise, or welfare.

In western Europe the ultimate claim of the liberal was religious. Liberal faith rested in origin upon the religious dissenter. Liberalism on its more important side was a criticism of the medieval world of all-embracing religious orthodoxy. Dissenters won a free right to express a religious opinion which was not the accepted or prevailing opinion. And that axiom was soon seen to have two consequences. Religion being what it is, the right to religious opinion must include the right to religious practice. And freedom of religious opinion is impossible without freedom of opinion. Liberalism might or might not be religious. It must demand the right to be secular. John Stuart Mill[3] remarked that it is

on this [religious] battlefield, almost solely, that the rights of the individual against society have been asserted on broad grounds of principle, and the claim of society to exercise authority over dissentients, openly controverted. The great writers to whom the world owes what liberty it possesses, have mostly asserted freedom of conscience as an indefeasible right, and denied absolutely that a human being is accountable to others for his religious belief.

If the right to be irreligious is won, then the institutions, privileges, customs, of a state and society must be dismantled, sufficiently dismantled at least, to prevent the state or society exercising pressure upon the individual to be religious if he wishes not to be religious. The liberal state, carried on logically, must be the secular state.

That is, a state in which government exerts no pressure in favour of one religion rather than another religion; a state in which no social or educational pressure is exerted in favour of one religion rather than another religion or no religion; a state wholly detached from religious (or irreligious) teaching or practice.

No such scheme could ever be carried out logically. Many liberals had no desire to carry it to logical conclusions. Though they seemed to stand upon ultimate principles, they wanted the freedoms necessary for a state and society able to meet the revolutions of trade and industry and education. Liberals often recognized the force of history and custom in the making of a society. The liberalism of the nineteenth century did not always lead to 'secular states'. The most we can say is, its tendency was always in the direction of 'secularizing' the institutions of the state.

In Christian countries divided in religion, a free market in opinions became a reality; on grounds of right of conscience, and duty of toleration, and principles of equity, and expediency in a world of disagreement. In the leading countries of western Europe it finally became a reality between 1860 and 1890. When, therefore, historians speak of a more 'secularized' atmosphere of public life in those years, they in part describe an eventual and inevitable consequence of toleration acts like that of 1689 in England. Toleration of dissenting opinion must lead to toleration of opinion. Equality of dissenting opinion must lead to equality of irreligious opinion. An atheist might rise in public and assail religion with bitterness; or print books to the same end which no censorship would touch.

Religion had been protected by an authoritative constitution based upon consensus. The consensus about religion had not markedly changed by 1860. What had changed was the constitution which once protected it. Liberty to attack religion rose less from decline of religion than from love of liberty. Men had loved liberty since they were able to think politically. *Everywhere they are in chains* – the romantic age sought its heavenly city in the mysterious dim land where all men should be free. Disillusioned by the corrupt issue of ideals latent in the French Revolution, they took up again the call to liberty because it fostered human development, even human responsibility and morality.

John Stuart Mill published his essay *On Liberty* in 1859, the same year that Darwin published *The Origin of Species*. He had been meditating it for some years, and conceived it as a tribute to his dead wife Harriet, whose ideas he thought it to fulfil. He was not concerned with the liberty of the individual against a tyrannical state, for that was no new problem in the world. His problem was unique to states with representative institutions: the tyranny of the majority over the individual or the minority. Seeing that 'the people' were coming to power, and suspecting that 'the people', even less than the old tyrant, would allow the right to differ in opinion, he laid down axioms about liberty, which were not to stand the test of time in practice, but which were imperishable in the memory of free Europe.

The only purpose for which power can be rightfully exercised over any member of a civilised community against his will, is to prevent harm to others. His own good, either physical or moral, is not a sufficient warrant. He cannot rightfully be compelled to do or forbear because it will be better for him to do so, because it will make him happier, because, in the opinion of others, to do so would be wise, or even right.[4]

No right to exercise power to moral ends? Is not the state based upon the moral health of its citizens? Mill exempted certain classes of human beings from the dogma. Children: 'those who are still in a state to require being taken care of by others, must be protected against their own actions as well as against external injury'; men in a backward state of society – 'in which the race itself may be considered as in its nonage'. Which of the peoples are in their nonage? 'Despotism', he says, 'is a legitimate mode of government in dealing with barbarians, provided the end be their improvement, and the means justified by actually effecting that end.' Is there such a gulf between the 'barbarian' and ourselves? He goes on: 'Liberty, as a principle, has no application to any state of things anterior to the time when mankind have become capable of being improved by free and equal discussion. Until then, there is nothing for them but implicit obedience to an Akbar or a Charlemagne, if they are so fortunate as to find one.'

He was confident that all 'civilised' nations had 'attained the capacity of being guided to their own improvement by conviction or persuasion'.

The idea of liberty had moved. Only a generation earlier it was seen as an instrument to justice; or to good government; or to the enterprise and prosperity of society; or to satisfaction of the consciences of dissenters. Now it was a quality of life; not an instrument, but a good in itself, a quality of man and of society which enabled moral personality, moral development, self-realization. A mature man is a free man. He has the right to be persuaded and convinced. Society is under obligation to listen to his opinion if he wishes to express it. Society is not just to tolerate individuality, to allow it because it can do no other. It should foster it. Our fellow-men press upon us and push us to dress in line. To the contrary, they should encourage our differences, not for the sake of difference but so that any man may be himself, sentient, thinking, choosing, responsible. So is man a civilized being, society a civilized society. We are not to let custom, or consensus, pick our way of life for us. Morally it is better for each of us to employ all his faculties to discern the right way for himself as an individual. Mill rose up to his lovely and lyrical hymn of praise for the individual human being; no man's copy; cultivating his faculties of sensibility and discrimination; seeking truth; contemptuous of convention; diversifying human life; becoming at last a noble object of contemplation, risen above the mediocrity which surrounds him.

A generation before, liberal governments were defended because they were effective. Mill passed beyond that utilitarian doctrine. Liberal governments, very likely, might be inefficient – but they have the highest moral end and therefore are good. He concerned himself little over tyranny or injustice, the truncheons of a secret police never rose over his horizon. The essay hardly recommended a political plan, and only touched upon the constitution. He asked instead for an open society, for a people willing to allow wide disagreements and – more than willing – he asked for a people welcoming different opinions, partly as the road to truth, partly as the nurturing of fertile ideas, and partly as the reflexion of moral worth among men and women with these attitudes. A generation before, political theorists supposed that freedom among men depended upon free constitutions. Mill began to tell them that free constitutions depended upon freedom among men.

No society could put into practice all the principles of this great essay and remain a society. But the essay is of the first importance as an illustration of the connexion between liberalism and secularization. The essay has been called the first modern exposition of a theory of the secular state.

John Stuart Mill's father, James, to his son's astonishment later, believed so confidently in the power of reason over minds 'whenever it is allowed to reach them, that he felt as if all would be gained if the whole population were taught to read, if all sorts of opinions were allowed to be addressed to them by word and in writing, and if by means of the suffrage they could nominate a legislature to give effect to the opinions they adopted'.[5]

This was not very realistic; at least, it was derived from faith and not from experience. The liberal mind (in this sense) was individualist. It looked upon the solitary conscience in its right to be respected. But men could not be wholly individualists if society were to survive; nor indeed if they were to be realists instead of thinkers in a castellated tower whose thought never touched the experience of mankind.

Across the doctrines of liberal theory – not contradicting them but knocking them about, forcing their restatement, changing their formulas – came the claims of social consciousness, reasserting truths about men and states which orthodox liberals were inclined to undervalue.

I am told to 'realize' myself. What am I meant to do? From the moment that the umbilical cord was cut, I began to form ideas from the air around me. Hegel called this pompously, suckling at the breast of the universal ethos. Intuitions (perhaps) are my own. But they are framed and guided and formulated by the experience of a world about the cradle. To 'realize' myself is to find a 'natural' or appropriate place among people, and my moral duties are the duties of a 'station', a vocation in the midst of people, even if that vocation is found to consist in criticizing those people. If it should prove that duty leads a man to assail all that lies about him, he formed his conviction of the duty from some perception of what lies about him.

No man is an island – man is a moral being because he is a social being – man is reasonable as he accompanies and learns from other reasonable beings – his life as mere individual is solitary poor nasty brutish and short, only in his group can he be free, and thinking, and civilized. This group or community is no construction of himself, nor of a moment. It is inherited, painfully built over generations, carrying a received tradition of law or constitution or convention, a community not composed merely of the persons which then compose it, with a will which is no more than the decision of the majority in number, but with a will of its own, a 'general' will, linking past with present and present with future, the continuity of a civilized city or state.

From Burke or Rousseau or Hegel onwards these insights were the base of intelligent conservative philosophies. But they could be adapted to liberal ends. And since they contained platitudes of experience, they were so adapted necessarily. Every liberal had to allow that freedoms must be narrowed if men were to be free. He could allow limits to liberty if they aimed at making more men free. He could not easily abandon the notion that every man is free to choose his own way, because this choice was now held up as the moral good of each man and each society. But social theorists knew that each man is not free to choose his own way. Mill expected every civilized man to decide for himself his philosophy, his politics, his morals. More conservative and more radical theorists knew that few men are capable of deciding such high matters; and that even if they could, they would leave out of account something of higher import still, the general consciousness and general opinion which is more than the sum of all our separate opinions or consciousnesses.

Society is impossible without law. Is society possible without some form of social discipline, that is, some form of moral consensus, for example, that the expression of racial prejudice ought not to be encouraged or sanctioned? According to Mill, the state has nothing to do with the public utterance of racial prejudice unless it is expressed at such a time and place that it is likely to cause a breach of the peace. The state has no responsibility to the moral principle, only the responsibility of preventing violence. For the good of freedom is a higher good than the various challengeable ethical goods sought by restriction.

But, said the social theorists, a people is not just a heap of men and women. It inherited an organization, a history, a loyalty, a piety, almost a personality. This has been created over centuries by people, partly by men who made conscious decisions, but more by unconscious or half-conscious movements within the mind of a whole people. Burke had even dared to say that society rests not upon reason but upon prejudice. We have not built our society by reasonable enquiry, with philosophers as our kings, but because we have loved our wives and our families and sometimes our cousins, reaching out in loyalty towards our clan and our nation and at last towards humanity, with the kind of self-interest which is like the self-interest within a happy marriage, resting more upon instinctive attitude than cold calculation. We have not invented institutions. They have grown. They are like plants, not like machines. They have been part of a long-inherited consensus. There is no such thing as a civilized man on a desert island. There are only civilized societies.

On the highest moral grounds Mill wished to unseat consensus – whether it be inherited religious attitudes, an agreement on moral principles, an acceptance of custom or convention, a reluctance to challenge prevailing axioms.

It is better for society, wrote Mill, if opinions disagree than if they agree. It does not matter how moral or immoral the doctrines proposed – there must still be the fullest liberty for expressing them. 'If all mankind minus one were of one opinion, and only one person were of the contrary opinion, mankind would be no more justified in silencing that one person than he, if he had the power, would be justified in silencing mankind.' For no one can say for certain that the solitary opinion is false. And 'even if we were sure, stifling it would be an evil still'. The only way in which we can know an opinion to be probable is when we can defend it by reasonable arguments against men who contradict it. An uncontradicted opinion cannot be well-founded. 'The beliefs which we have most warrant for, have no safeguard to rest on, but a standing invitation to the whole world to prove them unfounded.'[6]

The leading aim of these thoughts was to free anti-religious propaganda from the restraints still placed upon it by the laws of blasphemy. Mr Cowling has argued[7] that Mill was as far as possible from intending the destruction of a consensus in society; that on the contrary he saw that the existing consensus was breaking up and wished to replace it with a new (and, in Mr Cowling's view, equally authoritarian) consensus based upon the opinions of wise and reasonable men, like himself. Taking all of his books, and especially his younger books, we find evidence to support this verdict. But the effect of the essay *On Liberty* in isolation is the destruction of consensus, not the substitution of another consensus.

'He who knows only his own side of the case knows little of that.' Each of us is to examine his axioms, digging, testing, proving. Society is to examine its base, ceaselessly. You are to listen to the arguments against all that you hold most sacred, not in any crude form, but in their most penetrating, plausible and persuasive form. If you cannot find opponents to argue against you, you must imagine them, try to throw yourself into their minds, to perceive what could be their most powerful arguments. Religious opinions have become desiccated, hard, rigid, and at last lifeless because they have been put by time into glass cases which no man may touch. In this age, he says – and he means the coming age of the masses – 'the mere example of non-conformity, the mere refusal to bend the knee to custom, is itself a service. Precisely because the tyranny of opinion is such as to make eccentricity a reproach, it is desirable, in order to break through that tyranny, that people should be eccentric.'[8] Mill extended the sanction of eccentricity to include, for example, a liberty for polygamy provided that its practitioners placed themselves, like the Mormons, in an enclosure remote from civilized habitations; or a liberty to import opium into China, and therefore a liberty for persons, who wish, to smoke opium; or a liberty to allow a citizen to cross an unsafe bridge if he wishes, and a refusal to allow the policeman to do more than warn him of the danger. No opinion could be offensive to others if it did not hurt others. All opinions were better if they were challenged.

Mill took the scholar's axiom, that truth comes from the interplay of free minds, and applied it to society. Being a born philosopher, he saw the perception of truth to be the supreme good of society. His plea for eccentricity was not quite a plea to destroy consensus. He knew well that if all men are eccentric no one is eccentric. He was afraid of two kinds of consensus; the outmoded convention of the past, attempting to maintain itself when it had already lost the conviction of faith in rational minds; and the coming convention of the masses with their social tyranny over the individual. But his doctrines, if carried into effect by miracle, annihilated social consensus.

Conservative minds, the descendants of Burke, the philosophers who drew upon Hegel, disliked the destruction of consensus because it seemed to them out of touch with all experience of the way in which societies are formed and develop. 'We should consider', wrote the Hegelian F. H. Bradley, 'whether the encouraging oneself in having opinions of one's own, in the sense of thinking differently from the world on moral subjects, be not, in any person other than a heaven-born prophet, sheer self-conceit.' 'In respect of morality', wrote Hegel himself, 'the saying of the wisest men of antiquity is the only one which is true, that to be moral is to live in accordance with the moral tradition of one's country.'[9] My daughter asks me questions in her cot. What is authority? She forms a picture of the world. Later she finds reason to doubt her father or to think him wrong. A regius professor of history at Cambridge once gave mankind the surprising moral advice that the first commandment with promise is, *Children, distrust your parents*.[10] Still, when we have disbelieved our parents, we shall believe other authorities, thought to be reputable, on numerous subjects because we have no time to investigate, and in many areas no competence; on the Common Market, or prisons, or Ireland, or evolution, or psychology, or God. Our choice of guides in high matters depends in part upon the ability of those guides to convince that they know more than we. But it depends more upon the approach we make to such guides, whether we are attracted to one rather than another, are more willing to be convinced by the *New Statesman* than the *Daily Telegraph*, whether we have ears and eyes open to east rather than west. And this inward stand is framed by symbols which already inhabit the mind. When the stance is impervious to evidence, it is prejudice.

Fourteen years after Mill's essay, *On Liberty*, Fitzjames Stephen the lawyer published a reply: *Liberty Equality Fraternity*. This is a blunderbuss of a reply, that is, its leading qualities were not subtlety or refinement. But the book sets a point to the argument over the bearing of liberalism upon the secularizing process.

Society rests upon a consensus of shared opinions. No society can exist without a consensus of shared opinions, and among opinions moral opinions are the most important. How is that consensus made up? Is it really true that each of us can behave with the discrimination of a professor of philosophy like Mill, capable of determining what is true or false for himself? Nothing could be more absurd. Most of us are not capable of making rational decisions on the fundamental issues of our life, whether political, or religious, or even personal; rational in the sense of being based purely on reason, or on evidence, or on enquiry. And if they were purely rational decisions, to the exclusion of other aspects of our nature besides reason, they are likely to be wrong decisions. Mill, one might say, had a top-heavy brain. Carlyle thought that he was stuffed with sawdust. Stephen called him a book in breeches. By reason of his personal education and extraordinary abilities, combined with ignorance of the human race, he imagined men to be pure intelligence and even imagined women to be pure intelligence; so as to be able to make decisions of pure intelligence. It is an idle dream, said Stephen, to imagine that one man in a thousand really exercises much individual choice as to his religious and moral opinions.

Then how is a consensus arrived at? By a minority – a band of apostles, passionately convinced of the truth of what they have seen – slowly and steadily imposing their belief or their faith upon all the people. We do not understand, wrote Stephen, the sources of religion. What we know is that 'now and again in the course of ages' someone is inspired so as to set 'to music the tune which is haunting millions of ears. It is caught up here and there, and repeated till the chorus is thundered out by a body of singers able to drown all discords and to force the vast unmusical mass to listen to them.' It is as though the few men of vision speak words which find answering inarticulate assent among the majority of us who have no vision. 'To oppose Mr Mill's *simple principle* about liberty to such powers as these is like blowing against a hurricane with a pair of bellows.'[11]

So it is not true that civilized societies proceed by discussion, by rational enquiry, any more than it is true of primitive societies or children. Mill has too naive a faith in civilization. Consensus rests upon authority, upon a large measure of mere acceptance by the crowd, of what a few men say who are trusted and responsible. The dangerous consequence of Mill's theory is to destroy all trust in authority. He urges us to challenge every authority, whether we are capable of it or not. And the end-result is fatal to society, fatal to consensus, fatal to reasonable authority. The result of our accepting Mill's advice to decide everything for ourselves is not decision but indecision. Since we are mostly incapable of doing what we are told by Mill to do, we refrain from doing anything. His advice is good enough to demolish, not good enough to construct. That means, general scepticism in philosophy, general agnosticism in religion, and eventual anarchy in politics; scepticism in philosophy and agnosticism in religion, that is, *irrespective of the teaching being offered by philosophers or religious men*. The truth or otherwise is not here in point. Even if something is true the ordinary man is put into the situation where he cannot decide.

Here was an argument between a Victorian Conservative and a Victorian laissez-faire Liberal. The difference of axiom between them lies in the attitude to the mass of the people. Stephen thinks the mass incapable of conscious decision. Mill thinks that every individual in the mass must be treated as though he were capable of conscious decision. Mill thinks that all men are potentially wise and good. Stephen thinks that wise and good men are never likely to be more than few, and it is their vocation to guide the many.

Both these doctrines can claim backing from the religious heritage of Christendom. Christianity was realistic about men and women. Its phrases about *original sin* or *depravation* were built into structures of divinity or legends which blinded men to the experience of humanity on which they rested. Trust no individual with too much power, trust the mass of people not at all, the best we can arrange is always lower than the best that we can see, never give the other man a gun if you have no gun in your pocket, better to yield authority to the good than the many – the tradition of realism was founded in an experience of ancient Greek political animals and consecrated by a Christian perception of man unaided by charisma from heaven.

But Christianity also contained a gospel of hope for the human race; resting little upon experience, and much upon teaching received as revelation. Justification by faith looked at first sight like nothing but an appeal to the moral and spiritual feelings of a soul in its solitariness. But on it was founded the redemption of man, an optimism that, despite chains which bound him to hell, God could raise him up, to mount towards heaven as the eagles fly, to run and not be weary. *Out of the mouths of very babes and sucklings,* not to wise but sometimes to foolish, God may speak through child or ignorant, the unique value of each soul. 'It has been found', wrote David Hume, 'as the experience of mankind increases, that the *people* are no such dangerous monsters as they have been represented, and that it is in every respect better to guide them like rational creatures than to lead or drive them like brute beasts.'[12] The optimism about man found in the men of the eighteenth century, an optimism based upon faith and not upon observation, was not reaction against Christianity but restatement of part of its faith, sometimes (as restatements often are) one-sided and isolated from an earlier context of ideas. To think with Hume men did not need to believe, against all evidence, in the natural goodness of human beings.

From Stephen's point of view, the trouble about the nineteenth century was the inability of wise and good men to agree. Wise and good men were more disagreed about truth (though not yet about morals or politics) than at any time since the sixteenth century. But the point worthy of contemplation is the question raised by Stephen; whether a theory of liberal individualism closely associated with the origins and theory of democracy, must create a secularized *society* (and not only a secularized *state*) irrespective of the truth or falsehood of the philosophies or theologies being taught in that society?

Because anti-Christians might freely profess anti-Christianity and proselytize men to their lack of faith, it did not follow that churches would lose adherents. Men may gain the right to profess eccentric opinions (as in modern astrology) without a consensus showing the least desire to accept their dogmas. They would only start to desert their old opinions and adopt new if the new seemed nearer to truth; whether because they commended themselves to the intelligence, or because they were felt to be more in harmony with a desired way of life, or because they offered axioms upon which a new developing society could more easily rest. Therefore we ought to concentrate the enquiry upon new ideas, and a new social order, not upon a new political system. Stephen could hardly argue that moral consensus could be weakened without propagation of ideas.

2

In the years 1860–80 contemporaries were agreed that the tone of society in England was more 'secular'. By that they meant the atmosphere of middle-class conversation; the kind of books which you could find on a drawing-room table, the contents of the magazines to which educated men subscribed whether they were religious or irreligious, the appearance of anti-Christian books on bookstalls at the railway station, the willingness of devout men to meet undevout men in society and to honour them for their sincerity instead of condemning them for their lack of faith.

Later Victorians sometimes looked for explanation by machine. Some of them believed that they descried a machine which by its action confirmed the theory of Stephen: namely, the printing press of the modern newspaper. The Victorians asked themselves, was the modern newspaper secularizing in its effect – and if it was, as Pope Pius IX and others believed, why? Those who asked themselves this question, did not usually mean what we mean. They meant that gambling news received more space, or the sports pages turned men's minds to triviality, or information on stocks and shares was unhealthy, or reporting of divorce cases lowered the morals of the people.[18] Their attitude to men of the press was not our attitude.

Queen Victoria told Lord Palmerston that journalists were not to be received, and got one of those courteous but dusty retorts which made him the least flatterous of her prime ministers. In an English novel of 1856, entitled *Perversion*, the villain sank morally, downward and downward, until he reached the abyss of writing leaders for *The Times*. Two years before that even the historian Michelet congratulated himself on having grown up under the Empire, when *happily* (as he said) the press did not exist.[14]

Those who study leading Victorian newspapers in Britain are almost surprised that men asked the question whether the newspaper secularized by being a newspaper. British newspapers of that day lend little support, *prima facie*, to the theory. The press achieved freedom, true, because it was unstoppable; second, because it was needed by all parties. Men continued to argue, occasionally, that control was necessary to true freedom; that most people had neither information nor ability to form sound judgment upon great questions; that stability was precarious, and therefore an uncontrolled right to criticize was dangerous; that those who talked about freedom of the press hoodwinked themselves to the real freedom, which was the freedom of powerful men or corporations. To the contrary, it could not be denied that the press was 'the open eye of the people's mind',[15] that without it democracy was not possible, that it was the way of a people to self-knowledge, and the one liberal instrument which enabled society to advance by free discussion.

The press, as Marx said, reflects society. But society is now a mass of tensions, contradictions, opinions. Therefore the press becomes the means by which tensions frame themselves. Hence it articulates oppositions which until that moment were partly inarticulate and therefore partly concealed.

To articulate opinion is not to create it. Nor is it to leave it as it was. Men understand their opinions better when they articulate them. They not only frame their opinion into words, they form the opinion by framing it. Hence the press became the organ which for the first time turned a mass of citizens into political animals. As such it was an indispensable tool of democratic constitutions.

In framing opinion, it impassioned it. The growing mass of the people which read newspapers could follow politics only in outline. They did not want the details of political information from their journal, and if they got them they passed on hurriedly. They did not desire news about Parliament or foreign policy. They looked instead for symbols of the political struggle, for broad schemes, for attitudes, which were articulated less by news than by slogans. The citizen who newly became political wanted to take sides. He wished his opinion confirmed, supported, and made emotional. The new reader liked the chance of being indignant for his cause. Moral indignation became the simplest expression of an articulated viewpoint towards politics or society.

They took sides in the name of ideas. But the ideas necessarily remained misty. Only if they were general could they command a broad enough area of support among the people. When the country was radically and socially divided, as in France, the ideas were platforms of indignation and therefore negative. In France the scapegoat came to play an important part in some forms of public opinion. The classical example is antisemitism. A section of the French press, between 1870 and 1914, fastened upon the Jews, a symbol of passion which men felt inarticulately, and which the antisemitic press focussed for them and thereby infuriated. Anticlericalism in France was first, a feeling in republican bellies; secondly a way of holding together political parties which agreed on little else; and thirdly, a way by which the republican press could form, transmit, articulate and impassion, the feeling in the belly. This was possible because, like antisemitism, anticlericalism was anti.[16]

Realities not only needed turning into symbols. They could be understood better by a wide public if these symbols were made pugnacious. To interest crowds you must provide a fight. Only so could spectators be excited, take sides, become emotional, feel suspense, charge their moral convictions; only so could they be lured to go on reading; and only so would they cease to be passive, march with a leader, identify with a cause. No man is interested if he does not care. This was why the new national newspapers from 1860 onwards, though indispensable to the working of popular sovereignty, could never carry the load of popular sovereignty which optimists laid upon them. To carry all that load would have meant a capacity to interest all of us in a mass of tedious detail; and in the moment of such an attempt indifferent readers ceased to read and the instrument of popular education failed. The weight of the press was not argument but assertion; not the making of opinion but its strengthening. It confirmed viewpoints, brought like-minded men into association, and so made their opinion more potent in action. Since rival opinions were expressed more loudly and felt more forcibly, the result sometimes gave the impression of confusion. It is possible, therefore, that the coming of the press weakened (more than the coming of modern science) the established moral agreements upon which the consensus of European society rested; and with these moral agreements was integrated religion. It is possible that the coming of the press pushed ordinary readers towards a feeling of the relativity of all opinion and especially the relativity of moral standards. This is speculation, not to be derived (as yet) from historical evidence. But it looks possible. And according to one leading theory, the demolition of an established consensus in moral authority was fundamental to the secularizing process.[17]

The strength of the press was against, not for; criticism, not construction. It was adapted to show the ills of society, less adapted to showing remedies. Its searchlight fastened upon the inadequacies of the Church and helped the ecclesiastical reforms of the nineteenth century by exposing old abuses. It strengthened Whigs everywhere, even when it was Tory, because its genius lay in change, and not in preservation. It made fanaticism look more foolish by printing it. For all its function of breeding parties it made intolerance more disreputable. The rise of the ecumenical movement within Christendom was almost certainly connected with the new power of the press as well as with new means of transport. 'The press', said a celebrated English editor of the *Birmingham Post* in 1893, Mr Bunce, 'has tempered the Church in political ecclesiastical and educational conflicts; it has helped towards stimulating criticism, liberalising theology, and moderating sacerdotalism.' It has rendered, he said, an 'incalculable service in enlarging and defending the freedom of the laity'.[18]

But newspapers also followed opinion. The first duty of the newspaper was to survive, and enable its proprietors or shareholders to live. Therefore it must capture and keep a broad public. Since the broad public in Britain was Christian (even if not churchgoing), the newspaper could not offend the deeper convictions of that public. *The Times*, the weekly *Guardian*, the *Manchester Guardian* had no desire to shock convictions. They addressed themselves to a civilized Victorian group of educated men, and sought to present the religious aspect of life, among its manifold varieties. Both *The Times* and the *Manchester Guardian* carried penetrating, sometimes learned, reviews of works of theology. They seldom printed matters which disturbed any but fanatics. Those readers who were interested in divinity were given pabulum enough. *The Times* greeted the Revised Version of the New Testament (May 1881) with four leading articles, and by a review (by Henry Wace, who since 1863 supplemented the stipend of a London curacy by writing leaders and reviews for *The Times*). Charles Kingsley reviewed a book about travel in the South Seas and took the chance of 'rebuking levity' and 'having a hit at the missions of the Protestant Dissenters and the Catholics'. Newman's austere *Grammar of Assent* received a serious review; and R. W. Church was allowed to write two superb articles on the theologian's theologian J. B. Mozley. A remarkable tribute to the power of a newspaper's readers may be found in a letter by a very bold editor of *The Times* dated 11 March 1873: *'Erewhon,* I won't touch. It could not be reviewed as favourably as perhaps it deserves without alarming the "goodies"– and they are powerful.'[19]

The example of the British national and provincial newspapers (and of the German provincial newspapers) appears to show that the mere existence of the press was not, by mechanics alone, a secularizing force Men were more easily able to buy atheist literature if they wished. They were more easily able to buy religious literature. If it be assumed that religion is all illusion, and reasonable men need only to have this pointed out to perceive its truth, then the press as a mere communicator of knowledge – e.g. that Strauss or Renan existed – was an anti-religious force. One or two of the older histories of 'freedom of thought' worked upon this axiom. But no one now accepts this axiom. It bears no relation to what happened during the later nineteenth century. The press was a force for more than one kind of opinion. The Pope of 1889 was far more influential than the Pope of 1839 because the later Pope was surrounded by the press and the earlier Pope was not. Still, even in Britain men had the sensation that newspapers were a secularizing force.

Was it only that the most powerful man in the cathedral close at Barchester was not Bishop Proudie, nor Archdeacon Grantly, nor Dean Arabin, but Tom Towers, thundering from his newspaper office in London? Was it that the most powerful man in French Catholicism was not Archbishop Darboy of Paris (though Lord Acton thought him the most intelligent bishop he had ever met), nor Bishop Dupanloup of Orléans, nor Bishop Pie of Poitiers, but Louis Veuillot, layman and editor of the newspaper *Univers?* Was it simply that a new instrument of power came into society, and the wielders of that power were detached, did not spring from the ordinary sources of authority hitherto known? As the teaching profession rapidly became lay because schools were needed in numbers far beyond those which Christian ministers could supply, so the guides of public opinion became lay because only machines could reach out to members of a society grown urban. Journalists established themselves as a profession in the same decade when teachers established themselves as a profession distinct from the clergy. And some of the new journalists treated their medium consciously or half-consciously as though it was a pulpit. John Morley used the *Fortnightly Review* and C. P. Scott used the *Manchester Guardian* for preaching; in Morley's case, doctrine unwelcome to conservative churchmen. They served as the pulpit served three hundred years before; confirming the faithful, rebuking vice, controverting opponents, at once followers and leaders of public opinion.

For the new journalist was conscious of power. 'From the first', wrote Wickham Steed of *The Times*, 'I conceived journalism as something larger than the getting and the publication of news. . .I looked for and found in it a means of working out and applying a philosophy of life, a chance to help things forward on the road I thought right. . .While under modern conditions the making of a newspaper must necessarily be a business, the making of that which newspapers exist to print is at once an art and a ministry.'[20]

It is a large, indeed a noble, sense of vocation. We are reminded, at the opposite extreme, of the rebuke issued by the second congress of the third International to French proletarians: 'You keep the chief place in your newspapers for parliamentary trivialities and little happenings of bourgeois society. Those newspapers do not know how to become, and do not want to become, the true mouthpieces of the revolutionary anger of the masses.'[21]

A chasm sundered Wickham Steed from the third International. But they illustrate the proposition, that every journalist, if he was a serious journalist, wanted to proselytize; and that if a newspaper was a newspaper, that is, if it was more than a notice of information put up by a Roman quaestor or a commissar, it must intend some point of view.

'There is little doubt', it has been said, 'that the expansion of the press made the people of England sit a little more detachedly to religious commitment. It is not quite clear why that should be so.'[22] We seek an answer along the lines of a new profession of laymen, necessarily writing sometimes on matters religious or ecclesiastical and often from points of view more detached than any writers who previously wrote upon such subjects; a machine of communication by its nature not merely a machine to communicate information, but by that nature rather critical than constructive, tending towards the weakening of authority; whether that authority belonged to government and was clothed in trappings of power which, however capable of hoodwinking men, could not deceive the machine, or whether that authority lay in social axioms and social convention.

A conservative like Fitzjames Stephen was convinced that scepticism was the child of religious liberty.[23] Pope Pius IX was equally convinced. Stephen did not propose that since religion is untrue, freedom to criticize it makes it vanish. Nor did he propose that if the worse is given right to propaganda equal with the better, the worse always drives out the better, though his view of human nature was compatible with this belief. He did not contradict the question of Milton's *Aeropagitica*, 'Who ever knew truth put to the worse, in a free and open encounter?' He proposed instead that a religious doctrine is not a doctrine comparable with a philosophical opinion. To teach a man religion is like a parent teaching a child to be loyal, or sober, or honest. If loyalty, or sobriety, or honesty, become the sport of public debate and public contradiction, their moral force is weakened for those who wish to weaken them. And if the truth of religion becomes a matter of public debate in newspapers, the effect is not like a debate on the truth of utilitarian philosophy. Once religious beliefs are equated with philosophical opinions and so become matters of purely intellectual argument, scepticism has won. The vast majority of mankind live by *commonplaces*, half-truths to which they become attached and accustomed and which, without thinking deeply, they suppose to be true. Unlimited freedom of thought means that all these commonplaces are cast into a cauldron and men no longer have stable principles to guide their moral beings.[24]

We need not take so melancholy a view of the consequences of liberal theory. We need much more research into the social and intellectual consequences of those free rights of publication gained almost everywhere in western Europe between 1855 and 1890.

The newspaper was sometimes imagined to be the tool of direct government by the people, as though it fed every citizen with all the information that he needed and so enabled him to make up his unaided mind on each issue. If that were true, the newspaper would be a vehicle for that perpetual self-examination which John Stuart Mill wished to encourage. The advent of the national press would have created an infinite (and intolerable) sequence of introspections about all the highest matters known to society. But this was not true. For by its nature the newspaper could not serve that function. It could present news only in a selection with special attention to the pugnacious. And it could not enable most men to form an opinion on every point under discussion partly because it had not the means of presenting adequate information, and partly because most men could not be influenced and read the paper only to confirm what they already believed. We shall do well not to exaggerate the power of the machine in its impact upon the thinking of educated society about the mysteries of the soul.

When we contemplate a notion like secularization, we ask how and why certain ideas, several of them difficult or very difficult, impinged upon a lot of ordinary men and women not used to analysing abstractions. This aspect of public opinion has been studied in other contexts, like war and politics, and historians of the intelligence can learn from such investigations. What stands out is the necessity for symbols or, as they have been called, *stereotypes*; easily identifiable names or persons or pictures or issues. Most men – most educated men – do not understand *evolution*. The word can only be a symbol, a substitute for understanding, a point of adherence for a faith, which bears small relation to what happened (so far as scientists can discover that). The instance shows that the symbol or stereotype does not need to be definite, nor to offer a picture with lines that ordinary men can see. The most experienced of journalists tell us that 'at the level of social life, what is called the adjustment of man to his environment takes place through the medium of fictions'.[25] By fictions he did not mean lies. These symbols might be false, but they might be as true as the molecular models which scientists construct in laboratories to explain their observations. We act like men seeing through a glass darkly. Our world is too big and too complex to be understood. Yet we cannot move in it without trying to see what cannot be seen, and so we move with the aid of symbols or stereotypes, names or slogans. 'To traverse the world', wrote Walter Lippmann, 'men must have maps of the world. Their persistent difficulty is to secure maps on which their own need, or someone else's need, has not sketched in the coast of Bohemia.' They move not by what is, but by the picture which they form of what is from the little that they understand of what is.

Remembering the limitations of a machine, how it can only disgorge matter fed into it, we may put the case thus. The press reflects society. But society (for reasons not connected with the machines) became a realm of argument on moral and religious issues. The instrument did not create the arguments. But it sharpened, quickened, magnified, sent out to the furthest village in the land. If part of what we seek is the weakening of consensus in western European society, we cannot avoid asking about its mechanism and force. But not even then should we explain the nature of the matter fed into the machine.

3

During the middle years of the nineteenth century, churches, when old-established and conservative, stood against liberalism. Liberals wished to dismantle or adapt the ancient régime, of which these churches were part. The mortal enmity between the Church of Rome and Italian liberals was only a tense example of a clash which was found in Prussia, Austria, France, Spain and sometimes England.

In their attitude to conservative churches, liberals found it hard to stick to their principles. The predicament resembled that of Turkey in the 1960s, where the ruling groups, whose principles demanded free elections and representative government, could hardly bear to concede either because it would give power to the peasant electorate which believed least of all in liberalism. In the twentieth century some liberals have argued that they are bound to tolerate every opinion except that which seeks to destroy freedom, and therefore that the state may rightly, and consistently with liberal principles, suppress fascist or communist parties. A similar mentality afflicted the French anticlericals between 1870 and 1905, Bismarck in his Kulturkampf, and occasionally even the British government's attitude to the Irish. The Catholic Church, thought Lecky, claimed so extensive a dominion over men's souls and minds, demanded obedience, possessed agents in every parish, enquired into the secrets of the heart, dominated women, controlled schools, interfered between husband and wife or parent and child. Universal suffrage brings political power to this organization, and makes us realize that our fathers were not so wrong in making legal safeguards against Catholic power. 'When a large proportion of the electors in a nation submit to such dictation, that nation is very unfit for representative institutions.'[26]

Liberal principles were liable, in this way, to fade when confronted with reality. Among French anticlericals of the same decades were equal paradoxes or contradictions. In 1902 the leaders of the French radical party issued an election programme with this extraordinary paragraph: 'By suppressing religious orders, by secularizing ecclesiastical property in mortmain, and by abolishing payment from public money to the clergy, we mean to put into practice this decisive liberal formula – free churches in a free and sovereign state.'[27]

If liberals contradicted liberal principles in their attitudes to churches, then liberal principles could appear to churches as a defence against liberal governments. They claimed, they said, no peculiar privilege. Legal protection inherited from the past they abandoned with reluctance or with pleasure. They accepted that they now lived in a society where throne and altar could no longer be at one. But they claimed rights which liberal principles conceded to all men – right of meeting, and opinion, and free expression, right to proselytize or to hold property. Instead of regarding liberal theory as their enemy, they began to find it their friend. German Catholics appealed to it as early as the 1870s, French Catholics not until the 1890s. From the end of the 1880s Pope Leo XIII started a policy of encouraging Catholics to take part in democratic elections and democratically elected governments.

As the nineteenth century moved from the 1860s to the 1870s, liberal theory began to move away from its concern only with the freedom of the individual. In Mill's ideas freedom was still linked with economic freedom, the doctrine of non-interference with men's private enterprise. But as they began to be aware how political liberty for individuals was not at all the same as liberty for everyone, and that political liberty was compatible with many men being chained to servitude, liberal theory moved into its collectivist phase. Industrial development, left to itself, dug wider gaps between rich and poor. A doctrine which ended in the slums of great cities could hardly contain all truth. Industry must be controlled. Liberal minds began the long climb in which they abandoned all desire to confine state power within narrow limits, and came to advocate interference by government as the instrument to general welfare. Their ideas were not confined to economic arrangements. We shall not understand liberalism unless we recognize that it was always a moral doctrine. Terrible poverty breeds immorality and casts doubt upon the morality of the society. In a philosopher like T. H. Green, seeking to restate liberalism in a form which could mend poverty and slums, the Christian background of ideas, or at least, of moral impetus, provided the intellectual drive. Once, the aim of liberal theory was negative; to get rid of clutter, obsolete law, interference, privilege, restriction. Now it became positive – to accept restriction for the ends of morality and justice. Liberty was henceforth seen more in terms of the society than of the individual; less as freedom from restriction than as a quality of responsible social living in which all men had a chance to share.

Collectivist society resurrected old fears of absolute sovereignty. How could Mill's anxiety for the minority or the individual be met when everything rested upon the social power of a general will? A line of political theory directed attention to the groups within society – guilds, corporations, trade unions, professional bodies, clubs and churches; above all trade unions and churches. History proved that such groups were no artificial creations of a state but were spontaneous, self-generating.

In a collectivist society men saw how the freedom of the individual was protected as much by his membership of a group as by state law. There was new talk, or at least talk revived from the Middle Ages, of the state as a *communitas communitatum*, a group made up of groups. Harold Laski applied the doctrine to the experience of trade unions, Neville Figgis to the experience of churches. The life of these associations was pictured as inherent, not derivative; as group personalities; group-individuals with characteristics such that no external force could touch their nature without tyranny. Without these corporations the individual could never be free against the omnicompetent state. Figgis knew too much history not to be aware that corporations also could be tyrannical, among them ecclesiastical corporations. He did not think, in 1914, that this was a modern danger. He was sanguine. He did not think, in 1914, that a time would come when men would again, as in the age of the Reformation, want to increase' the power of the state to protect them from the power of corporations, but now from corporations secular not ecclesiastical.

By this unusual route churches became once again important to the theory of liberty; as houses of conscience, altars of a loyalty which was not loyalty to Caesar, realms where the spirit could be free though the body lay in chains; possessing rights which denied claims by a state to possess all the rights that are. Like the liberal, the Christian maintained the faith that legal right can be moral wrong and that a legislator cannot reject appeals to an ethical standard not derived from his laws.

47

3

KARL MARX

The theory of Marxism lies near the heart of the European problem of the secular. To consider Marx would be necessary in itself. It is the more necessary because of modern progress in Marx studies. Formerly men used to see Marx with spectacles of the tradition; influenced, consciously or not, by the eyes and formulations of Lenin, and still more by the eyes and formulations of Engels; inevitably by Engels, because of the nature of the association between the two men; and because Engels so long outlived his partner and continued to expound his mind. The original critical edition of the Marx-Engels corpus of work, edited by Riazanov, was stopped by the Stalin purges, and the Stalinist epoch fossilized intellectual Marxism. Only from 1957 has East Berlin published the fuller critical edition. Since the standard commentators fixed the tradition, the early writings of Marx, collected in small part from manuscript, cast a brilliant light upon his mind and philosophy.

He became thereby no easier for expositors. Did his mind change over the years and are the early texts reliable for his mature judgment? Engels wrote two books with Marx, they wrote regular letters to each other, consulted each other. No discovery of manuscripts could drive a wedge between the two authors. And yet Engels had the less subtle mind of the two. He made Marx simpler, or cruder, to make him intelligible. Despite the sympathies and common interests and friendships, the two men had different outlooks and qualities. To try to see Marx in himself has by consequence the complication, that it breeds contemporary disagreement about the nature, as well as the results, of the system. But it has the merit that, as the system looms less crude, the stature of the mind is seen to grow.

It is not my purpose to expound Marx. My purpose is to consider his mind in relation to our special theme; while I confess that in isolating one aspect of so philosophical a thinker, I risk misinterpreting by over-emphasis or by selection, especially in one who is sometimes elusive, and whose Hegelian modes of expression are foreign to our ways of thought.

The phrase '*opium of the people*' was written at the end of 1843. It appeared in the essay called *Introduction to the Critique of Hegel's Philosophy of Law*, in the only number of the *Deutsch-französische Jahrbücher* which he and his little group at Paris were able to 'publish. The context ran: 'Religion is the sigh of the oppressed creature, the heart of a heartless world, the soul of a soulless environment. It is the opium of the people' – not, as Lenin amended it, opium *for* the people.

If the phrase was new, and destined to power in the future, the idea was not new. As early as 1767 the French materialist d'Holbach used it in his attack upon Christianity: 'Religion is the art of making men drunk with enthusiasm, to prevent them thinking about the oppressions committed by their rulers.'[1] But it was the British and their Opium War of 1839 to 1842 which popularized the drug and its properties. Several of the romantic assailants of Christianity, including Feuerbach, glanced at the idea. At least three friends of Marx used it before Marx. Moses Hess had just introduced the bourgeois Marx into workers' associations and unions. In 1843 Hess published at Zurich essays in *Einundzwanzig Bogen aus der Schweiz*, in which appears the sequence, 'intoxicants like opium, religion, brandy', and the sentence 'A man who is miserable because he is a slave can be enabled by religion to bear it', but religion cannot give him the strength to free himself. Marx thought well of this book. Probably more immediate than Hess was Bruno Bauer, who used the idea more than once. In the Halle Jahrbücher of 1841 Bauer published an article on 'The Christian State and our Age', where he contended for a state neutral in religion and with its laws dependent only upon the rights of man. Bauer wished to demolish the idea of a Christian state; and in passing, explained how the theological aspect of state order had 'an effect like opium' in putting to sleep the instincts of men for freedom.

When Marx's phrase is not torn out of its context, this is no contemptuous condemnation, like that of Hess. The language is poetic, almost wistful. *Religion is the sigh of the oppressed creature, the heart of a heartless world, the soul of a soulless environment.* This is, after all, a Jew speaking. Jewish people, emerging into the light after centuries of injustice, were naturally among the radical leaders of Europe. We keep finding them, for intelligible reasons from their past, throwing up revolutionary leaders, being as a people gifted with their traditional love of books and their innate inclination to philosophical thinking. The influence of newly emancipated

Judaism is not to be ruled out of court in contemplating the rise of the secular state. Since religious division once kept their people under, they were disposed to challenge all of a European religious tradition. But in the inheritance of Judaism, their own religious inheritance ran deep. They might abandon the religion of their fathers and with it all religion; but seldom did they thereby come wholly to despise what once was constituent of their people. Marx thought religion a mistake, an illusion. He passed through a phase of hating it. But to be hated is more of a compliment than to be despised. He did not scorn or mock it. It was the consolation of an oppressed people; a necessary consolation; a consolation without which the people in its predicament could not live. You must abolish religion because you must abolish illusion and make men face what is real. But you cannot abolish illusion unless you change the environment. Give the world a true and real heart and you will not need this artefact of a heart, change the environment so that it has true soul and you will want no ghost of a soul. 'The demand upon men to sacrifice illusion about their state of life is the demand upon them to sacrifice the state of life which requires the illusion.' But now, at this moment, men are in this predicament. They find no soul in the world. They need soul, so they make soul in their image and likeness.

To identify religion with illusion is not complimentary to religion. But the value is not hollow. Drugs are sometimes useful to doctors, are sometimes necessary. Men, in their present condition, cannot help but have religion. He was grandson of a rabbi, and descended from a long line of rabbis. His father was not a practising Jew, and neither gave up a religion nor adopted one. Heinrich Marx was a deist of the eighteenth century surviving into the nineteenth. When Karl Marx was six, in August 1824, he and all the other six children were baptised. The next and last child was baptised after birth, two years later. The motives were more social than religious. For his father could hardly retain his legal post in the Prussian civil service without conforming, and had received baptism some seven years earlier, shortly before Karl Marx was born. But evidently the motive was not irreligious. Karl's mother did not receive baptism with her children in 1824 because she was the daughter of a Jewish rabbi who still lived. She was baptised after her father died during the following year.[2] Her husband took the view that it was right to have a broad, firm faith in the few simple truths of religion.

Karl Marx derived no spirit of revolution either by heredity from his father or by reaction against his father. Father by nature was an intelligent conformist. A famous letter of 10 November 1837 from Karl shows intellectual sympathy with his father and mutual confidence.[3] Academic reports on the young Karl prove interest in religious thinking. They gave high marks to an essay which he wrote on the text of St John 15.1–14, the vine and the branches. The schoolmaster said that it was 'a thoughtful, copious and powerful presentation of the theme'.[4] Jewish inheritance, and adolescent interest in Christianity, and no superficial study of its texts or theology, make it necessary to trace the process by which the young mind turned, within five or six years, to the moment of 1841 when at the age of twenty-three, he stood against all religion, and was a member of the group of left-wing Hegelians who cried for atheism and identified atheism with social reform.

Something is due to the high school at Trier which he attended. The headmaster was Hugo Wyttenbach, who taught history and inspired his pupils with liberal principles like the need for freedom of the press; for after a nearby demonstration in favour of freedom the police searched the school and found copies of speeches made at the demonstration. Something is due to Baron von Westphalen, a legal colleague of Marx's father at Trier, and himself Karl's future father-in-law. Westphalen interested himself in the able boy, took him for walks, read him Homer and Shakespeare, and introduced him to the radical thinkers of the age – especially Monsieur de Saint-Simon. It is typical of the intellectual history of modern Europe that the greatest of revolutionary thinkers owed his first lessons in socialist theory to a liberal German aristocrat.

Karl Marx started his university career with a year at Bonn (1835–1836) and devoted such time as he did not spend in sowing oats to writing juvenile romantic poetry which he wanted and mercifully failed to publish.[5] When he moved to Berlin in the autumn of 1836 he continued to attempt romantic poetry. The fragments that remain show signs neither of social ideals nor of irreligion. They deal in dreams, and mystical apprehensions. The turn away from religion appears contemporary with the turn away from romantic poetry. The quest for hard reality began. He had disliked philosophy partly as a confusion of words and partly as not poetic enough, as too tied to the understanding of the earthy. In 1837 he suddenly saw the point of the philosopher's enterprise. He became a convert to Hegel. The conversion was uncomfortable. He felt as though he was carried willy-nilly into the clutches of the enemy, his belly filled with a physical nausea at being forced to make an idol out of what was still detestable. He came uneasily into the 'Doctors Club', the group of young men who met in a café to discuss the problems of Hegelian philosophy.

Hegel died at Berlin in 1831, ruling German philosophy. He identified Christianity as the perfect religion because capable of representing true philosophy in pictorial form. Religion and rational philosophy have the same essence. This belief could not go unchallenged for long. Religious thinkers disliked it as heartily as rational philosophers. The argument soon centred upon the history of the gospels; a history for Hegel unimportant except so far as it was a picture of a moral world attainable also by enlightened reason, for religious critics indispensable to any form of Christian thinking, and for some philosophical critics not needed for reasonable thinking and therefore better jettisoned.

In the religious argument appeared the radical school known as Young Hegelians. This debate on religion conditioned the debate on politics and society which followed. Prussian censorship made it easier to discuss great issues in religious terms because it suppressed articles which conducted the same controversy over politics or society. But accidents of censorship did not cause the religious debate. All intellectual Germany argued over the relations of philosophy, religion, state and society. Several of the leaders of social theory in the Young Hegelian school began academic work in a school of theology. Even Marx started his career of authorship by planning (though not publishing) an attack upon the Catholic theologian Hermes who tried to produce a harmony between Kant's philosophy and the Catholic faith. They were men of the middle class, academic or intending academic life, unable to obtain academic posts because their extreme theories alienated moderate men, and conducting their debate in articles and journals which came more and more under suspicion of the censors.

The Young Hegelians did not begin by attacking religion. As faithful Hegelians they aimed at first to integrate a Protestant Christianity into their understanding of the world's progress. They moved far from this discipleship under the leadership of their most famous and able member, the theologian Bruno Bauer. In English-language history Bauer usually appears as a comic figure of scholarship, a man with bizarre theories of New Testament documents, the eccentric academic of his generation. Marxist historians dismissed him equally, because Karl Marx at last turned against him and confuted him at length. But we have lately been learning more about Bauer, and what we learn makes him less contemptible though not more attractive. At the International Institute of Social History in Amsterdam lies a vast complete typescript biography of Bauer by Ernst Barnikol, too vast for anyone to publish, on which Barnikol had been working for 41 years when he died in 1968. Two editors gave us selected materials from the typescript in a fat volume.[6] Bauer was the focus of the Young Hegelians. They gathered round him because they found in him a critic who dissolved the gospels into legend. They faded out as a group when in 1842 he was expelled from his lectureship at Bonn university.

In company with Bruno Bauer and his circle Marx began to be radical about religion. It looks as though he began by concluding that religion is false on academic grounds and only later inferred that the real case against religion is that it is socially undesirable. Between 1839 and early 1841 he wrote a thesis, for a doctorate of philosophy, on the difference between Epicurus and Democritus, a thesis presented at the University of Jena in April 1841 and successful in winning the doctor's degree. The preface to this thesis contains a celebrated quotation from Prometheus, celebrated also because Marx made it his own – 'In a word, I hate all the gods.' This sentence has been lifted out of context to show that in 1840–1 Marx 'hated' religion, like a man chained by Zeus to a rock in the Caucasus with a vulture eating out his liver. In its context it is less emotional; a cry for the autonomy of philosophy and a declaration that philosophy must declare man's self-consciousness to be the highest divinity. Into Marx's later attitude to religion came passion. But this passion would only come as the intellectual critique of religion changed into the social. The appeal to self-consciousness was straight discipleship of Bruno Bauer who put self-consciousness at the centre of his system of philosophy.

Marx now identified himself with atheism. In the summer of 1841 he went with Bauer to Bonn with the plan of editing a journal entitled *Atheistic Archives*. The plan failed. With Bauer he worked on a satirical pamphlet, *The Trump of the Last Judgment on Hegel*, which advocated atheism under the pose of ardent defence of Christian orthodoxy. As a direct result of this pamphlet Bauer lost his post at Bonn University and Marx perforce abandoned his hopes for an academic career. For disliking the Prussian government Marx now had private as well as public reasons.

In January 1842 Marx first mentioned the name of Feuerbach[7] when he wrote a little article on the argument over miracles. We are still meeting more a radical theologian than a social theorist. The question of religion was still mainly of intellectual truth, less of social effect. Feuerbach published his book *The Essence of Christianity* in April 1841. It was an attempt to strip Hegel of his argument to God from man's self-consciousness. God is an idea which makes personal the infinite aspect of man's nature. Man is divine, and so projects this divinity into supernatural Being. Knowledge of God is knowledge of the self, or rather of all human selves.

Ernest Renan had a saying that you should never believe a German when he tells you that he is an atheist.[8] In Bauer and even in Feuerbach idealism makes the zareba in which their minds move, and compels them to remain theologians while they assail theology, almost to remain religious men while they assail religion. The atmosphere in which Marx moved was still theological. The debt to Feuerbach has been exaggerated. He did not need to learn atheism from Feuerbach because he had already learnt atheism from Bruno Bauer and his own reading. But he learnt phrases, at least, from Feuerbach: the expression of the theory that God is illusion whereby man makes himself divine. But it was not until 1843 that the reading of Feuerbach's *Theses* encouraged him to apply to philosophy the critique which he had already used against religion, and so at last desert Hegel, and idealist philosophy. His age of philosophic materialism began during 1843.

From about the same time the critique of religion shifted its ground. Marx started by arguing, or at least by assuming, that religion was untrue. During 1843 the truth or untruth of religion ceased to matter. The controversies conducted so passionately by Bruno Bauer ceased even to be relevant. What mattered now was not the truth of religion but its social function.

This change of outlook can already be detected in embryo during the later months of 1842, while he was editing the newspaper *Rheinische Zeitung*. His experiences as an editor, struggling amid difficulties to keep a newspaper afloat, did not raise his estimation of the wild impracticable articles or reviews sent in by Bauer and other extremists. He began to see through the old slogans even to despise them. They concealed the vagueness of their philosophy under attacks on 'atheism', and this editor preferred less emotion and more thinking. 'I asked', he told Arnold Ruge, 'that religion should be criticized more within a critique of the political situation than the political situation within a critique of religion, because this approach fits better the nature of a newspaper and the education of the public, for religion has no content of its own and does not live from heaven but from earth, and falls automatically with dissolution of the inverted reality whose theory it is.'⁹ He had ceased to believe that philosophers would rationalize away religion by analysing its transcendent ideas. Religion *lives from the earth*, and men must dispose of it by attending to earthly needs.

Marx did not reach this axiom quickly. The publication of his early works, and modern discussion upon them, shows the development of his mind between 1839 and 1843. He learnt much from his new experience as a journalist and editor. He found himself forced away from the theoretical questions of metaphysic or Biblical criticism with which he began. His powerful mind gained the confidence to attack his masters Feuerbach and Bauer. Starting from the critique of religion he moved into the critique of the state. Yet the critique of religion and the critique of the state were still a unity in his mind. Since the existence of religion reflected the ills of state structure and consecrated tyranny, the critique of religion was central to the critique of the state.

In Germany and Britain Jews still suffered civic disadvantage. In 1843 Bruno Bauer published two essays on the Jewish question. He adopted a conventional axiom of mid-nineteenth-century liberalism, that the civil inequality of Jews rested upon the Christian character of the state. He proceeded to argue – it was characteristic of the wild logic of Bauer's mind – that no state could be emancipated unless everyone gave up religion. If Jews are to find equality they must surrender their Judaism while everyone else surrenders their Christianity. Then there will be a secular state and a secular society. Bauer thought that if you make the state secular, it will follow that society is secular.

To justify this curious doctrine – that if you make the structure secular the people in the structure will be secular – Bauer used language which at first sight is very close to the language which Marx himself would soon use. People used to believe that the motives of their actions were religious. They went on crusade, and supposed that they sailed because God called them to his colours. We know (*we* are the students of Feuerbach, the inverted Hegelians) that these motives are imaginary. Men act from their needs; then they sublimate their action by appeal to a higher cause. Therefore, today, they are acting in response to the kind of society which they find, a Christian state. Make the state non-Christian and they will have no desire to appeal to the same kinds of sublimation. The religion of society, for Bauer, is men's response to the structure of the state. Make the structure different, and religion dissolves. Therefore Bauer could argue the startling proposition that if you make a state secular you make all its citizens secular.

Marx considered long this theory of Bruno Bauer and reached conviction that it was in fundamental error. The United States proved that a constitution may be secular while religions flourish among its people. Something has been misstated in this theory of the relation between state and society; something misstated too in the way in which the place of religion in society is conceived. Marx reviewed both the essays in an article of February 1844.[10] The article, though obscure and over-subtle, was a landmark in the development of his mind.

Political emancipation is progress, great progress. But it goes nowhere near so far as Bauer thought. Bauer supposed that if you give every man civic rights you will get justice. Marx did not. He distinguished in his mind the structure of society from the structure of the state. Political emancipation means the power of the bourgeois. A state can be free without most of its citizens being free. And a state which is free will be best of all for religions and not worst. A democratic state, though outwardly secular, may be inwardly religious, because religion is the ideal, 'unsecular consciousness', of its citizens.

Here Marx began to play with these ideas destined to such power in modern intellectual history; the juxtaposition and contrast between religious society and secular society. The juxtaposition and contrast is still cloudy and vague. He was slowly thinking his way through to something vital to later social theory.

What makes a political democracy Christian is the fact that in it man, not only a single man but every man, counts as a sovereign being; but it is man as he appears uncultivated and unsocial, man in his accidental existence, man as he comes and goes, man as he is corrupted by the whole organization of our society, lost to himself, sold, given over to the domination of inhuman conditions and elements – in a word, man who is no longer a real species-being.[11] The fantasy, dream and postulate of Christianity, the sovereignty of man, but of man as an alien being separate from actual man, is present in democracy as a tangible reality and is its secular motto.[12]

It is an obscure paragraph. But it is a crux of this year which marked so profound a change in the mind of Marx.

The less important part is clear. Bauer thinks that if you disestablish all the churches you will weaken and throttle religion. On the contrary, so religion will live again. Of itself political freedom creates neither social freedom nor freedom from religion. And this proves the weakness in the idea of political emancipation. It does not do enough. Jews can be politically free and still devout Jews – therefore political freedom is not human freedom. Not just the political structure but the whole inward essence of society needs changing.

If we ask Marx how religion fits into this mysterious scheme of human life, we do not find so plain an answer. We best understand these paragraphs if we take them in the light of the other article which Marx published in that same number of the *Deutsch-französische Jahrbücher* of February 1844, the *Introduction to the critique of Hegel's Philosophy of Law*, the article where appears the celebrated saying on religion as the opium of the people.

Man makes religion. But he makes it because he cannot do without it. He cannot do without it because he lives in an ill-ordered society. Religion is the symptom of sickness in social life. It enables the patient to bear what otherwise would be unbearable. And because it makes the sickness bearable, it removes the motives for curing, the will to cure.

The article was a landmark because religion had now taken the axiomatic place in Marx's theory which for the rest of his life it never lost. Until 1843 religion was one of the opinions or errors which stood in the way of a people's society. Men must be educated out of it, as out of other wrong opinions, by enlightenment. The state would be reformed by reason. But now, from the end of 1843, Marx no longer believed in the reform of the state by reason, nor in the ending of religion by reason. Religion is not one theory which obstructs democracy. It is the outward sign of the innate conflict between state and society. Far from being a spirit of brotherhood, it is the essence of social division.

The over-subtleties of phrase and thought in his criticism of Bauer betray an inward uncertainty or confusion still surviving. Do you get rid of injustice by abolishing religion, or do you get rid of religion by abolishing injustice? Marx had just crossed the border-line on his way between the first of these axioms and the second. Little whiffs from the former axiom continued to hang, occasionally, about his papers. Still, religion was no longer judged on its truth or otherwise. That was assumed. It was judged on its social and political and moral consequences.

Religion was a *moral* evil – that is evident as the theory is stripped to its skeleton. This came to take so large a place in Marx that historians have speculated on its origins. Could a man reach the sense that religion is immoral merely by studying the philosophy of Hegel and then reacting against it? Historians have looked for hidden, more personal motives. They have argued from the language of Marx that he still felt, deep in his soul, social deprivation of Jewish infancy. 'The criticism of religion', he wrote in this same *Introduction to the Critique of Hegel's Philosophy of Law*, 'ends with the teaching that man is the highest being for man, and hence with the absolute demand to overthrow all circumstances in which man is a debased, enslaved, abandoned, despicable being.' It has been suggested[13] that as a boy and youth Marx reacted against the self-demeaning excess of courtesy by his father towards their betters, against the self-deprecatory manner inherited from a long tradition of Jewish social disadvantage. Might this have affected his attitude to Christianity? In Marx's old age one of his daughters persuaded him to fill in a questionnaire which amid numerous enquiries asked 'which vice you detest most?'. Marx put down the word *servility*. Certainly the note of passion sounded when Marx touched the 'creatureliness' of man. What are the social principles of Christianity, he asked in an article of September 1847 in the *Deutsche-Brüsseler Zeitung* when he engaged with the theory of Christian Socialism. 'The social principles of Christianity preach cowardice, self-contempt, abasement, submission, dejection, in a word, all the qualities of the *canaille*; and the proletariat, not wishing to be treated as *canaille*, needs its courage, its self-consciousness, its pride, and its sense of independence more than its bread.'

'The social principles of Christianity are cringing, and the proletariat is revolutionary.'

'So much for the social principles of Christianity.'[14]

We hardly need the theory of reaction against family servility. Hoping for an academic career, and intellectually convinced of atheism, he lost his academic future when Bauer was dismissed; and the Prussian government, object of his criticism, pleaded 'the Christian State', united throne and altar, and was unusually outspoken, even among traditional governments, in claiming religious sanction for itself and its ordering of society by monarchy, oligarchy and Church.

So Marx found his chosen career blocked by 'the Christian State'; and then found himself an exile from it, in Brussels or Paris or finally London. He remained an academic theorist. But his private experience must have added something to his moral repudiation of the contemporary world. Attentive readers of his early writings notice a hostility to Judaism as a religion, as well as the conviction of all his people that religion can be married to social disadvantage and even social injustice. One theme of much of his scattered thoughts on religion is the incompatibility between religion and the *freedom* of a human being. Jewish ancestry and origin are not to be dismissed in accounting for the international cast of his mind, or for the profound sense of estrangement in the relations of the world.

The onslaught upon religion is not an intellectual assault or critique, like that of the Enlightenment or its heirs among the contemporaries of Marx. The question is not whether religion is true or untrue but whether it is desirable or undesirable for society. In the critique of Marx is a powerful element which may justly be termed anti-intellectual. This element grew upon him, for a decade, as he began to preach a doctrine of philosophical materialism, 'dialectical materialism' as it would be called by his successors. The religion with which the argument engaged was less doctrine or way of life than social phenomenon, caused inevitably by social phenomena of the past and made inevitably to vanish by social phenomena of the future. No need to argue against religion. Otiose to controvert its adherents. Religion was the outcome of a failing and historic social structure, which culminated in bourgeois and capitalist society. As the structure collapsed in the relentless process of history, religion must collapse simultaneously.

For all Marxist historians the social cause of secularization must be far weightier than any intellectual cause. The social changes are not so much the origins as the necessary context of the intellectual changes. Men's ideas, Marx was writing in *The German Ideology* of 1845–6, arise out of their material life-process. 'Morality, religion, metaphysics, all the rest of ideology and their corresponding forms of consciousness, no longer retain the semblance of independence. They have no history, no development; but men, developing their material production and their material intercourse, alter, along with this their real existence, their thinking and the products of their thinking.'[15] If we want to write the history of the human intelligence, we turn to the history of production. If we want to change men's ideas, or to dissolve their illusions, we shall not do it in preaching atheism, or in undermining their beliefs by philosophizing. We shall change their conditions of work and life. To make religion vanish, we need not science but social revolution.

In the theses on Feuerbach of 1845, Marx wrote of Feuerbach that his work consisted in dissolving the religious world into its secular foundation. But 'he overlooks the fact that after this work is completed, the chief thing is still to do'. 'What else', asked the *Communist Manifesto* rhetorically, 'does the history of ideas prove, than that intellectual production changes its character in proportion as material production is changed?' Later in life he modified this extreme anti-intellectual version of intellectual history, and some of his successors modified it further. But how integral it was to his outlook may be seen by the refusal to discriminate between religions. It is religion which is disappearing. Whether one religion might be different from another or contain more truth than another, did not interest Marx. The doctrines of any religion are not relevant to the theory.

This theory that production determines intellectual progress must not be taken too crudely. In various texts Marx stated it as theory. But when he analysed actual cases of intellectual or technological change in history, he looked for various causes like any historian, and was only unusual in the weight which he gave to social and economic causes. When he wanted to account for progress in culture, or progress in politics, he did not immediately resort to the simple solution of new machine, new invention, new mode of production. *Historical materialism* is a phrase which Marxists applied to his theory of history, but which does not universally fit the way in which he used history.

Marx was a great maker of epigrams, like *opium of the people*, and his epigrams gave his successors plenty of chance to mislead themselves. Theoretical statements could sweep all before them – 'Religion, family, state, law, morality, science, and art are only particular modes of production'.[16] The difficulty is that neither his practice, nor the full exposition of his mind, can be confined within so strait an epigram.

Engels gave an address in 1883 on the grave of Marx in Highgate. He summarized Marx's discovery, which he compared to Darwin's discovery in these terms – 'the elementary fact, hitherto concealed under a veil of ideological nonsense, that men, before they busy themselves with politics, science, art, religion, etc., must first eat, drink, clothe and house themselves; and therefore that the production of the means of life, and so the degree of economic development, constitute the foundation for all the institutions of the state – legal ideas, art, even religious ideas – and not the other way round.'[17]

Marx talked in these terms, more epigrammatically than Engels. But gradually he introduced a little more flexibility into the language – the mode of material production in general (*überhaupt*) conditions the development of social, political and intellectual life.

To introduce flexibility into the doctrine was necessary to Marxist thought. For in enquiring into the nature of religion, they had too strong a sense of history to force the history of religion into a rigid pattern which made its development hang exclusively upon economic development. To say that economic facts *condition* development was not to declare that religion was always created by a material situation of production. Their study of primitive agricultural religion, or of medieval Christianity, was not doctrinaire enough to conform to the canons of dialectical materialism. Both Marx and Engels saw the forces and mysteries of nature in the religious instincts of primitive man. The turning of tribal or national cults into monotheism was confessed to be linked with the new social powers of wider trade and wider production and wider sovereignty. But history established no direct parallel between economic development and religious development. Christianity, like all great movements of the human spirit, was the work of the masses. From the old saw that *Christianity was a religion of slaves*, Engels inferred that Christ conquered the Roman world because the slave-rebel Spartacus was defeated and killed. The slaves tried to liberate themselves by violent revolution and were crucified. So they turned to an otherworldly redemption and Christ swept the labouring classes.[18] The economic and social motive was always pushed to the forefront of the historical ideas. But it was never made exclusive, as if to conform to a crude theory of materialism.

Perhaps – the question, like so many questions about Marx, is a controversy among students of Marx – he should not be understood so sweepingly as his epigrams. Perhaps he is not saying that religion, or intellectual history, is nothing but the outline of a changing production of material things; and the *prima facie* case for believing that he did not intend this lies in the simple observation that it is untrue, and that no close student of men could ever believe it to be true. Perhaps he only said, what more and more historians after him said, that in explaining intellectual or religious changes we ought always to be conscious of the social and economic changes with which they are connected; and more than this, that any history of ideas, as conceived by Hegel, independent of the history of men who framed ideas, is a chimera. The language of Marx can be wrested to this more restricted interpretation of his doctrine of intellectual history. It is not the natural straightforward meaning of all his epigrams.

Hegel conceived the external world of matter as the expression of the inward developing idea. When Marx abandoned Hegel's idealism, he inverted the notion, and consciously stood Hegel upon his head. The inward idea is the expression of the external developing world of matter. The notion that intellectual history or religion is the outcome of material production was one way of stating his reaction against Hegel's idealism. It hardly corresponded to facts of history when he came to examine them. But it accounted for some facts of history which the historians often overlooked. Intellectual history is tied to social history. Men's habits, men's mode of living together, men's needs change; and in that change they seek a new picture of the world about them, a picture which cannot but be in part an intellectual and in part a religious picture of the world.

The word which henceforth marked him was the word *alienation*, *Entfremdung* (or sometimes *Entäusserung*). In the *Communist Manifesto* Marx condemned the way in which German socialists used the word – French socialists criticized the money system, and then Germans added rhetoric, 'philosophical nonsense' of phrases like *The Alienation of Humanity*. This condemnation misled many people into believing that it was not a word of which he later approved. Historians have sometimes contrasted the early Marx from the later, as though the idea was confined to his immature state of mind.

The *Economic and Philosophical Manuscripts* of 1844 caused a long debate on the theory of alienation, the continuity in the thought of Marx, the contrast between young Marx and mature Marx, the nature of Marxist revisionism, and the debt which Marx owed to Hegelian philosophy. The manuscripts are brief, fragmentary and obscure, obscure not only because they are fragmentary. The more coherent section discusses *alienated labour*. But for all the enigma and imprecision, they are argued powerfully. No reader can mistake that he deals with a mind seeking to penetrate a mystery of social life, with no desire to hoodwink either himself or others by phrase or by rhetoric. As with so many of his early works, Marx showed no interest in publication. He wrote them to 'clarify' his mind; but the word *clarify* is not quite right, for it suggests a making simple, whereas Marx attempted the impossible of a theory of the world in its full range of complexity. Society is never at rest to be studied. It is always in movement, always changing. The complexity of Marx rests in some small part upon his refusal to freeze society or make it stand still in his analysis. He aimed always to catch motion, relations, difference and yet continuity. This aim made Hegel difficult enough. It made the less systematic Marx more difficult still. And as a writer he is notorious for using words of which the meaning seems to slide about according to the context. Engels once said that these inconsistencies in terms were necessary in order to express his attempt at understanding. Perhaps they were, and perhaps they were not, but even if they were it makes the interpreter's task no easier.

The idea of alienation began among Jewish and Christian thinkers. Men have fallen from grace, are alienated from God. In Christian thought they are redeemed through Christ and made fellow-citizens of the household of God instead of strangers. Hegel seized upon the idea and made alienation and its overcoming central to his theory of man's progress both as individual and as social being. Bauer used it to attack religion. Feuerbach stood the notion on its head. Religion, instead of saviour from alienation, is vehicle of alienation, symbol and expression of the way in which man is divided from the real world. Feuerbach thought of God as alienated man.

Marx took the word and used it loosely; or, at least, its precise meaning must be judged more by context than by definition. It is used in Marx's thought from early to late. It began with a philosophical tinge, relic of some moral assertion about men's souls in an estranged world. But already in 1844 it was linked with his deepening study of political economy.

Amid the obscurity we can say that man is alienated from his environment, and from that environment under four different aspects –

from nature
from himself as a 'species-being', that is, from humanity
from other men, his neighbours
from himself.

(Later, by the time of the *Communist Manifesto*, Marx abandoned the second of these aspects because he ceased to believe in a humanity apart from individual men.) Alienation is a series of opposites – natural man made unnatural, species-man made separate, gregarious man made solitary, true individual made untrue. How do you get rid of these opposites? Hegel would have talked of philosophical synthesis. But Marx, still casting his mind in the language and partly in the thought of Hegel, turned to man as producer, maker of his world and of himself by labour. *Alienated labour* is the key to understanding alienation. The observer sees it at simplest when he finds how in a capitalist industry workers cannot enjoy their work. They are not even masters of their work but servants. The alienation which they experience in work is not due to the nature of the work, but to the system which makes them subjects of the work.

The structure of society derives from the work which men do. In bourgeois society the worker provides goods, to serve not the needs of men but the needs of the market. Then, instead of men controlling goods, goods control men; so that, the more workers produce, the wider the gap between rich and poor. This ill-arrangement may be called the 'alienation' of men's work. A man's work is 'natural', part of the structure of living. Therefore the alienation of his work creates an alienation of man from nature, from his fellow-worker, even from himself. Economic nonsense pushed all social relations awry. Men and women become things and treat each other like things.

By remorseless development of money men lost their 'true' needs, humane needs, needs which men ought to need because they are men. Money and property straiten them so that all needs are reduced to one need, the need to have, the need to own. This is why the state of the future, by abolishing private property, will restore human nature. It will take away the obsession to have and enable man again to want what as man he ought to want. Senses and perceptions, blinded or stunted in our system, will be released so that again they feel and perceive. Their capacities will be freed. They will be again themselves. Nature and man fell apart when man made barriers against nature. In the coming society man will again be natural, an unalienated person in the stream of natural progress. Marx never defined the society of the future. No more than a Christian heaven could its picture be painted. But it was seen by faith as a world below where a wanting man does not want what harms his fellow-men, and where no discord disturbs the harmonies between man and nature or man and his fellow-men.

Religion is the soul of alienation. Because society is awry, it creates religion; an unreality of relationships to compensate for intolerable reality. Religion is an expression of economic facts and mis-facts. To regard it as the cause of the false structure is to invert the real sequence. It issues from the false structure. But religion is not mere symptom, not triviality. It *formulates* alienation, and then conse-crates it by making it seem to be necessity, by ascribing to it permanence, by teaching that it is natural.

The first form of religious alienation is detachment. Religion wanted to deliver us from ourselves, to overcome our natural instincts, to suppress our passions, as though all these were not part of human nature; so that man is made to feel, and to appear, divided being, war between flesh and spirit, battlefield between con-science and wickedness; and therefore the detachment to which it calls is detachment of part of the self from another part of the self.

The second form of religious alienation is the divine justification of social evil. It compensates the poor for their lot in this life by promising them better things hereafter. It accepts the givenness of rich and poor, the schism of society into rulers and ruled, and only expresses the moral hope that the rich will behave with charity. It tells sufferers that their oppression is the just punishment of their sin, or a trial by which God leads them upward towards himself.[19] Heaven and hell are indispensable to class society, because they produce hope of imaginary justice later and thereby emasculate longings for real justice now. Resignation is indispensable to class society because it makes men accept, not only inevitable as inevitable, but remediable as irremediable, division as permanent, strife as natural.

In this context came the *opium of the people* text. Reality is salvation. Men conform themselves to their predicament by fantasy. Strip away illusion, let man see man as he is. But you will not stop the illusion by teaching. You must change conditions which make illusion compulsive.

Revolution therefore must be against religion because religion is a part – an essential part – of the social structure which revolution must overthrow. It must criticize religion as needful to show men reality. But it will not need to fight religion, because it will create a society free of alienation and so deprive religion of its root. In a society cured of alienation no one will want religion. In Marx is none of the militant atheism which you find in disciples like Lenin. This atheism is far sundered from atheism of the century before, which denounced Christianity because it could not believe it true. Yet Marx always held that the criticism of all society begins with criticism of religion. He wrote so little about religion that some readers have doubted whether it was important to him. It always remained at the root of his thought on alienation. Not only can we say, where religion there alienation. We can say, where alienation, religion is at the heart.

Marxism was the most powerful philosophy of secularization in the nineteenth century. Its power lay not only in the unforeseeable sequence of events which came after, the Paris Commune, the impact of the Commune upon the International, the German socialists, and the growth of a revolutionary party in Russia. Its power was intrinsic: the systematic and original exposition of a theory of secular society, based partly upon philosophical axioms and partly upon theories of contemporary economics.

Like all seminal thinkers Marx had the gift of raising his writing above the controversy in which he happened at any moment to be engaged. Almost all his books and pamphlets issued out of a controversial, often a passionate, debate. At no time in his life did he fail in the duty to controvert somebody. But within the debate he was always able to point towards fundamental principles of social enquiry. Though he occasionally stated these crudely and almost always stated them obscurely, he never ceased to attempt to show why men erred when their theories were seen against axioms on which, at least according to Marx, they ought to be working. Sometimes this looks like the celebrated device of academics when, arguing upon an obscure point of the agenda, they seek to show how all history leads towards the precise policy which they advocate. But for most of the time it was more than this. It was an attempt always to go beyond the superficial and to grapple with underlying issues as he saw them.

Religion, for or against, is often passion, or used to be passion. By this half-Hegelian half-economic route, he arrived at an Olympian theory, where religion did not even need controverting.

2

Certain eminent theorists or historians saw Marxism as a new kind of religion, a Christian heresy. If that were right, we should have a case, not of movement from sacred to denial of sacred, but from sacred to another form of sacred; as once Christianity came among Jews of the dispersion and caused them to think it the fulfilment of Judaism, and so altered the history of mankind from one religion to another while the two religions yet stood in relation of child and parent. When we study the development of the idea of the secular, we keep running into the apparent paradox, that in so many respects the idea seems to owe its ancestry to certain aspects of the Christian tradition as Christianity tried to answer the needs of changing society. If Marxism were seen as a new form of religion it would be the most prominent example of this attribution of the secular to a Christian inheritance.

The case for this view might be put like this:

1. For all his attack on Hegel, for all his attack on theoretical philosophy, Marx never ceased to be marked by Hegelian forms of thought. The more the early writings are studied the more impossible it becomes to disentangle his thought from the heritage of Hegel. Since Hegel's philosophy is unthinkable without the double background in Christianity and the Enlightenment, it is impossible to deny Marx roots in the western tradition of thought, impossible to suppose that he could have appeared in any context except that which we loosely call Christendom.

2. For all his severity to French utopian socialists, even to Proudhon, he received from them the message of a working-class yearning for freedom and soon ripe for freedom, to be achieved only by the total reconstruction of society and therefore by revolution. These French socialists were far from being Catholic. Some of them, Proudhon above the others, made bitter onslaughts upon the Catholic Church. But they derived their moral stance, and something explicit in their moral argument, from appeals to Christian principles.

3. To think of Marxism as ethic is odd when many Marxists, including Lenin, exposed ethics as disguise for self-interest. 'Communists', wrote Marx in *The German Ideology* of 1845, 'preach no morality at all.' They do not urge men to self-sacrifice because they know that under conditions of the present system selfishness is the only means of survival. They say, change the system, and men will want to be unselfish.[20] But this is faith in a future ethic; and the motive of changing the system is nothing if it is not ethical. The Marxist social philosophy is ineradicably moral in intention, for all protestations to the contrary. Capitalism is condemned, not because rich men are rich and poor men are poor, but because it 'sanctifies', or cloaks, injustice, by turning some free men into slaves and other free men into tyrants. The economic system is arraigned in a court of law where at least half the charge, and that the half passionately held by the accuser, is moral. A man of books, Marx knew of men from books, and in his earlier years theorized over men on the basis of books. The academic lived in his tower of detachment. His moral concern has sometimes been charged with being concern for

abstractions, structure, groups, proletariat but not concern for Tom and Dick. But we cannot reduce the moral content by claiming that it is only general, still less by inferring necessary descent from him of a ruthless Stalinist collectivism in which he would have suffered by being last to conform.

4. Alienation was an idea taken directly from Christian vocabulary. The world is awry. Christians taught that it could come right only by Christ, would come finally right only in a future kingdom, and would always as this world remain under God's judgment. Marx taught that it could come right here and soon, by relentless developments in economics and society which must beget a classless and unalienated society. Nothing is common between these two contradictory doctrines, for even the language – a word like alienation – is used in different contexts and therefore different senses. But the world is awry and shall be redeemed – that at least is no irreligious idea. The whole idea of alienation is unthinkable without Christian and Jewish axioms, and the coming of its cure is sometimes expressed in terms which bear the scent of older language of redemption.

5. Marx taught his readers to feel the relentless and meaningful purpose working itself out through history, not against man's will but by means of man's endeavour, and yet determined for man by long and deep forces in society which no individual could resist. Marxist determinism was like Calvinist predestination in not overthrowing individual will or responsibility, and yet in making the actor powerful because he knew himself to be in the stream flowing towards that which must come.

6. Marxism had an eschatology, a vision of a future to come when we put the world to rights, defined with no more precision than the vision of a new Jerusalem, but apocalyptic in its force because it comes, must come, comes soon, cannot long delay.

7. To these points of doctrine had been added feelings. Here we have a body of thought based upon axioms which are only in a measure rational, structured with doctrine, and evoking faith and discipleship among its adherents. It is perhaps metaphorical, but seems to be no contradiction in terms to call a man 'a devout Marxist'. The enthusiasm of a convert can display the same sensations and effects as the enthusiasm of a proselyte in religion. It is not to be doubted that some of these instincts in human beings which religion satisfies are satisfied by Marxism. Religion without a god may still be religion.

If this view is taken, it casts doubt upon my present thesis, that Marxist theory is the most influential of all symbols for the process of secularization in the nineteenth century. It is not a view which I share. Because atheism has or can have religious origins, that does not warrant us in counting it religion. But what name we ascribe to an apprehension of the world is less important. If we contrast a former generation we cannot doubt that something drastic has occurred. Feuerbach had no god but was a religious man. Marx, who owed much to Feuerbach's theory, had no god but was not a religious man. A Russian refugee, who met him in his old age, reported a letter in which Marx used language most unusual for him. He was said to have written that *The religion of working men is religion without god because it seeks to restore the divinity of man.* The letter was not published until 1933, the original has never been produced;[21] and until further evidence we must think that a text so unlike the rest of the thought of Marx, in calling atheism a religion, is at the least a paraphrase and possibly a mistaken report. The language of the alleged letter could easily come from the mind of Feuerbach, but not from the mind of Marx. The change in attitude to religion is too transforming. 'If socialist writers ascribe a world-role to the proletariat', he wrote in *The Holy Family,* 'that is not, as critics pretend to believe, because they consider the proletariat to be gods. On the contrary.' That is one of several texts in this sense. Marx used religious language to describe non-religious processes, especially during his earlier years. He liked analogies drawn from religion or religious history. (The state as 'mediator', bureaucracy as 'jesuitical' or 'clericalist', democracy is to other constitutions as Christianity is to other religions, etc.) The force of all these comparisons needs more study. They remain nothing but conscious analogies.

3

Friedrich Engels wrote more about religion than Marx. He was communist before Marx, atheist not quite so early, though he also came to atheism by way of Bruno Bauer and Feuerbach and the Young Hegelians of Berlin. But no Jewish family background affected his attitude. Engels was the child of a devout middle-class family of the Wuppertal who believed every word of the Bible to be true and was sent to schools in Barmen and Elberfeld where the spirit of pietism reigned. We possess a devout and sincere Christian poem from him when he was sixteen or seventeen.[22] At eighteen he was sent to a house of business in Bremen to learn trade. From the time at Bremen are preserved a series of letters which he wrote to two brothers Graeber who were training to be pastors.[23]

These letters sometimes have the sadness of a man floundering as he finds that the faith of childhood is smashed and he must seek truth to set in its place. Personally he was forced to express independence of the narrow outlook of the home. Then a reading of *The Life of Jesus* by Strauss shattered his inherited axioms about the Bible. For a time he regarded Strauss as the mind of the age ('I only know one of our contemporaries to equal him in mind, force and courage'[24]) who brought light into intellectual chaos. For a time he tried to restate his personal religion with the aid of Strauss and ideas of myth. The debate in his mind took the inevitable form of a controversy between orthodox obscurantism and the free rights of reason. For a time he admired the religion of religious experience, and read in old mystical authors. But Strauss led him inevitably, as he directed so many others, to his own master Hegel. In November 1839 Engels told Graeber that he was on the point of becoming a Hegelian; and so he came to Berlin, the Young Hegelians, and Feuerbach. He refused finally to admit himself atheist until 1842. Why not, like so many radical thinkers among his contemporaries, like Comte or Feuerbach or Proudhon, think of a new religion to replace the old – perhaps a pantheism – perhaps a cult of humanity – perhaps a cult of work? It would not do. He was educated in pious religion of rare devotion and knew that it could not stand. Further quest for a true religion was doomed. 'All the possibilities of religion are exhausted' he wrote in 1844.[25] 'After Christianity, after the absolute and abstract religion, after religion "as such", no other religion could come. Carlyle sees that Christianity, whether Catholic or Protestant, declines irresistibly. If he knew the nature of Christianity, he would see that after Christianity no other religion is possible.'

The mental voyage of Engels, therefore, owed nothing to social impetus. He was the educated middle-class young man troubled intellectually by the new knowledge and the intellectual freedom of a world for which his childhood had not prepared him. No such problem could ever be purely intellectual, and we cannot neglect the need to assert an independence of a particular kind of home. But the problem as such was intellectual – the truth of the four gospels and the consequence of no longer knowing all of them to be true in all parts. Though Engels was a communist before he was an atheist, the intellectual quest came long before the social quest. Hindsight has seen in his attitudes to the Wuppertal workers the seed of a later communist. Phrases of his anonymous articles against pietism, *The Letters from Wuppertal*, has led to this theory – as when he calls the Wuppertal 'the true Jerusalem of the most hateful form of pietism which flourishes in various parts of Germany and saps the vitality of the people'; pietists as 'the employers who treat their employees worst'. But, again, a social attack was being used as stick to beat a religious group of which he now disapproved. Repudiation of pietism was in no direct way linked to rise of social conscience.

4

The approach of Engels to atheism was not the same as that of Marx and the arguments which the two employed to defend or advocate atheism were not the same arguments. It could not be otherwise when the one started as liberal convert from Judaism and the other as illiberal pietist. But the knowledge of their differences makes the student suspect any theory of an automatic sequence of logic from communism to twilight of the gods.

Marxism is a world-outlook into which, by design of its creator, is built self-criticism. Therefore it is as possible to write the history of the development of doctrine in Marxism as it is in Christianity. And within the generation of non-Russian Communists after Stalin's death, new young Marxists did not begin with the anti-religious prejudices inherited from the postures of the nineteenth century. Without wishing to baptise their philosophy they were less unwilling to listen to questions which religious men asked. Most of them still felt, as Lenin felt, that anyone who moved towards religion moved away from the truth about men and society. But their minds, or some of their minds, were not, like their predecessors' minds, sealed.

The old Marxism was at once a system of faith and an intelligent mode of diagnosing social ills. The circumstances in which it was born united the dogmas to the diagnosis and made them seem identical; rather as Christians once identified the rightness of their ethical system with precise adherence to the Athanasian creed. The old generation was more prone to blind faith in a Marxist world-outlook, to a simple and crude adherence to a series of bald propositions. The newer generations were readier to see the complexities of humanity, which metaphysicians once sought to express, and therefore to be sceptical or neglectful of the quasi-metaphysical axioms which they inherited, and to turn to treat the Marxist tradition more as a social tool than a body of dogma. Such a change may be ascribed, in part, to the fear of metaphysical propositions which mark the philosophers of the middle twentieth century. It may also be ascribed to the opening of minds, to a less blinkered sight of human beings.

So far as the new Marxism thought of itself first as a tool for the ordering of society, it made possible a dialogue with religious men. To the post-Christian age not all Marxist propositions appeared equally momentous in Marxist theories of society.

Some of these propositions are indeed important to any understanding of what happened to the churches in the nineteenth century. Churches, being of man and therefore made of the dust of the earth as well as the breath of the divine, are always entangled with the culture and structure of their age; and when the culture and structure of an age is shattered by new economic and/or new intellectual conditions, churches are liable to be shattered with the rest of the social structure. The working-man was going to become a standard-bearer of social progress. He was going to be less idealized than Marx sometimes imagined, but through him lay the road towards a classless society, or at least a non-hierarchical society. In the sense of relentless march onwards towards the light, which Marxism gave him, he was to have little or no sense of using the churches. His attitude to religion might be friendly or favourable or hostile; religion he could use; churches he hardly felt that he could use. The social movement of the nineteenth century would drive a wedge between religion and the traditional societies which religion enshrined and created.

All this was of the first importance in Marx. But there is one proposition which the hindsight of history disproves.

They had a vision; and in its manner, and for all its queer shapes, it was a vision of beauty and, it may be, at least in part, a vision of truth. But there was an untruth in it, perhaps more than one, but at least one untruth; namely that the vision expected fulfilment round the next corner. The next corner came, and then the corner after next, and then the corner next after next; and still the vision eluded their grasp. Some few were tempted to believe it a mirage, but others knew that their sight was authentic insight and therefore that they must press onwards, adjusting only their scale of time. But in adjusting their scale of time, they found that they adjusted more in their understanding of the world than their scale of time. Am I speaking of early Christians, or of Marxists of the nineteenth century and after?

For with the readjustment of time, was disproved a proposition about religion. Historical hindsight showed as groundless the belief that religion is the reflexion or symbol of an alienated society and will vanish away with the social structures which gave it birth. This proposition appears to be, not merely groundless, but no necessary part of a communist theory of society.

Marx himself would have flatly denied that it was no necessary part of his theory. He believed it to be the heart. And the question arises, whether it was central only to Marx's mind because he was Marx and because he had the personal and intellectual history which was Marx's; or whether, in the predicament of Europe in the middle nineteenth century, it was a belief central to the process of emancipating the working-man.

A great historical process does not depend upon the choices or minds of single individuals, however eminent or however original. Such minds give new impetus or new expression to stages in a process of social development and public opinion which far transcends the isolated contribution even of a genius. The Reformation would have happened without Luther. But without Luther it would not have happened in the way it happened. And since the entire protest focussed itself upon the protest of a single monk, the nature of Luther's protest helped to colour and articulate the nature of the general protest. Though it was necessary that the Reformation came, it was not necessary that justification by faith should be so explosive an idea in the way it came. To Luther's experience the moment in the tower at Wittenberg was central; and because Luther was central to the Reformation, the text *the just shall live by faith* became the ground of Christian reform.

The parallel raises a question for our subject. The rise of the working-man, urbanized and industrialized, depended not at all upon Marx. But because Marx provided an explanation, less superficial than any other explanation offered until then, of what was happening; and because of the Paris Commune and its aftermath – Marx became, for large numbers of German working-men, as identified with their hope for the future, as Luther had been identified with the hope of reform.

The question to which I have tried to lead is the question whether the irreligious character of the working-class movement was essential to its nature, derived from roots deeper than any to which we have yet penetrated; or whether this irreligious character was in a manner as 'accidental' to the historical process as justification by faith was 'accidental' to the Reformation; accidental not in the sense of being a thing of the surface only (for it permeated the process), but in the sense of depending on the experience of men who for quite other reasons stood at the heart of the process, or who were believed by many to offer a true diagnosis of what was happening.

Putting the question in a sharp form: was Marxism anti-religious because Marx and Engels were anti-religious? Or was their anti-religion an expression of an anti-religion which in no way depended upon their private views, but was (in some way still mysterious) necessary to the social aspirations of the working class? A reliable answer to that question would make a difference to the possibility of fruitful dialogue between Christians and Marxists of the present day. And from our point of view, it would help us to see our way into one of the most difficult of all problems in social as well as religious history.

In 1874 Engels[26] quoted the case of a Spanish disciple of Bakunin who maintained that it was against all Socialism to believe in God, but that the Virgin Mary was a different matter, every good Socialist should believe in her. Even if the man was as legendary as he sounds, the story forces upon the mind the same puzzling question. A lot of the working-men of the nineteenth century had religious experience and neither the world nor human nature could change overnight. How did it come about, that despite the natural and agelong inheritance, it should seem to be necessary to good Socialism, focussing so many of the aspirations of the working classes, to accept a metaphysical doctrine, the non-existence of God, which at first sight had nothing to do with Socialism?

5

The word *reaction*, as applied to politics, was a word of the nineteenth century. In the 1860s and 1870s we find propagandists talking of 'the reactionary nature of Christianity'. This feeling, that God was on the side of oppressors, how widespread was it? In Bruno Bauer, and then in Marx and Engels, atheism and social reconstruction became in course of time inseparable. How far was the link due to the particular views of a group of Young Hegelians in Berlin, and how far was it necessary to the social conditions of western Europe in that age?

Communism was not atheistic in origin. In November 1843 Engels published a little essay called 'The Progress of Social Reform on the Continent'.[27] He surveyed socialists of western lands and found curious differences according to nation. English socialists usually attacked religion and suffered from the prejudices of a Christian people. French Communists, though citizens of a nation famous for begetting free-thinkers, were Christians, and appealed to the Bible and the sharing of the early Christians in common property. German Communists, headed by their founder, Wilhelm Weitling, likewise appealed to Scripture, and stood close in outlook and sympathy to the French. This religious appeal of early German Communists puzzled Engels, for he keeps referring to it. One of their favourite axioms he reported adversely, *Christianity is Communism.* He tried to account for it by remembering that the French word *religion* had not so much the sense of *going to church* as of conviction or feeling.[28] He visited a club of Communists in Paris and was introduced by a Russian. 'These people ... say God is a secondary matter, and can work with us on all practical schemes, saying "Well, atheism is your religion".' Engels came back, with surprise, to this phrase of French Communists, *atheism is your religion.* He spent the years 1842 to 1844 in England, learning not only about the condition of the working classes but about the teaching and practice of Robert Owen and his socialist disciples. He studied various groups of 'Christian Communists', usually small puritan and eccentric groups stemming ultimately from the Anabaptist tradition of the Reformation. During the winter of 1844 to 1845 he even wrote an essay on these groups of communist Anabaptists and published it.[29] He aimed to answer critics who accused communist society of being a wild and impracticable dream. It was neither wild nor impracticable, for it existed already and worked in various places and among various peoples. Most of them belonged to Christian sects. Their beliefs, wrote Engels with natural dogmatism but implausible history, have nothing to do with their communism. If anything these beliefs in God must make communist society more difficult to achieve. If these religious groups achieved it, how much easier will it be for men whose minds are free from the restraint of their beliefs? And the student of the communist groups sees how they live at a higher standard while they do less work, have more leisure to develop their minds, and behave more morally than their neighbours who have property.

Here was direct connexion by way of example between Christian sects with common property and the first ideas of a communist

75

reconstruction of society. The creed of the Christians was conceived to be irrelevant, even harmful. What mattered was their proof that men could be happy, happier, without private property. Engels, disciple of Strauss who overturned the truth of the gospels, could never appeal to the Bible for texts to defend communism. But he could and did appeal to the example of men who did appeal to the Bible.

Almost at the same time as he made this study of sects in the old Anabaptist tradition, he published the article,[30] already referred to, on continental socialism which he wished to explain to English-speaking socialist readers. He singled out Saint-Simon, whose school 'shone like a meteor' in the sky, for a moment, and had now vanished; Fourier, more scientific than Saint-Simon but still mystical; Cabet and his 'Icarian Communism', which has gained the allegiance of 'the great bulk of the French working classes'; Lamennais and Proudhon, the last because he defined property as theft. For all their diversity these French apocalyptic movements had common characteristics. Their appeal took various forms, some bizarre, some self-contradictory. But they invariably combined three elements; an apocalyptic belief that the Kingdom of God could be brought to this earth; a belief that all institutions must be reconstructed to that end; and an appeal to the Bible and primitive Christianity as the authority for reconstruction. 'Religion', wrote Saint-Simon in his *Nouveau Christianisme*,[31] 'must guide society to the great end of bettering as quickly as possible the lot of the very poor.' Luther might have told the popes and cardinals that they had explained the faith enough, the preparatory work was done, now they had the greater and more satisfying work of organizing the human race after the fundamental principle of God's righteousness.

Cabet stood much nearer than Saint-Simon or Fourier to the French working class, and the attitudes of his group were less coherent. But they conformed to the common characteristics of these early French social reformers. 'You can even say', wrote Cabet,[32] 'that communism is a true religion; for there is no religion which unites men more than the doctrine of brotherly love or fraternity... Perhaps you could even say that nothing is more essentially religious than communism.' Cabet looked with unusual attention at the primitive Christian community, decided that Jesus was an Essene and that Essenes held property in common. 'I add this: according to Jesus, the apostles and the Fathers of the Church, Christianity cannot exist without communism. No one can be called a Christian who is not a Communist.' The Kingdom of God which Jesus came to establish is not in heaven, as afterwards priests taught wickedly, but here.

The German Communists were not different. Moses Hess converted Engels to communism during 1841; and Hess identified the triumph of radical socialism with a new Jerusalem to be created in western Europe, an opinion which under the influence of Marx suffered vicissitudes, but which was at last sublimated when he became one of the earliest founders of Zionism. Wilhelm Weitling,[33] the tailor from Magdeburg, was regarded by Engels as the founder of German communism, and like the French believed that *Christianity is Communism*, and that the reconstruction of society was the coming of the Son of Man in judgment. Engels called his message 'the new gospel'. In 1845 Weitling published *The Gospel of a Poor Sinner*, in which (not for the first time, but important in the series of such representations) Jesus appeared as a Communist. One of Weitling's poems for children has become famous:

> I am a Communist small.
> Because my Lord's no call
> For money, then I ought
> In faith to ask for nought.
> I am a Communist child.
> Strong in my faith so mild,
> Because my God I know
> To the Workers' League I go.[34]

Weitling was in the Anabaptist tradition, and consciously appealed to the revolutionary chiliasts in the age of the Reformation. Sometimes the old sectarian tradition overlapped curiously with the new aims of barely conscious workers in modern industry.

To represent Jesus as a Communist was not new when Weitling wrote. Extremists in the French Revolution talked of the *sansculotte* Jesus. But Weitling, without the glory of the literary style of a Lamennais, had a fire which imparts to *The Gospel of the Poor Sinner* something of the strange emotions of Lamennais's *Words of a Believer*.

He called it a gospel written by a sinner. 'Come, all ye who work and are poor and depressed and oppressed. If you want freedom and justice for all mankind, this gospel will give you new courage and new hope.' What gospel? Trust not those who tell you that all will be well in the future world. We hope that all will be well in this world. 'We do not hope for pie in the sky and eternal life while nothing gets better here below. We hope that this life will change and get better soon.' 'Lamennais, and before him Karlstadt, Thomas Münzer and others, showed how all democratic ideas sprang from Christianity. Religion must not be destroyed, but used to free humanity...Christ is a prophet of freedom.' It was no gospel of miracles, no gospel which minded contradictions in the Bible text. Jesus was an Essene with a revolutionary aim, to overthrow the Roman and priestly authorities and institute community of goods; St Luke 6.20 and 24, 'Blessed are ye poor for yours is the kingdom of God.' 'Woe to you that are rich now. . .' The early Christians sold all their property and lived in common. Religious feeling, wrote Weitling in his conclusion, 'can be put to powerful use in the service of communism'.

The religious element present in early Communists like Weitling was a sign that the working classes possessed at least residual religiosity. A little of the appeal was directed towards middle-class sympathies. But most of it was aimed at working people in industry. From the manner in which communist evangelists framed their appeals, it looks as though, by 1848, most labourers were friendly to religion and critical of churches; friendly to religion especially as basis of morality and foundation of social justice, critical of the churches because they did not look as though they stood upon the side of social justice and therefore because some of their teaching was erroneous.

To see a chain of cause and effect is to go too far. Communism as a word was derived from a Christian memory and authority. Its first vague beginnings were part of a long heritage of Christian discontent. But it only began to be made precise when thinkers who rejected Christianity seized upon it as the word which expressed their hope for social reconstruction. Marx and Engels did not develop a seed which they found. They took an existing word, deconsecrated it, and made it a name for a new system of social thought. But they made their communism out of philosophical theory, not (yet) out of economic theory. Marx and Engels both identified themselves as communists before Marx began his long enquiry into the economic base of society.

Weitling, however, showed how there were motives of prudence for emphasizing the Christianity of communism. Like the Chartists in England and Cabet in France, Weitling saw that the fundamental appeal to the worker was a moral appeal and therefore a religious appeal, morality being inseparable from religion in European society as then constituted. Men attacked communism as immoral and un-Christian. Its defenders must show how it was an authentic outcome of Christian truth. *The Gospel of the Poor Sinner* was intended to show the world that this workers' movement stood upon texts of the Scriptures. But no one could use the Bible so passionately as Weitling used it, without being sincere in total commitment to both Christianity and communism. Among German Communists, among English Chartists and among French Utopians, the two attitudes to the churches lay together, sometimes in clear rigid opinion, sometimes confused and mixed, but always present: first, churches are middle-class affairs, and parts of Christianity are the weakness of the churches (hell, miracles, garden of Eden, etc.), and therefore we can attack Christianity to weaken the institutions which depend upon it. Secondly, to gain our objectives we need the help of sympathetic members of the middle class, and especially we need to appeal to their moral insight, and therefore we seek to show how the workers' programme represents their better moral and religious convictions.

The one school sought to demolish the Bible as a step to demolishing churches; the other to show how unfaithful to the Bible were the churches. The one school accused Christians of following, the other of not following, Christ. Only Marx stood aloof; much nearer the first group than the second, but convinced that Christianity would not fall by intellectual attack but for quite other reasons.

The feeling that atheism and socialism were akin was very slow to win the European working-man, and probably it never won more than a relatively small number of dedicated theorists or preachers. Its advance coincided largely with the acceptance of Marxist theory. But it did not depend on Marxist theory, for we find it among labour programmes in both England (very slight) and France (strong), and in neither country was Marxism very powerful.

6

Marx wrote in German, and was understood by Germans, though he was too intellectual a theorist to be understood by ordinary German workers. Until after 1870 Lassalle was more influential than Marx. Lassalle was himself killed in a duel over a love-affair during 1864; but his ideas, in which Hegelian idealism continued to flourish, lived on among his followers and contained more than a touch of old Utopianism with its religious appeal to communism. In the year 1873 it chanced that Lassalle's birthday 11 April fell on Good

Friday, and the leading article of the Lassallean newspaper *Neuer Social-Demokrat*, number 43, was headed 'Death and Resurrection and made comparisons between the one Messiah and the other. In Stuttgart the Social Democratic evangelist Dreesbach shocked Christian ears at a public hall by claiming the Sermon on the Mount as the foundation of socialism. The Lassallean press continued from time to time to cla'm Christ as a Communist.[35] The newspaper *Neuer Social-Demokrat* called the hill, where many Paris Communards were shot, a Golgotha, and was prosecuted in the court for blasphemy but acquitted. The Marxist wing of the movement was not pleased with this use of religious language.

For already the Marxist stream of thought in German socialism was growing, especially after the publication of *Capital* in 1867. In 1869 August Bebel and Wilhelm Liebknecht, both Marxists, founded at Eisenach the Social Democratic Party. The newspaper of this wing of the movement was the *Volkstaat*. By 1872–3 the rival newspapers and speakers clashed over rival programmes or philosophies (universal suffrage as the panacea or not, revolution by political act or by economic inevitability, the place of trade unions, etc) and among them the link between socialism and religion. *Volkstaat* denounced these religious comparisons between Christ and Lassalle – 'Christ, if he ever lived, which is doubtful, was as little a socialist as Lassalle was a Christian.' 'The humility that blesses its enemies and rebukes resistance and lets itself be crucified has as little in common with the wild revolutionary pride of the proletarian as a chairman's wand with the powder-blackened guns of the heroes of the Paris Commune.' 'With the last Christian the last slave shall be free.'[36]

During the 1870s, the Social Democrats were a relatively small and extreme party and gathered adherents by noise. August Bebel their leader committed himself to Marxism in 1868. By 1871 he was making blood-curdling assaults upon God and religion, both in the Reichstag and on political platforms. 'If we bury heaven and its authority', said Bebel in the Reichstag on 17 June 1872, 'then earthly authority soon collapses, and the consequences will be republicanism in politics, socialism in economics, atheism in religion.' During his months in prison in 1872–3 he devoted his time to educating himself in Marx, and Darwin, and Büchner's materialism, and Dühring, and Lassalle, and Buckle's *History* which, he tells us, 'captivated' him most of all.[37] He came out convinced that to make workers socialists you must make them atheists. His speeches were directed as much at men of compromise in his organization as at the middle class.

During 1874 there was therefore hot argument whether Christianity and socialism had anything in common. *Volkstaat* assailed those who claimed that men of the red flag were 'true' Christians as guilty of folly and cowardice.[38] It issued an epigram which became famous – 'Christianity and socialism are as against each other as fire and water.'[39] Bebel took up the cry in a pamphlet against the Catholic chaplain Hohoff. *Volkstaat* piled up the contrasts – trust in God versus trust in the self, ideal of service versus ideal of independence, world-renunciation versus world-acceptance, working to win heaven versus working to win bread, a vale of tears versus a home of happiness. This cry was welcome to church leaders trying to prevent their members from sliding away into working-class movements. It was taken up by the chaplain Hohoff, by the militant Protestant pastor Richard Schuster, and by others. Germany was sufficiently Christian to make it an easy weapon to discredit the young Social Democratic Party. But Bebel and several of his colleagues were not moved by the arguments that these attacks lessened the general appeal of the party.

In 1874 the Lassallean and Marxist wings of the Party agreed to unite, and in 1875 adopted the Gotha programme, a political platform which was unwelcome to Marx and others for its compromises. The Gotha programme incorporated the phrase *religion is a man's private concern*. The phrase had the merit that it could be interpreted variously. Members of the Party could argue that it left them free to be as religious as they liked, and sanctioned the view that a man could be at once a good Socialist and a good Christian. But the context of the clause was more negative. Bebel and his men preferred to see it as a statement that religion should be eradicated not only from public life but from public influence. In 1875 they were still in the full tide of their assault upon Christianity and clericalism. Their extremism in this as in other respects was not diminished when Bismarck made socialism illegal by the law of 1878, a ban which did as much as any other external act to encourage Marxist thought in the leadership of the party; in the same year, as part of his attempt at reconciliation with Germany, Pope Leo XIII by the bull *Quod Apostolici Muneris* condemned socialism, communism and nihilism as incompatible with Catholicism. For a decade the bull made life more difficult for pious Catholics who on political or social grounds wanted to associate with the Social Democratic Party.

By 1891 the atmosphere changed. The party was again legal. It was a wide-based party, returning many members to the Reichstag, with a broad appeal to popular support, and needing the alliance of Catholic peasant voters for its political ends. Over revolutions and social policy, it became of necessity a more central and progressive party. New moderation was reflected in ideas of the compatibility or incompatibility between Socialism and Christianity.

In 1891 the Party Congress at Erfurt readopted the clause *religion is a man's private concern.* But the negative overtone was in part lost, and it was frequently understood to mean that any man who wished to practise his religion was free to do so. Members who did not share these views saw how the party lost by crude onslaughts upon religion. Wilhelm Liebknecht said at the Halle Congress of 1890, 'Instead of squandering our strength in a struggle with the Church and sacerdotalism, let us go to the root of the matter. We desire to overthrow the class state. When we have done that, the Church and sacerdotalism will fall with it, and in this respect we are much more radical and much more definite in purpose than our opponents, for we like neither the priests nor the anti-priests.' 'Those among us who declare war on religion...do but strengthen the enemy.'[40]

At first sight it looked as though socialism and irreligion had been united; as if in Germany a situation prevailed such as would have prevailed in Britain if the Labour Party in its origins officially adopted an irreligious philosophy. In the catalogue of the library of the socialist newspaper *Vorwärts*, Bebel's pamphlet *Christianity and socialism* had this note appended: 'Very suitable for distribution to the masses, especially in Catholic countries.'[41] But after Erfurt in 1891 Bebel and his disciples could not carry the body of the movement in their sense.

At party congresses motions against religion kept being proposed. But they kept failing for lack of support, kept failing because their backers were but a handful. At Berlin in 1892 it was proposed that every candidate for Parliament must give an undertaking that he had left the Church – but the motion found no seconder. At Cologne in 1893 appeared motions to alter the clause *religion is a man's private concern*; to delete it, or to substitute some such phrase as *religion and its doctrines must be fought everywhere that they oppose the progress of knowledge or try to keep men in political or economic slavery* – the motions were discussed by two speakers and Congress then insisted on passing to the next business. The delegate

Katzenstein attacked Bebel – 'The reporting throughout Germany of Bebel's speech on the state of the future has been harmful to us because of its ending: "We leave heaven to the angels and the sparrows." No! We leave heaven to those who have faith in it. Many a comrade has felt himself run cold in his inward religious feeling at hearing these words' [Protests from the audience]. At Munich in 1902 a delegate demanded that, to prepare for the next election, party workers should try to emancipate voters from religion, especially in Catholic areas. He needed twenty votes to get onto the agenda and got two.

Here is a speech made by the delegate Fendrich, at the Party Congress of Hanover in 1899:

A delegate has made an attack on a fundamental article of the Party – our honourable comrade Bebel. [The article that *religion is a man's private concern*]. . .Bebel said yesterday 'The bourgeoisie is as atheist as any of us.' I refuse to be taken for an atheist. This has nothing to do with the party (Bebel interrupted: 'I wasn't thinking of you.'). . .We have continually to suffer from these personal opinions expressed by Comrade Bebel speaking as an official representative of the party. Only the other day there was a court case at Karlsruhe when the president said clergymen might lawfully warn their flocks against Social Democrats because it is proved that the party fights religion. For such people the personal opinions of Bebel, contradictory to article 6 of our party programme, are naturally very welcome. I demand that in future he abstain from such attacks on the fundamental principles of the party. [Cries of '*very good*'.]

Bebel did not repent. 'They tell us not to attack religion', he said at the same Congress. 'I tell you we do too little, not too much.' Yet the complaints kept coming in that such rabid speeches undid years of patient propaganda.

The atmosphere within the party remained very different from the atmosphere of any other socialist party except the less important Socialist Party in France.

Just before the end of the century two pastors joined the Social Democratic Party. They were both exceptional. One was Christoph Blumhardt, an excitable Swabian chiliast who looked, long before his time, for reconciliation between Marxism and Christianity. The other was Pastor Paul Goehre, who had already a name as a theological student when he worked in a factory and published his experience as *Three Months in a Workshop*.[42] The adhesion of two pastors to the Party caused a sensation. That makes a contrast with Britain because British priests or pastors were often Socialist and if they lost some members of their congregation gained others. Goehre explained to the Chemnitz Socialists how it was that he, though a pastor, joined the party, and afterwards printed the speech.[43] It is curious:

I declare at once, first, that even as member of the party, I have no intention of ceasing to be a Protestant Christian, as I understand it; that as a Social Democrat I will remain Christian in my understanding of Christianity. I rely on the party programme: *Religion is a man's private concern.* I know that this will elicit a smile of disdain on the faces of more than one of my new political friends. My religious attitude will be thought by them a blemish, a survival of my past, a broken egg-shell from the past. . .I have in perpetuity stripped myself of my functions as pastor. I see in the Social Democratic Party only a political party.

He promised he would only speak of his religious opinions if they were attacked, or if he were directly invited to expound.

Apart from that they will remain private to me. And no misgiving shall take them away. I have the absolute conviction of finding myself, in religion, on a better road than a good number of my new party comrades.

It is impossible to imagine such a speech being made by a minister in England or Scotland. The reason appears to be, less a difference in the psychology of the worker than in the attitudes of the socialist leaders, or some of them; on the circumstance that Marx was a German; and on the history of the German working-class movement in its context within a conservative state. It was a background to become of the first importance in the development of Russian Communist theory. The background suggests that the difference between Germany and (say) Britain lay less in any inarticulate attitudes of working-men than in the different politics of the situation. Confessedly, the politics of the situation might be different in part because the underlying attitudes were different.

Just after the turn of the century Rosa Luxemburg was probably the only serious rival to Lenin as a contender for the leadership of European communism. She was Jewish, liberal and non-practising, and of Polish origin. In 1905 she published at Cracow a pseudonymous dissertation on religion, posing under the name of Józef Chmura,[44] and entitled *Socialism and the Churches.* When the revolution against the Tsar began, why did priests preach sermons against the revolution and against socialist workers? Social democrats never attack the clergy, never assail men's religious beliefs, regard conscience and opinion as sacred. No one has any right to attack the religion of another. The clergy ought to help Social

Democrats. Both stand for freedom of conscience. And their social ideas are akin. Social Democrats want liberty, equality, fraternity, why do not the clergy welcome them? Jesus Christ loved the poor, the clergy should bless those who work for the poor. But the clergy help oppressors, and preach resignation to tyranny, and place themselves in pagan contrast with their gospels. Communism was an apostolic practice. The Fathers of the Church struggled with burning words against the growth of social inequality in the Church. But as the Church became wealthier its leaders grew silent. The clergy became allies of the nobility. The Church is kept going by the labour of millions of exploited people. No wonder they support the Tsar.

Coming from the hand of a woman so central to one wing of the Social Democratic movement, the pamphlet was important. Not a word in it is against religion, not a word against Christ. The onslaught is directed against churches because they have been faithless to Christ who did great good in the world. The pamphlet is in the direct line of the old Chartist or old Utopian Socialist three-quarters of a century before – assail the churches because they are irreligious, not because they are religious. It is a far cry from the social theory of Marx and Engels, or the speeches of August Bebel. But it burns with the passion of so much of the political worker during the nineteenth century, that however religion was good, and to be used, and propagating ideals on which justice and freedom were founded, yet the churches could not be used because they were pillars of the structure which must be destroyed.

7

If men believed their situation intolerable, they bowed down under it if they saw it incurable. If they had vision or faith in a remedy, they wished to overturn the system which made them feel their lives intolerable. Through the extreme revolutionary strand of European thinking ran the wish to destroy what existed, especially if it posed a claim to authority. Followers of wild men, disciples of Babeuf or Bakunin, anarchists or Nihilists, they hated priests not so much because they were religious as because they claimed authority. The Anarchist Congress at Geneva in 1882 issued in its manifesto these world-denying phrases:

Our enemy, it is our master...We fight against everyone invested with power or who wishes for power, any kind of power whatsoever...landlord ...employer...state...every abstract authority, whether called devil or

God, in the name of which priests have so long governed good souls. . .Our enemy is the law. . .[45]

In all revolutionary thinking which wanted revolution for the sake of revolution, and which, unlike Marx, had small faith in economic inevitability, this strand appeared. It was destined to a long history. As late as 1923 Leon Trotsky told the students of Sverdlov University that the revolutionary must be deracinated, and must annihilate in himself every barrier against revolutionary acts, whether the barrier lay in religion, or morals, or legality. 'Therefore', he said – and the *therefore* is important in discerning the motive for irreligion – 'we regard atheism, which is part of materialism, as an indispensable constituent of the revolutionary education of a terrorist.'[46] That is: religion hampers freedom of action, especially freedom of moral action; and for our purpose, we must have men who stop at nothing in the cause.

No one must attribute this attitude to the ordinary working-man of the nineteenth century. Revolution for the sake of revolution had as little appeal to him as to landed aristocrats. But here among anarchists we see in an extreme form what may be faintly discerned in other more moderate and more conservative men – throw off God (not because anyone has disproved him but) because we are against authority and God is part of authority, supreme in authority. God was moral code. God meant resignation, and resignation meant acceptance of tyranny. God was a bar to violent acts. God looked to be on the side of squires, or of bourgeois. God comforted men who ought to be uncomfortable. Down with God – let us see whether we cannot find men who prove that he does not exist. Men were resolved to be 'free'. They would break the bonds of kings, of aristocrats and oligarchs and plutocrats. Must they, in throwing off their bonds, throw off their religion simultaneously? Ever since the early eighteenth century, when first sounded talk of strangling the last king with the guts of the last priest, the link existed among certain schools of radicals. That link was almost made canonical in the French Revolution by Hébert and then by Robespierre. Between 1865 and 1890 German and French politics made it, not near to canonical, but near to popular. Or, if not popular, it was such that preachers of atheism were heard gladly by some halls full of labourers, heard gladly for political reasons and not for religious.

Authority – suddenly it was an ill-sounding word, not only among fantastical Russian exiles. As far apart as was possible from Bakunin and his anarchists, Sainte-Beuve wrote in Paris, elegant, satirical, dilettante, exquisite and disdainful. In a speech of 19 May 1868 Sainte-Beuve told the French Senate that French minds must be freed, 'above all else', from 'absolute authority and blind submission'.[47] But this was the critique by a liberal; and the liberals' intellectual motive against authority over minds had a different origin from the social critique of authority among working-men.

If dukes go to church, will peasants go? If rich men go to church, will poor men go? Do social inferiors always imitate their betters? If powerful men go to church will weak men conform? Is general society less secular if prime ministers, diplomats, stockbrokers, generals, and bishops go to church? In all the sophisticated countries of western Europe, during the nineteenth century, the answer to these questions was, astonishingly, doubtful. Rich men (unless very rich) went to church, poor men (especially if very poor) stayed at home. Social prestige had less consequence in determining our problem than might be predicted. The worship of God appeared not to be an act which caught by fashion, like wearing a crinoline or growing a beard. Fashion, in this matter, is subsidiary, an aid to a movement which lies deeper down in the social consciousness. Machiavelli has been blamed for telling us that a prince who wants to stay on his throne must at all costs *seem* to his subjects to be religious. He did not suggest that this 'religion' of the prince would advance the religion of his subjects.

4
THE ATTITUDES OF THE WORKER

I

In the third chapter we met the question whether atheism and the drive towards social betterment or social revolution were linked, in a manner, fortuitously; by historical accident or juxtaposition; represented in the central place of Karl Marx in the intellectual history of working-class ideas. I now wish to illustrate the same juxtaposition in other sources, from men of different backgrounds.

I take the case of British working-class atheism.

The French Revolution begot by sympathy men who identified atheism, or deism, or at least the destruction of the churches, with liberty. The tradition of Tom Paine thenceforth survived continuously in English life. The atheists were not precisely working-men. But they were in touch with working-men, and formed groups which contained working-men. They were small groups. Nothing in the history of English working-class atheism in the first half of the nineteenth century resembles in the least the beginning of a popular movement. They would almost have been as quaint as table-turners or phrenologists, had their leaders been less vociferous, their pamphlets less noisy, and their cause less directly bearing on high matters which troubled educated men. The 'free-thinkers' of 1840 differed from the 'free-thinkers' of 1740 in two ways. They were lower in the social scale, and they associated their religious cause with a social cause. If Chartism or Socialism declined, they declined likewise. If Chartism looked dangerous, they looked to the magistrate less contemptible. And when they are said to be few, they nevertheless could draw. During 1845 Southwell held audiences of a thousand in the Hall of Science at Manchester. In the year before, Emma Martin addressed a crowd of five thousand in the market-place at Leicester; a larger crowd no doubt, partly because she was refused the Assembly Rooms, and partly because she was a woman. But in January 1846 the publisher of atheist literature complained to Holyoake that: 'All the pamphlets issued against superstition or religion for years past lay on the shelves like so much waste paper.'[1] In the last years of the 1840s they found it difficult to keep many groups going.

The more deeply we study atheists (or anti-Christian) working-men during the nineteenth century, the more surprising the conclusions, and the more our investigations overturn or weaken hitherto accepted axioms about the way in which secularization happened. Of course we have not yet proceeded far. But at the moment it looks as though we shall need to revise some guesses drastically.

'Secularism', wrote W. N. Molesworth in his impressionistic *History of England*,[2] new edition, published in 1874, 'was embraced by thousands and tens of thousands of the working classes. The success which attended the attempts made to propagate it was due partly to the fact that great masses of the working classes, especially in the large manufacturing towns, were already lost to Christianity, and had, in many cases, almost unconsciously adopted the ideas which Mr Holyoake fixed and shaped into distinct doctrines.' − 'Almost unconsciously.' A vast multitude of 'almost unconscious' adherents of Mr Holyoake. Probably more influential than Molesworth was the famous judgment of Engels in his *Condition of the Working Classes in England in 1844* (1892 edition, p. 126) − 'almost universally a total indifference to religion, or at the utmost some trace of Deism too undeveloped to amount to more than mere words, or a vague dread of the words infidel, atheist, etc. . .' If these contemporary judgments are authenticated, it would be of the first importance to our subject. It has been accepted, and propagated, by a tradition of subsequent books on the working-man of the nineteenth century, a tradition of historical repetitions.

The first revision, is, that this is not true; at least not in the sense that Molesworth intended a century ago. Dr Edward Royle examined the generalization in his book, *Victorian Infidels*, written out of a careful examination of the archives and publications of the secularist groups. It can at once be said that he demolishes the thesis. The secularists were always a small minority, or series of minorities. Not that a minority of this kind can be neglected. Like all such minorities, they can be shown to have influenced many more men and women than those willing to commit themselves to membership and to activity. But their activities hardly touched the mass of the population. They resembled independent chapels in more than their mode of life, for the social groups to which they appealed were those just above the real labourers. They were artisan, shopkeeper, weaver, shoemaker, small bookseller. Holyoake and several other leaders had no desire to make the movement working-class. On the contrary, they were always trying to extend their influence by making it more respectable; even raising the price of tickets for their lectures in order to exclude. They were men of the coffee-house, and the coffee-house was no natural home of the poor. This is part of the explanation for the tiny number of atheists, or *active* assailants of Christianity, reported in those decades by home missionaries or parish visitors. Where the audiences were large, they contained many, often up to two-thirds, who came to be amused and not to learn. Of course, this does not mean that the ordinary labourer was a religious man. Often he did nothing at all about religion. This observation caused Horace Mann, in his homiletic preface to the report of the religious census of 1851, to describe him as an *unconscious secularist*. Dr Royle (233) thought that the phrase *unconscious Christian* would be quite as accurate a description; or at least, if I put it more negatively to suit myself, quite as inaccurate a description.

There is one fundamental objection to the theory that Holyoake and his like articulated the inarticulate atheism of the British working-man. It is very simple; that all the group, from Holyoake to Bradlaugh, tried to dissociate themselves from atheism when they wished to propagate their social doctrines.

Socialist propaganda, they found, suffered from its association with atheist propaganda. They could more easily persuade men to join them in a social programme if they refrained from simultaneously persuading them to join a theological programme. The British working-man might or might not attend church or chapel, but shrank from speakers who attacked subjects which he instinctively or by tradition felt to be sacred. The cooperative movement, starting with the burden of a name for atheism, freed itself from the imputation as it extended. Even Holyoake said that he no longer wished to be called an atheist, 'since the public understand by that word one who is without God and also without morality, and who wishes to be without both'. He wanted not to use the term *infidel*, 'since Christians understand by that term one who is unfaithful or treacherous to the truth'.[3] 'We object', said Holyoake on 20 January 1853, 'to those terms which have the effect of condemning us before we are heard, and causing the public to regard us with foregone disapprobation.' Nothing is so revealing for the attitude of the working-man than such a sentence from so redoubtable a controversialist.

In connexion with this shift to moderation, or perception that we need not offend unnecessarily, or sense that we shall get our aim more easily if we cooperate with others who disagree in theology, or confession that truth does not prevail in this world merely by being shouted, Holyoake put into the English language that new word linked to our study: the word *secularism*. In June 1851 a friend and backer, the lawyer W. H. Ashurst, advised him to call himself a secularist, with the special object of freeing himself from the imputations of atheism and infidelity. At first the word *secularism* needed explanation to his readers; the *Reasoner* was described as a journal concerning itself with this world – 'the issues of which can be tested in this life'.[4]

During the middle 1850s the first 'Secular Societies' were founded in various towns. They were nearly all weak. Several of them depended on the influence, energy or money of one man. They rose and fell, languished and were reformed; with irregular meetings, occasional Sunday school, an occasional library, open air assemblies, market stall, tea-parties, brass-band, bazaar. They hired a room in a public house, or a coffee-house, for there was a puritan strand about these groups and many of them were linked with the temperance movement.

They were an offshoot of the socialist inheritance. Old Chartist groups provided members. In some areas the continuity with Chartism is obvious. Some of the groups, especially in the West Riding, were almost wholly political and scarcely at all irreligious. The subjects which agitated an open-air meeting of 2,000 secularists at Hollingworth Lake near Manchester in June 1858 were the bill before Parliament for the equality of the Jews, Sunday recreation and boats on Hollingworth Lake.[5] If they were secular, they were not very secular, in the original sectarian sense. Though chapels and churches regarded them as enemies, their structure, outlook organization and philosophy resembled nothing so much as a loose structure of independent chapels. They ministered to much the same personal needs and to much the same social groups. They served the want for private friendships, a moral cause, a common work for good and instincts for religion. Bradlaugh always dressed so that he could be mistaken for a nonconformist minister, or even a Roman Catholic priest.

The secularist movement touched top in England in 1883–5. Thereafter it declined. Why the date? The common theory is that between 1880 and 1886 Britain established with pain the right of an atheist to take his seat in Parliament. I committed myself in print to the theory that in those years the working-man came near to identifying his cause with one whose distinguishing mark was atheism.

Contemporaries took the same view. The Gladstone papers in the British Museum contain a letter from a Liberal M.P. of a Welsh constituency to every clergyman or minister in the British Isles; to the effect that the defeat of the Affirmation Bill by the House of Commons 'has seriously advanced the popularity of Mr Bradlaugh among a very active section of the working classes previously opposed to Atheism. It has enormously increased the popularity and sale of his works. It has, we fear, by causing him to be regarded as the Champion of Popular Rights, converted many working men from a position of neutrality towards Religion into its active opponents; and it is calculated to promote the creation in this country of that class of bitter, proselytising Atheistic Communism which is already so dangerous to law and order in Continental countries, but has hitherto been rare in our own.'[8]

So, did the fight over Bradlaugh almost make the working-man an atheist? Or was it something quite different? The more carefully we examine secularist groups the more they look like a little religious denomination, even though their *raison d'être* was anti-religious. And then we remember how statistics, whether of France, or England, or Germany, show church attendance and number of ordination candidates beginning at last to fall in just those middle years of the 1880s. In short, did the rise till 1883–5 and then the downward turn of secularism have nothing whatever to do with secularization, but was simply a sign that this was one church among others and shared the common and contemporary fate of all theological institutions? And if a Welsh M.P. at the time threatened that the refusal of Bradlaugh turned the worker towards atheism, perhaps he knew nothing about that unknowable side of his country, and like a good Liberal politician was merely doing his best for the next Affirmation Bill.

The comparison with a sect goes further. The kind of trouble which a preacher of secularism suffered in mid-Victorian England was the trouble suffered by Primitive Methodist preachers a generation before, or by ritualistic priests soon afterwards. Drums beaten to make them inaudible, windows smashed at their place of meeting, fists flying, yells and hoots and spitting – the English mob enjoyed itself by treating revivalist preacher or atheist lecturer or Anglo-Catholic ceremonialist with fine impartiality.

Statistics of Primitive Methodism prove how it advanced swiftly during the age of rabbling, and how its first turn downwards in numbers coincides in time, more or less, with the end of mob attack.

Statistics of Anglo-Catholic advance and retrogression are less clear. But they are enough to suggest that the age of mob attack coincided in time, more or less, with the age of quickest advance in ecclesiastical power. It might be less that persecution caused advance, than that advance caused persecution. It would be gross to call persecution the sole cause of advance. Yet these comparisons may after all suggest that the blood of martyrs, especially when blood flows only from fisticuffs or flying glass, is the seed of the Church.

This leads to a further reflexion. The old Christian state was dismantled by Christians for the sake of keeping the people Christian. This is well-known about the campaigns for disestablishment in Victorian England and Wales, Scotland and Ireland. Most of the men who tried to separate the Churches from the State, wanted to make society more Christian even while they made the State more secular. This axiom applies to other matters besides the Church-State nexus. Secularists campaigned to make the State more secular. Affirmation Bills, laws of blasphemy, laws of evidence, these had to be passed because secularists protested. But they were passed because Christians saw that they must be passed; partly on grounds of justice and morality, partly on grounds of expediency for the welfare of the people. To the extent that political structure was secularized during the nineteenth century, it was secularized, for the most part, by men without desire to make society more secular; and in some part by men who had the opposite aim.

2

The next axiom to consider is the thesis of direct link between secularization and the nature of a man's job.

You work as an agricultural labourer. You are surrounded by nature, you see daily bread growing under your hand, you are a man of open air, you live a simple uncomplicated life, you have a sturdy relative independence, you have work with a measure of interest and variety, you are well-known to all your neighbourhood and your conduct is subject to comment by neighbours, you fit into the background of revolving nature, sun and frost, spring and autumn, you commune with wet and with wilderness.

Then you move into the town because you hear rumours that the streets are paved with gold. You become anonymous. You are in a crowd. You have no neighbours, no one comments. The customs of your family and your village fade. You are an individual. You earn more money, have the freedom of a money economy. Your mode of life is withdrawn from nature, you drink water from a tap instead of a spring, your milk is bottled on the doorstep instead of squeezed from the udder. You inhabit a little house in a row of little houses as alike as postage stamps. You have a job in a factory where you know neither the owners nor the employer, your new job is impersonal. It is monotonous. You tend the machine hour after hour, unreflecting, yourself a less reliable screw in the works. A curtain made out of city streets and the nature of city employment, has fallen with a crash to divide you from the gods of home and hearth and the gods of field and forest, the things of eternity which are known in quietness.

So the Industrial Revolution divided men from God. Men become melancholy if they are deprived of their higher ideals. But they have the compensation that while brooding on the iniquities of men makes men sad, brooding on the iniquity of machines is never disagreeable.

And this theory or feeling, nostalgic as it is, begins to look as though it may be false; or at least, that we should go warily before we trust it.

The statistic on which it rests is proven. Larger the town, smaller the percentage of persons who attended churches on Sundays. This statistic is liable to variation and even exception, according to country, parts of the same country, or social conditions. Still, it is a proven statistic. No longer is there room to doubt it. Whether or not decline in churchgoing is a sign of secularization (and it probably is), bigger towns were a cause.

To this general theorem, riders are needed. (1) If bigger towns were a cause (as they must be), they were not an immediate cause, nor perhaps an inevitable cause. The second quarter of the nineteenth century was an age of rapid revival of religion in all the countries of western Europe. It was also an age of rapid movement of population from country to town. We cannot assume without further enquiry that if you are living in a town you are more likely to lack a feeling for the sacred.

(2) Did those persons who failed to go to church in town go to church in the village, or were they the sons of such persons? Were the unchurched masses of the slum a heap of unchurched individuals from villages, or had their religious outlook changed by the single fact that they sank into a mass in the slum? Has the worker never gone to church since he was permitted not to, or did he only cease to

do so when he became a townsman? Evidence for an answer to this is hard to come by.

Here are some reflexions which have so far been brought to bear: The slum dweller of the later nineteenth century had no sense of guilt in not attending churches or chapels. If he professed atheism he might be aggressive. But mostly he professed no such thing. He took no notice, unless he listened amusedly to a street orator. When minister or district visitor called on him, he might proffer faint excuse. But his attitude needed no excuse, the excuse was but courtesy. Religion was not and never had been for the likes of him. This indifference was assured, it came with neither guilt nor bitterness as companion. From this assurance long tradition is arguable.

Secondly, villages were less utopian places of Christian worship than romantic historians supposed. In the villages was variety. The size of unit lent more weight to the influence of individuals, squire or parson, form of land tenure, history of the parish and of the parish church. Investigation into town versus country does not consistently leave a comparison unfavourable to town.[7]

A remarkable instance can be shown in the deep countryside of the state of Mecklenburg in north Germany. Here was a land of forest and agriculture and small towns. The Church had the backing of two godly princes in succession. Almost no denomination but the Lutheran existed, so no one competed for men's souls or jarred men's ears with obsolete jangle. Church government was guided, was almost controlled dictatorially, by Theodore Kliefoth, a Lutheran minister of learning, devotion and administrative ability. Everything was favourable to the Church. And by the third quarter of the nineteenth century some of the churchgoing statistics are the lowest in Germany, and the Land contained as much anticlericalism and religious indifference as any Land of Germany, more than some urbanized and sophisticated areas. It was a Land with more sense of entire classes of people alienated.[8]

In Mecklenburg, it happens, a different breach existed which will concern us in the next chapter; a breach not specially of towns or villages. For the moment I use that Land only to illustrate our inability to make universal the axiom that Christianity flourishes better in country than in towns. Apart from the well-known evidence of the primitive church, and the well-known evidence of the contemporary church, a modicum of evidence from the earlier nineteenth century may even suggest that the religious revival of those years was in part assisted, and not wholly hindered, by the flight to the towns.

Secularist groups were almost all in towns. But not all. In County Durham the village of Cockfield had for a few years a strong little society founded on New Year's Day 1856, and drawing members from surrounding villages. The examples of Mecklenburg, and such examples as Cockfield in Britain, prove hostility to the churches among countrymen. Was, therefore, the town important in this affair simply because it was number, or also because it was a different way of life? Was secularism more prominent in towns solely because villages could not provide enough people to make a reasonable meeting?

The statistic is ineluctable. Larger the town, smaller the percentage of churchgoers. Therefore some people at least who went to village chapel or village church failed to do so when they moved into Bolton, or Newcastle-on-Tyne, or Glasgow. A pointer to folk-memory of religion may be seen in the practice of religion by those in the cities who were otherwise indifferent. Not only baptisms, marriages, funerals were regular. On one, or two, days in the year crowds who never otherwise went near the church appeared at a service. These days were rustic days, not urban in origin. The harvest festival was one. In the depths of London men who never saw a wheatsheaf besieged the church door to give thanks for the harvest. The custom is only explicable by some half-conscious folk memory. The other day was New Year's Eve, or Watch Night. In the late 1860s the new Anglo-Catholic vicar of St Alban's Holborn refused to have a New Year's Eve service. He said that it was not a Catholic custom and had no warrant. He and his curate went to bed. A crowd of men assembled outside, perpetually ringing the door bell and shouting up, 'Ain't you going to have a service?' The curate got leave of the vicar, opened the doors, and the people filled the church. In each following year they announced no service, rang no bell; and each year, without being summoned, poor men filled the church.[9]

Not Christmas, but New Year's Eve. In England, and perhaps in Scotland, the Christmas feast moved downwards in the social scale. But no English middle class attracted working-men to New Year's Eve services. It was a feast of the people. Though Wesleyan Methodist ministers helped its propagation, it was imposed by no ecclesiastical authority. The Watch Night Service at St Mary's Bramall Lane, Sheffield near the end of the century, used to get more than 2,500 people.[10] It was not particularly a feast of the country rather than the town. But like harvest festivals, it points to subconscious continuity in the mind of countryman father and townsman son.

Throughout the century the Victorians built churches, more and more churches, in the towns of England and Wales and Scotland. Their enquiries showed the unchurched condition of the working-man, unchurched because no church stood within range of his habitation. They believed, or some of them believed, that you need only build churches, and find ministers, and the loss would be made good, the breach repaired, the worker would come again within the fold of church or chapel. Our century, seeing ugly churches standing empty because the Victorians built so many, doubts the axiom which caused them to build. We have small cause to be superior. Our denominations still pursue immigrants with churches and chapels into new areas, new housing-estates.

Does a people lose touch with God if it lives too far from a church? But how far is too far? Outside a journey of half an hour perhaps – if you wish to be there. The explanation of the middle nineteenth century for loss of faith lay in the failure of 'church extension'; that is, the inability of the churches' machine to adapt itself quickly enough to new areas, new suburbs, new towns. Old parishes had rights from the distant past. Like the popes' temporal power, old rights could not cheerfully be sacrificed. New parishes were hard to create, hard to run when created. The population of Paris rose by nearly 100% between 1861 and 1905, the number of parishes by about 33%, the number of priests by about 30%.[11] The comparable statistics for London and English cities are familiar. Babies of vast parishes were baptised and never saw church or priest thereafter. The collapse of religion (if it collapsed) was in this view nothing but the consequence of the collapse of the parochial system. In 1892 the abbé de Broglie published a book on *The Present and Future of Catholicism* in which he said that the cause of loss of faith was not intellectual scepticism but the failure of an old administration to cope with new numbers.[12] Did God depend upon the parochial system?

The big town of 1850 was not well prepared to receive its influx from the country, prepared in any way, whether by its laissez-faire philosophy of government, or in drainage, sanitation, police courts, food supply, parks, bye-laws, housing, schools, nurseries, medical care, cemeteries, hospitals, fire engines. New people strained the resources of towns near to breaking-point, and like all else the churches were neither ready nor able to cope with the flood. There is a case for believing that the events at the end of the century were but the nemesis of that failure; just as, on the physical plane, the slums of the cities were the nemesis of failure.

Was it town alone, or was it also industrial town? Was it the habitat only, or also the nature of the employment? For example: nearly half the 'regular' secularist societies known from 1837 to 1866 were in Lancashire and the West Riding.[13] Both were areas of textiles, spinning or weaving. Was a man likely to be attracted to a secularist group because he was a mill-hand, and the nature of his work or way of life had something to do with it? Or was it simply the large number of persons who lived in these areas, and nothing whatever to do with textiles or mills?

Natural scientists rule in their investigations that simpler explanations are to be preferred above complex explanations provided that they sufficiently explain the observations. Social historians have talked of the consequences of 'industrialization' for our problem. They have not meant that new machines created towns, and that towns created a new way of life or, rather, extended a very old way of life. They have meant that the kind of work which new machines demanded took the human race further from God than the work done before those machines were invented. We cannot rule out such a theory. But it needs evidence in its favour. For the moment we note only that new towns, *qua* towns not *qua* industrial towns, are a simpler explanation of an observation; and they are alone sufficient to explain what we observe of British working-class secularism in the 1850s and 1860s. A lot of people in a heap had more (metaphorical) weight than a lot of machines and change of employment; though no one can deny that a lot of machines were needed to heap together a lot of people.

Examination of people's occupations, like weaver or coal-miner, shows as yet no pattern that a man was more likely to be secularist by reason of an adopted employment. That might not be true of the middle class, especially the intellectual, later in the century. (At least, persons opting for civil marriage tended to come from certain marked professions like writers[!]). So far as we have gone it is true of the working class throughout the century. The secularist movement crossed the trades and occupations with no discernible pattern. The company which a man keeps of course affects him. If you live with an apostle you have more chance of becoming an apostle. It does not appear, so far, that the company which a secularist kept was (by reason of his secularism) identifiable, in any respect, with the trade which he practised.

The nature of the employment might be conceived, and has been conceived, as influential by reason of its ugliness, or boredom, or sordidness, or meaninglessness: the man with the spanner to give the nut a single turn through an infinite number of nuts.

We cannot find tests for this. We appeal to feeling.

A Wordsworth, a George Macaulay Trevelyan, experienced feelings, which they could not doubt or question, about the moral effects of natural beauty around them. Trevelyan felt this so deeply that he devoted a substantial part of a life of generosity to preserving the Lake District as a haven of peace for the people of England, and the countryside around Cambridge as a haven for the people of Cambridge. Men admired the sturdy independence and moral fibre of the Tyrolean mountaineer compared with the materialism of the occupant of a Viennese housing-estate. Are souls of the hills and fields naturally more open to the things of spirit? You and I have a feeling, which we hardly like to define publicly, that our universities are better universities because they are set in noble and historic cities; better universities in the sense that we do not merely find the cities pleasant places to inhabit, we suspect that we can look for truth a little more sensitively because we are surrounded by so fair a landscape; or suspect at least that if we cannot look for truth more sensitively, we ought to be able to do so. Reason tells us that the books in the library, or the equipment in the laboratory, are more momentous than the architecture of library or laboratory which perhaps have nothing to do with the matter. Still, our feelings are hard to deny; compounded as they are of affection for a home and pride in a place where monuments speak the long story of men's passion and men's nobility.

Eloquence sometimes means that the speaker is short of evidence. There is no evidence whatever that persons in monotonous occupations were less likely to be religious than persons in interesting occupations. There is no evidence that Europeans who settled in the fairest places of the earth, like the beaches of Tahiti, were more likely to behave morally than workers in the Black Country – not at least by reason of their environment. A man might be forced into a monotonous occupation and a squalid environment because he was poor, because he struggled for material existence. We shall get further by looking at the poverty and the struggle for existence than by looking at the monotony in the trade. No one has yet found evidence to suggest a diminished sense of the sacred, as well as a diminished refinement of the palate, because potatoes come in a packet of crisps instead of being lifted from the soil, or meat comes from a tin instead of lumbering up to be slaughtered. Unless that is, our feelings are evidence. Unless, that is, the coincidence of timing is evidence – that men seem to diminish their sense of the sacred (if they do) about the time that fewer of them sowed and reaped the harvest.

Urbanization and industrialization: twin cumbersome nouns fundamental to the study of secularization. You cannot have big towns without industry. But in other respects, on present evidence, we ought to focus our attention more upon the first process than upon the second, in seeking explanations for what we try to understand.

A man emigrates from country to town. It matters that he moves into the town. He has changed his community – that is important whithersoever he changes. He changes type of community. It matters more where in the town he settles.

A big town of the nineteenth century was a laissez-faire institution. Like all such institutions, faced with movements of population, it generated ghettoes. You could move only into that part of the town which catered for your pocket and your habits. The town was a class society. The analysis of churchgoing in big Victorian towns, so far as it has gone, points to a dependence on the nature of the area. Churchgoing rose in areas where the houses were larger; areas where more domestic servants were employed; areas where the garden attached to each house was a little larger; areas where the occupants of houses had leisure or desire to go out of their houses to other public occasions, political meetings, clubs, assemblies, lectures, art or theatre. Therefore, with regard to this phenomenon of working-class secularization, we need to focus on the ghetto, the old Victorian slum, the streets inhabited by no one but the poor.

Within the class area of the city lived the European working-man. He was somewhere between unconscious secularist and unconscious Christian. He did not at all object to people who were rude about clergymen and churches, he usually objected to people who were rude about God. So far as he was an unconscious Christian, he respected marriages in church and funerals conducted by Christian ministers and approved babies to be christened; and for the rest did not mind if his wife engaged in further religious practice and might even expect it of his children. So far as he was an unconscious secularist he had a feeling that church ministers were agents of the

Tory party, and that to attend church (except at harvest festivals) would be a departure from the social custom of his equals and friends, would turn him into an eccentric, if not one liable to the accusation of trying to ape his betters.

One thing which has begun to stand out is the strength of class feeling; not so much class feeling in the sense of class warfare, not in the sense of hostility to other classes or other areas of the city, but in the sense of solidarity. Clergymen concerned with the slum, or district visitors caring for the poor, sometimes blamed the movement of population within the area, the here today and gone tomorrow, which stopped anyone knowing anyone else and prevented the organs of social and municipal life from creating a community out of the casual inhabitants of a group of streets. But the characteristic which stands out even more to us is less the casualness than the solidarity of the population.

I remember walking a little street of East London, about the year 1943, and coming across two women fighting, surrounded by four or five women screaming at them to stop. I thought that masculine intervention was in place – you must remember that I was quite young. Nothing could have been more mistaken. Both the pugilists, and all the spectators, united against me. When I withdrew downcast, they resumed their quarrel with ferocity undiminished by the interlude.

This is the solidarity which we find in the Victorian city. I thought that I had a right, if not a duty, as a member of the human race. They knew that I was an outsider, not a member of the community, and therefore with no right to interfere, a busybody. There was a magic circle. Why was religion without the magic circle and not within?

The problem of clothes is notorious. Some of the poor made excuses that they could not go to church because they had no clothes. Occasionally ministers urged them to come 'as they were'. No use. They felt ashamed, they said. In 1882 the vicar of All Saints in Newcastle-on-Tyne had a success. He persuaded the parish to come 'as they were', and all the women came with their heads in shawls. Five years later all the same women were wearing bonnets in church. The churchwarden said 'they can afford bonnets now, but they are the same heads'. I have doubted[14] whether this was the explanation. Reverence was sacramental in their minds by a measure of respectability. They liked to appear in torn trousers even less than they liked to see the vicar's surplice in tatters.

Reverence and respectability, not always a comfortable juxta-position. Clothes were a symbol of something more than shame at not having the customary outward form. Churchgoing was not part of the way of life practised by a coherent community. In becoming a churchgoer a man (less so, a woman, though partially so) became an oddity in his social station. Like a convert gathered out of the world, he felt to his comrades, and even to himself, special; and this special quality came near to looking like an attempt to contract out of his class, since the coherence of the community was essentially a coherence of class. If you became a churchgoer or chapelgoer, you hardly seemed any longer a member of the working class. You were respectable, and the working class did not feel itself respectable. Therefore, if you practised going to a church or chapel (unless you were, for example, an Irishman or a Jew with an ethnic reason for professing your religion) you felt a nonconformism from your environment. Consequently the working-man, if he was religious, usually associated his religion with decisive outward acts, hot gospel, teetotalism, no smoking. It was not, so to speak, a natural, easily acceptable background. It had to be gripped. The worker had a mind for the concrete. He was hardly interested, not at all interested, in theory. Questions of truth did not loom large in his mind, hardly loomed at all.

Let me now apply what I have said to three questions vital for us:

First, Marx's theory of alienation. This theory contained two elements: the oppressed framing a god to make oppression bearable, the oppressor propagating a god to prevent the oppressed from other and violent remedies. So far as the theory consisted of the former thesis, very little in present studies of the nineteenth-century worker supports it. He felt indeed a gulf dividing him from the world outside his community. He felt part of a class, distinguished from other classes in society. But he hardly used God to comfort himself. For he hardly used God.

Secondly, the question which I put, whether the profession of atheism was necessarily an offshoot, even a basis, of the campaign for social betterment, or whether the link was fortuitous. In Marx social betterment was the centre, atheism a necessary part. But when we turn not to the bourgeois but to working practitioners, the link is not so clear.

A theological doctrine and a passion for social reform can lie side by side in the mind. One need not arise from the other. They can be undigested within the personality. Or they may be brought into harmony by philosophical reasoning, by systematic effort. Or, finally, they may be in entire harmony within the mind, a unity in philosophy and way of life. Because a man is a social reformer and an atheist, it does not follow that his social reform springs from his atheism, any more than among Christian Socialists it followed that their socialism sprang invariably from their religion. In a social campaign we expect representatives of every earnest group, from Roman Catholic cardinals to secularist lecturers. If you were a secularist lecturer like Bradlaugh the link depended much upon your response to your audience. If you orated at a meeting for the Liberal party, you played down atheism, left it to one side as irrelevant or as likely to lose support, because you wished to persuade the many. If you lectured (preached?) at a meeting of secularists, you blasted churches with every gun in your armoury; and one of your guns was the social record, the passive philosophy, the *be-resigned-to-your-lot-even-when-your-lot-is-hell.*

On present evidence, then, the answer must distinguish between the individual mind and the European social situation. In individual minds like Marx or Bebel atheism was essential to socialism. But nothing in the general social situation, nor in the attitudes of workers responding to that social situation, made the link necessary, provided we exclude for the moment the subject of the next chapter, namely, the political situation.

Thirdly: the European working-man was interested in bread, and drink, and the next meal, and the pub on the corner. So far as truth meant a concern with abstract ideas, he was too near subsistence to care much. The secularist controversy, though an argument about truth, did not thrive on truth. The older Holyoake grew, the more intellectual his arguments and the smaller his influence. Bradlaugh taught the movement that if you wished men to pay attention, it profited more to beat big drums than to blow upon flutes. It was hard for secularist leaders to bear, but the worker was too tired for education and came, if he came, because he wanted entertainment. They spread their light more by catering for men's leisure than by appealing to their minds. The churches were not different.

3

From time to time men accused churches of being on the side of oppressors. The question whether religion was used as part of 'social control' is interesting and difficult to test. At its crudest it asserts a conscious use of the other world to compensate for the injustice of this world. We trample on the poor and make life bearable for them by the illusory comforts of religion. We keep the poor from stealing unjustly acquired property, or from assailing despotic bourgeois governments, by threatening them with hell.

No one, perhaps, could quite believe the theory in so crude a form. But these notions are not to be ruled out of account merely because they are misty in themselves and were stated crudely. They were widely held by the philosophers of the eighteenth century. Voltaire's line of poetry, written in 1769, *If God did not exist, it would be necessary to invent him*, was a pithy version of the theory that without religion social structure will collapse. It came, as the climax of a passage on the hereafter, as the sacred bond of society, the consecration of justice, the brake upon criminals and the hope of the righteous. Voltaire was rude about Meslier, the curé who preached Christian gospel for twenty years and then left three manuscripts of 366 pages as a testament to tell his parishioners that he believed none of it. Why? – asked Voltaire – they cannot read – and if they could read, still why? 'Why take away from the common people a salutary yoke, a fear which is needed because only thus can secret crime be stopped? Belief in future rewards and punishments is a check which the people needs.'[15]

About hell we have a curious contrast. Social workers among the poor reported that hell meant nothing to them, they laughed at it. Parents and employers believed that retribution was powerful by way of a deterrent, and that hell was particularly important in its impact upon the poor worker. The link in men's minds between atheism and immorality, however, did not depend upon this belief. It is not always easy to determine which came first, the wish to protect religion or the wish to protect morality. When a Victorian said that atheism leads to immorality, we cannot be sure whether he wanted God to be worshipped and therefore prophesied ill if God were not worshipped; or whether he saw the weakness of law and wished to bolster its sanctions by those of another world. The second, rougher, notion of social control by religion, in a raw form of the theory, can only be proved of persons who themselves had no use for God but still wanted God taught to the working classes. But the first and more Christian attitude could never separate the desire for worship from the desire for goodness, for God was most glorified by the pure in heart and the righteousness of social life.

In 1864 a legal judgment in the English Judicial Committee

allowed a clergyman of the Church of England to teach or at least to hope for the ultimate salvation even of the wicked. The judgment provoked a public declaration of belief in eternal hell, signed by 11,000 clergy. The thought surrounding this declaration has been analysed.[16] 'I am sure', wrote Dr Pusey to Bishop Tait of London on 25 June 1863, 'nothing will keep men from the present pleasures of sin, but the love of God or the fear of Hell; and that the fear of Hell drives people back to God, to seek. . .Him, and in seeking to love Him first because He delivered them from Hell, then for His own sake.' From this and other utterances Pusey, as could be predicted of so religious a mystic, was plainly afraid, not for society, but for men's souls. Whether society broke or not, did not concern him. He feared for the damnation of immortal souls and shrank from the prospect that the Church was guilty of this loss by failing to speak truth. In this group were many clergy whose real concern was not hell but the authority of the Bible. If you disbelieved hell you disbelieved the Bible and if you disbelieved the Bible you lost God. Very little direct evidence suggests that instructed middle-class citizens believed in hell and taught it to their children mainly because they wanted to keep their children or the servants in order. This was as true of Calvinists as of high churchmen. Often we come across the feeling that even if one did not believe in everlasting torment, one ought to be reticent about saying so. Bishop Lonsdale of Lichfield, a level-headed sober man, most Anglican of Anglican types of mind, was once asked about it by a lady in his diocese. She reported him as saying, 'I have a hope for men beyond this life, but I am afraid it would not do to preach it, people are careless enough.'[17] Nothing suggests that he consciously thought of social control. The word careless hints at the contrary. What concerned him, as it concerned Pusey, was an eternal home.

Then we find evidence that the poor in London slums mocked at hell. A middle-class worker among the London poor wrote in 1886 that 'the popular doctrine of hell' was scorned by working-men and did not deter from sin. Of secularist charges against Christianity this was the easiest to make stick. Some reputable men believed that the dogma of hell, as traditionally taught, was chief cause of infidelity in England, and that nowhere was the gulf wider between what was taught in the pulpit and what was believed in the street.[18] These are opinions which no one had then or has now any means of testing.

We find two other opinions – first, that the teaching of hell was useful as a deterrent to children; and second, that it was specially suitable when preaching to the ignorant. George Lansbury's mother normally took him to a parish church. But if the children behaved particularly ill, she would take them that Sunday to a small Primitive Methodist chapel where they would be sure to hear of hell.[19] Many Victorian nurses, if we may judge by autobiographers, took the same view. Here was direct connexion believed to exist between belief in terrible retribution and formation of moral habits in an unformed character. But when we turn to the defenders of hell-fire preaching as especially suitable for the poor, we do not find the same attention to the utility of a deterrent; not at least without immediate reference to eternity. What can we infer from the circumstance that ministers who preached vehement sermons about hell often got larger congregations than ministers who never mentioned the subject?

The worker was not articulate. He read newspapers (sex and sport) but not books. If he were among the minority actively hostile to the churches, and if he were touched with secularism, he read a few books. But in Britain the author whom he read most of all was Tom Paine. The arguments with which he beat the churches were derived from a book valid only against the narrowest forms of Biblicism. The kind of question which he liked to ask was, who was Cain's wife? It had little in common with quest for intellectual truth. The typical convert to secularist doctrine was either an ex-Methodist who got to hate the God of the Old Testament, or the social reformer persuaded that churches were lackeys of tyranny. He was no scientist. His arguments had nothing whatever in common with refined upper-class arguments over Science and Religion. So far as can at present be discerned, Darwin and Darwinianism had no direct influence whatever in the secularization of the British working-man, and probably not much in that of any other worker of the nineteenth century. In Belgium the books he read were Eugène Sue, Victor Hugo's Les Misérables, and a few revolutionary hand-outs.[20] Very few of them knew anything of Marx. Marx was difficult. He was an intellectual's intellectual. He had to be made crude to bite at all. He was made very crude, especially on the Continent.

5

THE RISE OF ANTICLERICALISM

The vaguely anti-church attitudes of the worker combined with neutrality towards religion. He did not identify churches, which he might attack or scorn, with religion which he might well respect even though he shrank from practising its rites.

What begins to look as though it matters is the politics of the situation. Where you have anyone like Jenny Geddes, the throwing of a stool at the preacher, and especially the accurate aiming of a stool, causes stances to alter; a party to form; a party marked by attitudes to religion as well as politics, indeed a party where the attitude towards the religion is near the heart of the political attitude. A religious protest is taken up into politics and becomes a party cry, and then is found to gather broad support because it stands for a secular political objective and not only for the particular religious protest. Men in the mass live by simple objectives, and public repute or ill repute is one of the most transforming of political forces. Not the stool, but the politics which surrounded the stool, shifted in time the religious outlook of a people. We are not to despise mere politics in our problem. The social scientists look for social statistics. Intellectual historians look for bumps in philosophy. Let us consider whether mere politics has anything to say to us. And this is the more necessary to ask since the word *anticlericalism* is like the word secularization in being coined during these years to which I draw attention.

Early in the eighteenth century a Frenchman wanted to strangle the last king with the guts of the last priest; that is, he regarded throne and altar as the two pillars of the prevailing order of society which he wanted to overthrow. This sentiment is found, not always in such anatomical language, in moments of European crisis. When the Communards danced in a few (but by no means all) Parisian churches in the spring of 1871, and dressed up in chasubles or stuck pipes in the mouths of statues or used the altar as a bar, for the most part they just had a good time. But when a more serious and more bourgeois orator rose among them, he might, like Gaillard at the

Church of Notre-Dame-de-la-Croix, tell them, 'we have to cleanse society in the blood of the priests and the aristocrats'.[1] That was an eighteenth-century sentiment. 'Beware', said the father of Count de Montgaillard, 'Beware of a woman if you are in front of her, a mule if you are behind it, and a priest whether you are in front or behind.'[2]

To the middle twentieth century, where priests are expected to be of the left and to encourage revolution in South America or southern Africa, this is a more surprising juxtaposition than men of the nineteenth century found it. Here, for example, is a speech made by Archdeacon Christopher Wordsworth, son of a Master of Trinity, nephew of a poet, soon to be Bishop of Lincoln, at a Tory meeting in Reading on 1 February 1865. He engaged to define Conservatism:

What, gentlemen, is Conservatism? It is the application of Christianity to civil government. And what is English Conservatism? It is the adoption of the principles of the Church of England as the groundwork of legislation. Gentlemen, I say it with reverence, the most Conservative book in the world is the Bible, and the next most Conservative book in the world is the Book of Common Prayer.[3]

The Church the mainstay of order – that is the conviction common to both sides; both of the revolutionary who wants to overthrow order and therefore the Church, and of the conservative who wants to maintain order and therefore the Church. The religious revivals of the nineteenth century, evident in all countries of western Europe, did not depend upon faith in the political usefulness of Churches. They did not even depend only upon the background rattle of ghostly tumbrils on the streets. But this shadow of social ruin was quite important as a religious force. We can the more easily understand it when we remember how in our time Nazi terror forced many western Europeans back to enquire into their moral principles and thereby contributed, for a time, to a revival of religion.

Within this feeling among conservatives different strands can be detected:

First, the feeling that religion alone gave the fundamental moral principles which enabled society to cohere without corruption, failure of trust, or dissolution through civil tensions. Could you trust the grocer to serve you right measure if you relied only on the compulsions of the law? You preferred your grocer to go to church. That is less crude than Voltaire's *not before the maids* but it is a crude way of describing a more subtle feeling. Occasionally it can be seen to exist even in so crude a form. For example, in the 1870s, the people of Marseilles, by whom we may doubtless understand the middle classes of Marseilles, were said to have no confidence in lawyers unless those lawyers went to church; and accordingly in holy week each year a black procession of men of law appeared, almost a parade.⁴ So it was described. But when we remember our own processions of judges at the opening of term, and our sermons at the opening of assizes, we wonder whether the citizens of Marseilles may not have simplified motives, and that the people, not excluding the lawyers, wanted to bring the exercise of such responsible power before a supreme court and a supreme responsibility.

Second, the morality of *noblesse oblige* in new form, appropriate to coming democracy. You had better use your wealth, or your power, morally or you will be overthrown by those whom you treat with injustice or with indifference.

This line of thinking can be detected within all the Christian Socialist movements, though of course the deeper thinkers among Christian Socialists repudiated the paternalistic notions inherent in *noblesse oblige*. But it was not confined to Christian Socialists. On 14 February 1883 H. P. Liddon preached in the cathedral at Oxford to a congregation of Christ Church undergraduates, and was evidently conscious that soon they would inherit much money:

There are, perhaps, some young men among my hearers who a few years hence will dispose of considerable fortunes. Depend on it, brethren, that much even here depends – nothing, perhaps less than the safety of the social structure in this country – on the way in which you will understand your responsibilities. The strength of communistic theories, here and everywhere else, consists, not in any solid truth on which they rest, since generally they do but cover a single background of tangled fallacies, but in the failure of so many among the wealthier classes to understand the true relations of property to life.⁵

That is, you rich men had better be aware of your moral duty or you will not long be rich.

It was rather like the preaching of Salvian in the early fifth century – or even of Israelite prophets in a state of siege – you had better amend or you will be destroyed – a preaching inevitable and expected in times of looming disaster. In Liddon, or his type of preaching, there were two differences: first, the disaster of Salvian, or of Jeremiah, was of a different scale; the disaster which loomed in Liddon's mind seems to us to have been such an unconscionable time coming that we can hardly understand how middle or even late Victorians, secure men in secure world, expected disaster round the next corner; and secondly, the appeal of Salvian or Jeremiah was rather more to heavenly powers. Liddon was an otherworldly man. But here his preaching appeal was to this world. Repent, or else. . . not that God will overthrow, but the people will overthrow. We cannot however be so certain, as at first sight might appear, that Salvian and Jeremiah meant something much more 'otherworldly' than Liddon.

Both these attitudes are easy for us to understand, even for us to share. The third strand is less easy. Society has a due order. This order is given by God, or by circumstances, or both. Without that due order society cannot cohere. To say that all men are equal is to say what is false, it propagates a dream, a dangerous illusion. It tells men to be discontented with their lot when their lot is inevitable. Therefore religion is the only force capable of sustaining society against this threat. It teaches men vocation in their due place. It shows how they are to be resigned, how a man ought not to hunt wealth or run after power; how he who sweeps a room 'as for Thy laws, makes that and the action fine'.

'Catholicism', wrote Guizot once (and Guizot was a Protestant) 'is the grandest and holiest school of respect that the world has ever seen!'[6] So late as 28 December 1878 the new Pope Leo XIII issued the encyclical *Quod apostolici muneris* condemning the 'sect' with the diverse and 'almost barbarous' names of Socialists, Communists and Nihilists.

They say that authority comes not from God but from the people, and the people is subject to no divine sanction and will obey no laws but those which suit itself. . .God has set up different orders in society and as for princes, obedience is always due to them unless they command what is against the law of God.[7]

Fourthly: the state of the future looked like being a sovereign, omnicompetent state. John Stuart Mill wrote his essay *On Liberty* to protect men against the tyranny of coming democratic majorities. This same feeling is found among churchmen at least from 1870 onwards, until Neville Figgis gave it a theoretical basis in his *Churches in the Modern State* of 1914. Order gave better security for freedom. On 16 November 1878 the right-wing deputy, the Comte de Mun, spoke in the Paris Chamber of Deputies:

The Revolution. . .puts the human reason as Sovereign, in place of the law of God. From this flows all the rest – especially the pride and rebellion which is the source of the modern state. The State has taken over everything, the State has become your God. We are not willing [he said to the Republicans opposite] to join you in making obeisance to this idol of a state. The Counter-Revolution, that is the opposite of what you stand for. It is the doctrine which founds society on Christian faith.[8]

This link between Church and social order appears in many places of Europe. Modern research has examined the relation of Prussian evangelical leaders to the extreme right-wing stances of the Prussian government during the 1850s and 1860s. But it was a Swiss of 1867–9 who said that a worker without God, and without hope of another life, would remain dissatisfied with his wages however high the wages.[9]

At the centre of our problem lies the Syllabus of Errors, appended to the encyclical *Quanta cura* of Pope Pius IX in December 1864. Its last section condemned *errores qui ad liberalismum hodiernum referuntur*. The last proposition of that last section condemned the doctrine that the Pope 'can and ought to reconcile himself with progress, with liberalism, and with modern civilization'.

Historians of the twentieth century have minimized or neglected the Syllabus. They see that it was not a papal bull, but an appendix; that it was afterwards interpreted variously, and that even the Pope himself approved in conversation a lax or minimizing interpretation; that it sprang out of a political situation of the moment, when the Pope lost his lands after a thousand years of ownership, and ceased to be relevant when the politics ceased to live; that the fight over it concerned the doctrine of authority in a particular church, that is, was a matter only of theology and not of European politics. Such estimates gravely mistake the European importance of what happened. The Syllabus was symbol of something bigger, namely, the stance of the Pope in the age of Garibaldi and the Risorgimento. But no one ought to neglect the consequences in European opinion of that stance.

Europe – not perhaps in Spain; not in all of Italy; but in Britain, France, Germany, Austria, Belgium, Holland, Poland, Switzerland – Europe saw the Pope condemn liberalism – whatever that was, the Pope condemned it. And without precisely defining liberalism, or defining it in diverse ways, Europe saw that this was the irresistible force of the age. The Pope sat on his throne like Canute amid the incoming tide. But the Pope looked not merely ridiculous. Ethical ideals were associated with the slogans of liberalism, words like liberty and fraternity, freedom of conscience, tolerance, justice in the way of equality before the law. Many western Europeans had the sensation, not just that the Pope was wrong, but that he was morally wrong.

You did not need to be Protestant to feel this. Sir John Acton (as he then was) combined a devout Roman Catholic faith with a critical mind. The recently discovered Ampthill Papers record some extraordinary utterances of Acton during his visit to Rome during the early part of 1867. They are recorded in letters of Odo Russell, the envoy of the British government to the Vatican; a friend of Acton who saw him often. Here, as only one example of several, is a conversation recorded by Odo Russell on 12 March 1867.[10] I put it from the *oratio obliqua* of the record into direct speech:

ACTON: I cannot conceive a man like you discussing, admitting the possibility of the continuance of the Temporal Power. It is unworthy of you to admit such a contingency when the duty of every honest man is to upset it as soon and as completely as possible.

RUSSELL (*astonished*): A sensible secretary of state instead of [Cardinal] Antonelli could collect and secure [the] sympathies of foreign governments and get [a] guarantee from the Powers of a continuance [of the Temporal Power].

ACTON: (*replied in a long and eloquent condemnation of the Papal government, and ended with these remarkable words, which made Cartwright bound from his chair, and made Mrs Craven fold her hands in prayer to supplicate him to stop*): I pray to God that I may live to see the whole of this Fabric destroyed, and the Tiber flow with the blood of the massacred Priests.

(*On our all exclaiming, he repeated these words in a solemn voice and and with great stress.*)

Russell asked for explanations. Acton, in a very long conversation, said,

The Church cannot be reformed and become what it ought [to be] and what I want it to be, unless it be destroyed and rebuilt. I want the liberty of the press to destroy the Inquisition, and control the morals of priests, etc. . . .

Russell challenged the wisdom and the realism of what Acton said. The argument ended in Acton accusing Russell of 'falling into the Cant of Diplomacy'. 'You forget Divine Interests for mere human patchwork. Your views', he said disdainfully, 'are those of an ordinary man of the world.'

Here was a Catholic burning with anger against the Pope's stance and the political structure which begat it; an anger mostly composed of moral indignation.

The first Vatican Council of 1869–70 was afterwards seen to be concerned with the theology of faith and ecclesiastical certitude. That was not what was believed at the time, not even perhaps by the Pope. At the time it was believed to be concerned with the question of questions, whether liberalism and Catholicism could be reconciled. We find its consequences running all across Europe; in the discomforts between Ireland and the British Government, in the conflict between Poland and the Russian Government, in the politics of education in Belgium, in Bismarck's Kulturkampf and above all in the French political strife after 1871. Gambetta's famous quotation of his friend Peyrat, 'Clericalism, that is the enemy!' came in a speech (4 May 1877) reflecting on the entire Catholic posture generated by the Syllabus.[11] From a republican stance it had a touch of truth. The working-men of Europe looked for hope from the extension of the vote, probably from universal suffrage. And in 1874 Pope Pius IX, who became talkative in his old age, gave some French pilgrims a special blessing on their efforts against the 'horrible plague which affected human society', namely 'universal suffrage'.[12]

The French conflict was as much a political as a social battle. This is one of the reasons which leads me to think that sociological schools of history have not the exclusive answer to our problem, and that quite old-fashioned political history can have consequences in social change.

2

Were Churches on the political right in the nineteenth century only because of the politics of the age; liberal theory versus the inherited structure of the past?

Probably not. The base of Christianity lay (because the base of religion lay) in the family. Religion was close to the institution of the family. The household gods of the ancient world, the icons on the shelf of the Russian peasant, the little statues of St Mary or St Joseph, were ritual first of the family, and so of the tribe, the clan, the city and at last the state. Revolution in the nineteenth century knew of the state and the individual but not much of the organisms between. It exhorted sons to throw off the yoke of their fathers and of custom. To be religious was to be like a man inheriting a trust from the past. To be converted was to accept a bequest from the past. This inheritance was made real in the present, adapted, altered, made relevant, criticized and reformed. But still it was inheritance. Religion was part of continuity in the family. It helped to conserve moral values. It could never baptise with total cheerfulness a system or a philosophy which damned continuity, the stream of civilized inheritance. Religion was at its most powerful when men stood by the open graves of their father or their mother in a churchyard.

In one of Bourget's novels, *L'Étape* (1902), Jean Monneron, child of a republican anticlerical, was converted to Catholicism. He said to his friend, 'I've decided to become what all my family was for centuries. I want to get back, down into the depths of France. I can't live without my dead.'[13] This was no discovery of the nineteenth century. 'After God', wrote St Thomas Aquinas in the *Summa*, 'a man owes most to his parents and his country. If it is the duty of a religious man to worship God, his second duty is to revere his parents and his country.'[14]

Beyond the family, extension of the family, lay the community, the town, the state. As religion lay near loyalty to the family, religion lay near loyalty to the state, and was usually an element constitutive of continuity in the life of the state. Catholicism was part of the continuity of France (even of anticlerical France), Lutheranism part of the continuity of Germany or Sweden, Presbyterianism part of the continuity of Scotland. Religion and patriotism often lay together in a moral attitude. We find men who appear to be patriots because they are religious, other men who appear to be religious because they are patriots. Like non-jurors of the seventeenth century, some of them had a religious and not merely a political commitment to monarchy, and to legitimacy; just in the age when legitimate monarchs fell fast.

This religious sense of continuity and inheritance therefore had another consequence. Loyalty to the past stood for due order in the present. Not only, not even mainly, because the churches claimed to stand for a fixed body of truth, a harmonious philosophy of life, and an objective standard of private and public morals. Its ritual was a base of social custom. *Remember the days of old, consider the years of many generations; ask thy father and he will shew thee; thy elders, and they will tell thee...As an eagle fluttereth over her young, taketh them, beareth them on her wings; so the Lord alone did lead Jacob, and there was no strange god with him.* (Deuteronomy 32, 7–12.)

The words *clericalism* and *anticlericalism* have an interesting history. The first instance of clericalism given by the *Oxford English*

Dictionary comes in the *Saturday Review* for 1864: 'A living protest against clericalism.'

We are not surprised to find the word appearing within a year or two years of the first uses, in our sense, of the word *secularization*. Both words were needed by critics, with their sense of light versus darkness, rationality versus obscurantism. In the first decade or two the word was used normally about French politics, as for example in the *Daily News* of 11 February 1870 when the Haute-Saône is 'a stronghold of clericalism'.

But the first usage found, in May 1864, was not about France. It was a *Saturday Review* leader (1864, 470) against the Pope's Munich brief, castigating the inability of the Roman clergy to comprehend the movement of modern intelligence, lamenting that *the lesson taught by Galileo is still unlearnt*, comparing the Pope to Bishop Wilberforce of Oxford with his endeavours to silence historical critics of the Bible, and regretting that the brief caused Acton to end his *Home and Foreign Review*, which, wrote the leader, has been 'a living protest against clericalism, obscurantism and administrative despotism'. Note the juxtaposition of nouns.

The words *anticlerical* and *anticlericalism* followed a little later. They were probably Belgian in origin, and so passed to France. But the French coined them no earlier than the English. They do not appear in Littré's *Dictionnaire* of 1863. Even in that year, and from a positivist author, the entry for the word *laïque* is very short, and has neither pejorative nor metaphysical overtone. Littré first included *laïcité* in the supplement of 1877.

So the word *anticlerical* was a word which identified churches, or rather the Roman Catholic Church, with antagonism to modern liberties.

We must therefore distinguish anticlericalism as it came to embitter early modern mass societies from anticlericalism as it was since clergy were ordained. Every profession has its critics; politicians, professors, lawyers, schoolmasters, soldiers or builders' mates, all have their caricaturists and witty denigrators; every profession with a claim to influence has enemies; every man who tells you to be good is liable to prying investigation to see whether he practises what he preaches and Molière-like ridicule if he does not; a caste, separated from the rest of society by unusual customs, like enforced celibacy, will have novelists dramatizing its adulteries; anyone with an effect upon the passions and kinships and agonies of man, in marriage or sex, in babies or children, in suffering or death, may be feared as an outside intruder. These feelings were not new to the Catholic or anti-Catholic nineteenth century. They had always been the dark underside of a work which could be the most rewarding, in personal terms, known to man. It was not the priest's business to be obscure, nor even to be quietly conformist. It was his vocation to be followed or resisted, hated or beloved.

That was not new. What was new, in a mass society, was the political element which enabled the old antipathies to come out of the ginshops and bars and beery ditties, and become a programme against a governing party in the State.

Anticlerical movements in the modern sense did not exist in the old structure of throne and altar. They existed in modern democracies or incipient democracies:

where the peasant population was Catholic or partially Catholic;

where universal suffrage was introduced, or about to be introduced;

therefore where a religiously based political party was powerful at the poll.

It does not matter, absolutely, whether the Catholic party was liberal or Syllabus-bound. In Belgium the Catholic party accepted all the principles of 1789. They played the political game according to liberal principles and won their spectacular triumph immediately after the introduction of universal suffrage. When in power they were a Catholic social party – developing the welfare state for the worker. Yet their power fostered the rise of anticlerical opinion.

Unquestionably, however, a Catholic party in a less educated country produced more violent anticlericalism, partly because it produced more violent Catholicism. In Spain the law for universal suffrage was passed in 1890 at a time when more than 40 per cent of the people were still illiterate. That meant, a very conservative peasant population; and consequently very conservative church leaders. The gaining of popular votes by a liberal party was necessarily accompanied by assaults upon church power. The old alliance of throne and altar, though still standing nominally, could no longer protect Catholics against these assaults, and therefore Catholic leaders engaged in power politics to protect their endowments or their privilege in education. Because Spain was more clerical than Belgium, the anticlerical movement was more bitter. But in both cases its full flowering was due to the coming of universal suffrage.

The anticlerical movement in politics *used* the Syllabus. But it did not depend on it. It needed the rallying-cry of anticlericalism to rally voters who agreed on little else. It is the aim of a political party to gain power. Faced with a Catholic political party in power, or threatening to gain power, it needed to attack its roots not only in politics but in religion.

The rise of democracy created special novelty in the old problem of the relations between Church and State.

Before Marxists attained power in Russia and China, the proposition was widely believed, government likes religion. Wanting honesty and service, it hopes that religion helps to make honest men who serve. But government is ever aware that religion is unpredictable and that prophets are hard to control. To rule men needs compromise. In face of the sacred is always an unbendable will. Government likes religion to bless its acts, crown its dictators, sanction its laws, define its wars as just, be decorous master of national ceremonies. And since on grounds of religion religious men may criticize acts or laws or wars or modes of waging war, government prefers quietness and contemplation to excess of zeal. Though religion is important to government, it does not value excess of religion. It is happy with general morality, reasonable and moderate, but is uncomfortable with too much enthusiasm.

In the 1880s the journalist and philosopher Paul Desjardins founded a vague little religious group in France. A republican anticlerical expressed his alarm:

'It's dangerous, this machine of M. Desjardins.'
'Why?'
'A religion could come out of it, and not an old tired religion but a new just-born religion, that is an adult religion, for religions have the special quality that they are never more adult than when they are just born...'
'Well?'
'Well, this will embarrass government.'
'Why?'
'I'll bet you, it will embarrass government. Anything with a strong moral life has a will of its own. Anything with a will of its own embarrasses government.'[15]

Democracy allowed freedom of propaganda to the various groups in the State, and among them the Churches. Churchmen feeling their freedom, and realizing that they competed in an open market of opinion, were open, zealous, popular, aggressive. The Ultramontane movement in the French Church had for an outward aim the lifting up of the Pope's power. But underneath, it was a devotional movement at the level of parishes, placing Catholic life before a half-educated public, making religion warm, emotional, exciting, colourful and ardent. Ultramontane priests and laymen had no desire to make religion quietly acceptable among the people. They pursued a more uncomfortable goal. They wanted to make disciples, if possible, and if not disciples then antagonists. They wished to be followed or to be attacked. No one could be neutral about a saintly Ultramontane priest like the Curé d'Ars, or a violent Ultramontane journalist like Louis Veuillot. They divided men into sheep and goats and meant to.

Anticlericalism was a function, not of the weakness of the Catholic Church, but of its growing power in a modern democratic society.

Until after 1870 the stance of the French worker is difficult to analyse. Anticlericalism only began to be a French word in the 1860s and some historians have contended that until the fall of the Emperor Louis Napoleon in 1870, French general society was no more divided over religion than British or German. It is easy enough to find reports like that of the prefect of Haut-Rhin on 15 June 1828. 'The people, above all in the countryside, is but for a few exceptions religious and attached to the government.' A mob of 1830 sacked the archbishop's palace at Saint-Germain; but we can tell nothing about the attitude of the working-man from the émeute. All over France mobs moved as though to down the Church. In the Paris revolution of 1848 the crowds by contrast seemed very Christian, with clergy blessing trees of liberty. A famous story told how the crowd got into the Tuileries palace and started throwing furniture out of the windows. A young man ran to the chapel to save the sacred vessels and crucifix. When he got into the mob, men shouted at him menacingly. So he held aloft the crucifix, and cried above the din, 'If you want to be saved remember this, you can be saved by Christ alone!' And the surrounding mob shouted: 'Yes, yes, he is Lord of all!' and everyone whipped off their caps and escorted the crucifix and vessels in unceremonious procession to the Church of Saint Roch where the curé received them solemnly. George Sand tells of a demonstrator whom she saw crying: *Up with the Republic! Up with equality! Up with the true republic of Christ!*[16]

From these stories and other information of the kind some historians inferred a big change in French mood after the revolution of 1848, and argued that with the blessing of the Church on the dictatorship of Louis Napoleon from 1852 the churches began to lose working-men. But from a pro-Christian mob we can safely deduce as little as from an anti-Christian mob.

The deeds of 'anticlerical mobs' are instinctive. The demonstration which gets out of hand is a demonstration against government. An infuriated crowd would like to batter down palace, or Houses of Parliament, or castle. But these homes of government, unless they are the Bastille or the Winter Palace, are too stoutly defended for crowds with sticks and pistols to attack. Government commands what troops are near, and first takes care of itself, and rings fortress or chamber with bayonets. It cannot quiet the city but can only survive till reinforcements come. Yet a crowd in control of a city must do something if it is sufficiently angry, for example if demonstrators or bystanders have been shot by a volley from police. It cannot disperse. Its hot emotions have to find outlet. If leaders can be found, and weapons acquired, and soldiers made sympathetic, they can find their outlet by erecting barricades in the street and so begin revolution. If weapons cannot be acquired, it is too probable that intelligent leaders, political leaders, cannot be found, for any sane politician sees that the émeute has no future but repression. The mob then has no leaders but men of the streets with stentorian cries and lurid aprons. It must wreak its wrath on something which is helpless, is regarded as public property, and is associated with government.

This is the characteristic situation for an 'anticlerical riot'. There may be a further element. In a few known cases – for example, the Paris revolution of 1830, preeminently the Barcelona 'tragic week' of 1909 – commanders of one side or the other diverted the fury of the mob to churches or church property for the sake of preventing them from attacking palace or Parliament and therefore from facing troops. In Paris the police consciously helped to direct the crowd to attack the archbishop's palace in order to save the king's palace.

In Barcelona more than one intelligent man to whom the crowd looked for political lead diverted the smashing into churches and convents so that the demonstrators should not make hopeless assault upon an armed garrison; that is, politicians, knowing that the mob must do something and seeing that revolution was vain, turned the passions of the people into a fury which ended in arson and destruction but only in a few deaths (three priests, of which one accidental), instead of a pitched battle with many deaths.

When however we speak of 'the passions of the people' we are not to take this literally. Those organizing the demonstration are always a small and powerful group. The circumstances and the way it is handled by authority drive to their aid the sympathies of many. But when the demonstration goes wrong, and turns to mindless violence for the sake of release, the destruction is wrought by a few hundred people, never more, but watched by interested spectators. These spectators are very passive. They treat it like an outing, as in our days they flock round a crashed aircraft. They do not join the stone-throwers but neither do they help the attacked. The parish priest of one of the Barcelona churches lay in danger for several hours from a small group of young men setting fire to and breaking his building, and at last died of injury or fumes or shock – but during those hours no spectator raised a finger to get him out.

When we say that the mob needs a defenceless target associated with government, we touch upon the general politics of the country; conflict of liberal versus conservative, sense that the churches are friends of the conservative. In both Paris and Barcelona, three-quarters of a century apart, those who wished the churches or archbishop's palace attacked, merely needed to pass round the rumour that weapons of counter-revolution were stored in churches or monasteries. Most destructions in such riots are wrought in slums or working-class areas – for churches and convents and manses are the only buildings in those areas which are class-less and therefore not part of the mentality of the ghetto.

The sacred must have something to do with the crowd psychology. Rioters talk sometimes of wealth concealed in churches. But much more wealth lies in banks, and crowds never selected banks for consistent attack. Nor is looting an explanation. To raid department stores would be more profitable than snatching chasubles from vestries or breaking tombs in cemeteries to see if rings are on the dead. But in the circumstances I have described, members of a mob are far more likely to do the second than the first. The quality of outlet, which is the essence of the moment, is met, not by stealing for private gain, but by knocking down something regarded as sacred. Pollution of 'the holy' is a need of the moment of crisis.

From the heat of such crisis it is evidently unsafe to draw conclusions about attitudes to religion among the general population. Earlier riots which destroyed churches – Lord George Gordon in England of 1780, several of the 'Protestant' riots in German cities at the beginning of the Reformation, bear marked parallels with so-called anticlerical riots of the nineteenth century.

The evidence of religious attitudes varies greatly according to province or department or even suburb. We owe a debt to Gabriel Le Bras and his school because more work has been done on local differences in France than in any other country. Much more remains to be done. But investigations point to differences, reaching back into the past, between one region and another. There have been suggestions that a difference in religious practice can be discerned, for example, between those on the right bank of a river and those on the left, though both banks were in the same diocese and the same kind of parishes. If this were so, old historical reasons, long vanished from the realities of the present, ought to be working – a war, a bishop, an old frontier; the influence or non-influence of a group of parish priests – we can guess at a variety of motives or we can guess at mere chance. The deeds of men in the past live extraordinarily into the present; for sometimes in nineteenth-century France the division between better and worse practice of religion ran along an old and no longer existing frontier between one-time dioceses. Someone must have done good, or someone must have neglected, someone was beloved or someone despised, back into the eighteenth century or even into the age of religious war. If once a group had to fight for its religion, its posterity seem more likely to value it inarticulately. Descendants of exiled French Huguenots in Germany or England formed lively enclaves of religious practice, for their family history was conditioned by a one-time allegiance, at high cost, to their faith. In just the same way, in France of the nineteenth century, Catholics were quite likely to be more devout in places where once Protestants were strong.[17] Some of the differences between one area and another reach back at least into the seventeenth century, probably into the age of the Reformation, perhaps into the Middle Ages. We keep being surprised to find how undying are the dead.

These differences were not only due to individuals and their effect in groupings, and the effect of groupings upon large areas. Calamity or prosperity could evidently matter, civil war or civil peace, exploitation or justice, administrative neglect or capable government. Whatever such events affected French religion in centuries past, one event of the past dwarfed all others throughout the intellectual and social history of the nineteenth century; the French Revolution of 1789, or (even more) the French Revolution of 1793. Men were guillotined, drowned, expropriated and murdered; and other men attained freedom, equal rights before the law, modest prosperity and self-respect. On the one side killings and terror, on the other justice and democracy – the children of revolutionaries or counter-revolutionaries could hate the Revolution or love the ideals of the Revolution, and France was rent through the nineteenth century.

Almost steadily, the Catholic Church of France stood, and looked as though it stood, upon the side which was not the side of the Revolution. Men might say that liberty and fraternity were Christian ideals. Rebel priests like Lamennais might demand that the Pope baptise revolution. Some bishops were more democratic and occasionally more republican than many of their people. But in nearly everyone's mind the Revolution stood, first, for the demolition of the old Gallican Church of France; second, for the kidnapping of the Pope and confiscation of his inheritance; third, for atheism or rationalism, that is, for anti-Catholic thought as well as anti-Catholic practice. The breach in the national soul was healed at odd times by men and occasions – as for a moment in Paris streets during the revolution of 1848. But for nearly all the century, at least until 1891 and really until 1914, Church and Revolution sounded antipathetic terms. And this was not just because the word Revolution stood for violence and illegality, since the word Revolution also stood, in the minds of many, for justice and freedom.

This overwhelming event of the recent past made the atmosphere of French religion different from the atmosphere of contemporary Germany or contemporary Britain. *For our purposes* it may have been a more important difference than the circumstance that Britain and Germany were Protestant by majority and France by majority Catholic. Still, France was Catholic. Catholicism of the Counter-Reformation was hardly more embattled than Protestantism of the Reformation. In the eighteenth century the age of reason allowed the hard lines of old entrenchments to dilapidate, and dismantled the battlements. During the eighteenth century many French clergy were liberal, educated, far from obscurantist. The Revolution killed this more liberal spirit within French Catholicism as it killed Gallicanism. Even Protestants of Germany and Britain felt a need to look to their weapons again, to revive dormant practices, to be uncompromising in loyalty. Catholics of France felt the same need but with anguish. The task of keeping pace with a world that changed ever more quickly was made harder. For to some French Catholic leaders, keeping up with threatening modernity was like trying to run fast enough to keep up with the Gadarene swine.

In Protestant Britain and Protestant Germany religion was decked in many shades and colours from militant ultra-orthodoxy to watery agnostic religiosity. Men had no vision of a gulf impassable between Christian and un-Christian. It was easy for pious Englishmen to enjoy if not to revere Matthew Arnold or George Eliot. In Catholic France – though this is much less marked in the first three-quarters of the century – a man was Catholic or he was not. In Paris and Alsace lived numbers of Protestants. Hard Catholics deplored Protestants as they deplored atheists. We find devout Protestants among the leaders of later anticlerical skirmishes.

The Ultramontane movement among French Catholics was more than a campaign to increase the authority of the Pope in order to sustain the independence of the Church in a democratic and no longer Catholic State. But its ardour included love of the Pope, support of the Pope, desire for Roman liturgy or habits or architecture in France. And from 1815 the Popes were threatened by Italian revolution and Italian nationalism. To help the Pope meant voting for the Emperor Louis Napoleon because from 1850 until the war of 1870 he sustained the Pope's independent State with French bayonets. But it meant far more – supporting the Syllabus, distrusting representative government, attacking liberty of the press or of conscience; standing in short against 'the Revolution'.

Until 1870 France was a country of tensions, but not much more agonizing tensions than could often be found in Germany or Britain. After spring 1871 the word tension is too weak. The Paris Commune, with its massacre of hostages and pollution of churches proved to half France that the Pope was right. Justice and modern liberties were opposites. The French political right moved further to the right, the left further to the left.

But the political right was Catholic.

In the later Middle Ages pilgrimages became a people's devotion, at once travel and penance, holiday and self-sacrifice. The Reformation and Counter-Reformation attacked their abuses and decried their popularity. In the middle of the nineteenth century pilgrimages revived and by the 1870s and 1880s attained unprecedented numbers and popularity. The reason was simple: modern transport, steam by rail and by sea. Protestants began to make visits to the Holy Land where, as of old, tourism married piety in happiness. Catholics began to make visits to Lourdes, or Paray-le-Monial, or La Salette. The railway allowed the people again to say their prayers at the holy places of which they read in books or heard in sermons. The Catholics found it a revival of Catholic devotion. And when American and British and German Protestants visited Bethlehem or Nazareth, at first they hardly realized how they shared a religious instinct present in the early Christians.

Between 1871 and 1876 pilgrimages in France attained extraordinary numbers. 50,000 people and more would say their prayers at the shrine in Lourdes. They were warm, cheerful, expectant of miracle, emotional, brash; and they could be offensive to reasonable or unCatholic passers-by.

Vast crowds of Catholics gathered round a sanctuary – they moved the participants and fortified them. But in the France of the 1870s they easily put on the face of demonstrations. They were indeed demonstrations, like a Labour procession on Mayday, though with different objectives and thoughts and destination. As demonstrations, they were politics. So indissoluble was the union between Catholics and the political right, that speeches or sermons of bishops at a shrine could call for expiation by France of republican sins, for the return of the French monarchy, or even for the restoration by force of the temporal power of the Pope.

In these conditions God was a political slogan, anti-God another political slogan. Some of those who went on pilgrimage to the shrine of Our Lady at Lourdes in 1875 performed an act as much political as religious. Conversely the incorporation of anticlerical planks in the platform of republican or socialist parties owed more to political tactic than to irreligious necessity. They united parties agreed on little else, and afforded an apparent policy instead of a real policy. At times less extreme republican politicians hardly minded whether they were anticlerical as long as they were thought anticlerical. When Marshal MacMahon dismissed the republican Assembly on 16·May 1877 and summoned the de Broglie cabinet, half France was moved when Gambetta (16 June) told it falsely that the coup was a coup d'état of priests, that the new government was a government of parsons.[18]

An obscurantist body of religious men, obscurantist in large part because they were religious – versus a society marching towards light, liberty, social well-being – was that what it was? The very word *Kulturkampf* was invented by Virchow to mean struggle for civilization against obscurantism. Or, a body of religious men, who saw truths of human nature, and stood for all that was moral and civilized against modern materialism – versus a society plunging towards the tyrannies of social chaos – was that what it was?

The question of religious versus non-religious had never been so potentially divisive in the human spirit. At least Christianity would have to search into its truths. For it was now in a world where some men had motives of passion, and not mere motives of the lecture-room, for proving it untrue; and other men had motives of passion for holding religious doctrines to be true whether they were true or false. For local reasons the conflict in France was more agonizing. But it stood for a European religious predicament.

Here is a manuscript letter, now in the British Museum, from Archbishop Manning of Westminster to his friend Gladstone, who was then prime minister of Britain, and dated 13 November 1871:

> ...Of this I am sure as of the motion of the earth. My belief is that faith is gone from society as such; morals are going; and politics will end in the paralysis of the governing power. The end of this must be anarchy or despotism. How soon I do not know.
> France is there already: Italy will be: and England will not stand for ever. I have been a fearless Radical all my life; and am not afraid of popular legislation, but legislation without principles is in strict sense anarchy.
> I see no principle now but the *will* of the majority; the will of the majority is not either reason or right.
> My belief is that Society without Christianity is the Commune...What hope can you give me?[19]

Jesuits had a long reputation in European history. In the age with which I am concerned Jesuits were banned from Switzerland, Germany and finally France. Whether they behaved so as to deserve these prohibitions was hardly ever investigated. They had a history. That history was identified with what was now called the politics of the Syllabus.

Most of the 'ills' of the first Vatican Council were charged to them. How many of their members held opinions which agreed with the opinions of liberal imagination is not known and now is not knowable. But the slogan, the once-gained repute, was powerful.

Speeches were made in the French Assembly with extracts from Jesuit casuistical theologians, as though these concerned French politics of the nineteenth century. In 1876 a number of candidates for admission to the Paris Polytechnic were proved to have gained a previous knowledge of an examination paper – and they were candidates who came from the Jesuit school in the Rue des Postes. Because of French history, and because of the politics of that age, the matter was taken up in the Chamber, and students demonstrated outside the house in the Rue des Postes.[20]

In this kind of strife, where a nation was divided, each side had an interest in portraying the other by its extreme party. It paid radical controversialists to pretend that the journalist Louis Veuillot, who wrote among much else that Luther had been better burnt, was typical of Catholics; and radical controversialists had this extenuation, that Pope Pius IX approved Veuillot in person and much (though not all) of what he wrote.

Catholic fighters had an interest in representing radicals as Jacobin, or as shooters of hostages or polluters of churches; and they had this extenuation, in the number of pamphleteers, from Karl Marx downwards, who defended or applauded the behaviour of the Commune. The slogan was what mattered. It bore a relation to truth. But, like the organs of the press which popularized it and lived by it, relation to truth was not the most important thing. It gathered a party, and articulated an attitude to social and political affairs.

In one aspect anticlericalism in France rose out of a problem which concerned religion only indirectly: the question of Church and State. Since churches existed, they had not found it easy to determine where the rights of God and the rights of Caesar began and ended. If they claimed the power to draw the frontier as they thought fit, they might end by frustrating the capacity of the secular authority to govern, as with weaker states in the later Middle Ages. If they allowed king or parliament to draw the frontier, they risked handing over an inviolable conscience to politicians who looked only for the expedient. Church and State had always rubbed along with a measure of friction, occasionally issuing in explosive crises, usually kept within tolerable limits by luck and by compromise.

Representative governments posed the problem of this frontier between Church and State in a new form. It made customary forms of compromise impossible. The old world regulated its give-and-take with the less discomfort because government was avowedly and openly Christian, whether Catholic or Protestant. Churchmen accepted restrictions on liberty which government proposed because government itself owed allegiance to the Church. But no representative government could be openly Christian in the ancient way. Even if king or prime minister were devout or saintly (and it was not certainly in the interests of democratic government that a prime minister should be saintly) government must be neutral, must treat religions impartially; and to treat all religions impartially is to treat irreligion impartially.

By its nature representative government was weaker because it could be overturned by slight swings of opinion. Therefore it began to have a difficulty in controlling all corporative institutions within the state – industrial companies, trade unions, press, professional guilds and churches. Power diminished in the centre as government came to be government by consensus, and fragments of this power descended on any group which guided opinion. To control a church in the interests of government, or what was alleged to be good government, could not be achieved by the quiet old-fashioned methods of acceptable Concordats (except so far as their legal provisions survived from the past) or by bureaucratic device. Churches were too free for such time-honoured machinery to be effective. If they were to be controlled by acts of Parliament, that meant ultimately by public opinion. The Kulturkampf in Germany, whereby Bismarck sought to limit the power of the Catholic Church in Germany, was a series of acts of Parliament; carried through, however, only because public opinion by majority supported them and failing ultimately because public opinion refused to support them further.

The modern Church preached in the market place. Its power could be limited only by attention to the market place, and no longer by quick decision in the ante-room of a palace.

3

Some historians have classified nationalism as a 'rival religion',[21] especially if these historians wrote their histories of the nineteenth century during the age of Hitler. Whether or not that has any truth – and those who knew Nazis cannot quite deny it – its doctrines were not all in harmony with those of Christianity. It bade men sacrifice themselves for their country, not for their fellow-men. In its more fanatical form it disliked whatever savoured of international brotherhood.

Makers of dictionaries, who tried to explain *nationality*, left their definitions shadowy and vague. The thinkers of the nineteenth century tried various formulas. They agreed that race was important, but not exclusively so, for the Scottish or Welsh could be as nationalistic about Britain as the English. They agreed that language was important, but not exclusively so, for Alsace spoke a German dialect and adhered by national feeling to France. Since the nineteenth century was the age of an idealistic philosophy, they usually agreed that nationality was an inward principle, a spirit, the soul of a people. Even when they were prosaic utilitarians, they were not content with a prosaic definition. The Encyclopaedists of the eighteenth century sometimes reduced the idea of nation to the number of people inhabiting an area of land and wanting to be ruled by the same government and not by other government. The utilitarians of the nineteenth century confessed that so bald a statement neglected what mattered most – the common sympathies, loyalties, or affections which turned groups of men into *a nation*. As cause of these common sympathies, they attributed much to history; that is, to the social structures created by past events, and to memories in the consciousness of a people.

It was once an axiom that the best government was simply the best government; that if a government established justice, and cared for the welfare of the people, nothing else about it mattered. On this axiom Vienna and London established empires during the entire nineteenth century and after – successfully, so long as the people whom they ruled were themselves content with the axiom. Even in the states which young nationalism made revolutionary, the workingman was surprisingly difficult to interest in patriotic rebellions. Polish middle-class patriots, when planning force against their Russian masters, were vexed to find how little the Polish labourer seemed to mind being subject to the Russians provided his food and wages were secure. Italian middle-class radicals, who mistook the Papal states for the worst governed State in Europe, were grieved that Italian labourers in Central Italy cared not at all whether they were governed by priests provided that they were governed well. Not everyone who thought about these matters believed that liberty and nationalism went together. Even at the end of the century Lord Acton weighed the national state and the multi-national state, and decided that the best state was that which (like the British or Austrian Empires) gave a liberty to several different nationalities. The old international ideas of Christendom married more easily to states which were not identified with one nation or one race; according to the old and wise saying, *ubi bene ibi patria*.

The middle class did not believe it, in France, or Germany, or Northern Italy. 'The peoples', wrote Mazzini, 'will only reach the highest point of development of which they are capable when they are united in a single bond ... Every people is bound to constitute itself a nation before it can occupy itself with the question of humanity.'[22]

The word *nationality* became fully established in the languages of western Europe only between 1815 and 1848.

The states of western Europe became nations as their people became more educated, and therefore more politically conscious; as the press established its public and diminished the ignorance of national and international events; and as the railways diminished distances within a state and throughout Europe.

The enemies of nationalism were: first, racial minorities, which preferred rule by a benevolent despot to rule by a nationalist majority; secondly, international socialism as it began to develop – 'workers of the world, unite'; thirdly, churches, especially the Papacy.

4

Christianity was international. Religion as a social fact was not, or not necessarily. A racial and oppressed minority kept itself together in its Church. Its culture, language, and national feeling were expressed through its religious allegiance. If it was not permitted political leaders, it turned to religious leaders. The Rumanians survived as a national unity under the Turks by focussing their common heritage in the Orthodox Church. So the Greeks. The Irish and the Belgians expressed in their Roman Catholicism not only their religious faith but their cultural and political differences from Protestant Britain or Holland. In Poland, divided among the powers, Catholicism crossed the frontiers and joined with race and language in allowing Poles to express their sense of unity. German national feeling was in large part historical; and for the Protestant majority Luther was the chief symbol of the German inheritance. In northern Germany the Reformation was bound with national consciousness. Reformation festivals at the Wartburg were national as well as religious celebrations. When the question came to the front whether Austria or Prussia should take the lead among the German states, Catholicism was an obstacle to Austrian hegemony. In Russia, despite the existence of Catholics and a few Protestants, nationality and holy Orthodoxy could look to be the same. When the Tsar forced the Ruthenians to sever their allegiance to Rome and become Orthodox (1839), he aimed to Russify as well as to make Orthodox.

Scotland, lacking representative institutions, looked to the General Assembly of the Church of Scotland. Presbyterianism performed in Scotland something of the function performed by Roman Catholicism in Ireland.

Even subject peoples might be divided by religion. Serbs and

Croats had common political interests against their Austro-Hungarian rulers, and their languages were so akin that they could understand each other. But the Serbs were Orthodox and the Croats Catholic. Religion, rather than race, divided them. Some Czechs were heirs of Hus and others were heirs of the Counter-Reformation, and these inheritances generated different attitudes to Vienna. The Rumanians in Transylvania had an Eastern Orthodox mode of worship, but some of them were disciples of the Orthodox Patriarch, and others belonged to the Uniat Church dependent upon Rome; and again the attitude to the Austro-Hungarian government differed. The particular forms of a religion might matter politically. To be a Christian was to be international. To be a Protestant or a Roman Catholic or an Eastern Orthodox was to be less international.

Christianity and nationality stood in tension. On the one hand the national religion helped to make, and was felt to make, part of the national consciousness. On the other hand Christianity proposed to cross the barriers of race, and unite men in an order of charity. With the Epistle to the Colossians it declared that there was neither Scythian nor Greek. Yet simultaneously it enabled the Scythian to feel more conscious of not being a Greek.

The Pope experienced this tension more agonizingly than any other Christian leader. For the rise of nationalism during the nineteenth century cast him into a political predicament which was intolerable. In the spring of 1848 Italians rose to a war of liberation against the Austrians. They believed Pope Pius IX to be a liberal who would see the moral righteousness of such a war, expected him to put himself at the head of the movement, and had grounds for confidence that he would allow the army of the Papal States to join the forces of revolution. The Pope was the ruler of a political state and therefore possessed among his options the possibility of declaring war. He was also the head of a religion of peace, and could he therefore declare war? The Austrians also were sons of the Church. In an allocution of 29 April 1848 Pius IX solemnly declared that as supreme pastor he could not declare war upon a people which were his spiritual sons; and thereby drove many Italian nationalists into disillusion and anti-papal feeling. Never had the two functions, of secular ruler and spiritual pastor, seemed so incompatible in a Pope. Either he must become more Italian or he must become less. He chose to become less, with consequences which affected all Christian history of the nineteenth century and after.

This conflict – between the rising nationalism of peoples in modern states and the international ideals of Christianity – only became open ānd extreme during the twentieth century. Nazis hated Christianity because pastors and priests talked of a loyalty higher than loyalty to the State, of an authority beyond the authority of the leader of the State. But the difficulty between Churches and growing German (or Italian) nationalism reached back into the nineteenth century. Even in France the conflict of anticlerical and Ultramontane could be represented in these terms. 'It is rare', said Gambetta in a terrible phrase, 'for a Catholic to be a patriot.'[23]

Nationalism could express itself in religious ways. It was an extension, sometimes a corrupt extension but still an extension, of a man's loyalty to his family, which was integrated to his religion. Therefore nationalism sometimes valued religion. But if so, it valued Christianity for reasons which Christians did not always welcome. It valued religion because it was part of the national heritage, and because it articulated the sense of national community. 'Without community of religion', wrote that not very religious German the historian Treitschke, 'the consciousness of national unity is impossible, for religious feeling is one of the primitive instincts of human nature'; and in writing that he had no desire to hark back to the Thirty Years War and abandōn tolération of different Christian denominations. He wanted to exclude Jews from the German community, or at least to regard them as too few in number to make untrue the statement, 'we are a Christian nation'. 'The co-existence within one nation of several religions, involving irreconcilable differences of outlook upon life, becomes unendurable after a time; and can only occur in a stage of transition.' But though he wanted to talk of a Christian nation, he would allow no talk of a Christian state. 'The state is by its nature a secular institution.'[24]

A man like Treitschke did not think these opinions to contradict his religious feelings. He sat loose to Christianity, yet always retained something Protestant in his make-up. Unlike Nietzsche or the philosophical thinkers who represented one aspect of this age, he had no sense of revolt against religion, no sense of repudiation of Christianity because it was internationalist, though he repudiated Catholicism partly because it was internationalist. But some observers of these men criticized them for immorality and doubted their religion. When in 1864 Treitschke published an essay inviting Prussia to swallow up the little states of Germany, his father, an old Saxon general, accused him of immorality and wrote him a letter asking him how he stood with regard to religion.[25]

If a nation was a moral good; if its power, and progress, and unity, were not only a moral good, but the supreme moral goal of the age, then war must have a place in a nation's destiny, conceived even as an ethical destiny. The theory of a moral attitude to war has received attention lately, for the obvious reason that men tried to analyse the background of Nazi militarism. Gerhard Ritter, Meineke, Krieger, R. W. Sterling and others sought to reconsider the moral basis of power in its historical development and to understand how some nationalists of the middle nineteenth century came to advocate war as an indispensable means of moral progress for the human race; rather as some radical thinkers of the middle twentieth century advocated revolution as indispensable to moral progress.

The origins of this attitude go back beyond the two unifications, German and Italian, of the mid-century. The European conquests of Napoleon created a fear of super-power, and renewed emotion for national independence. 'Every nation', wrote Fichte (though uncharacteristically), 'is intent on spreading the virtues peculiar to it as far as possible, indeed if possible to incorporate all mankind. This desire stems from a drive implanted by God. On this drive rests the community of nations, their friction one against the other, and their progress.'[26]

Hegel took the moral ideal into his system, which combined transcendent and rigid concepts with practical and down-to-earth concern for the realities of political and international life. The state was primary, the individual secondary. The state, not the Church, is 'the reality of the moral ideal'.

Morality is not an individual act but a social, and therefore the individual 'achieves objectivity, truth, and morality, only so far as he is a member of the state'. Religion had no longer the supreme place in the turning of moral ideals into practical behaviour. It had a necessary place, but subordinate to the state. The state is the divine will, working as the spirit develops the world's true form and organization.

The state's highest duty is 'to perpetuate itself'. There is no moral judge to which the law of the state must bow, apart from the ultimate judgment of the historical process; and for the progress of a state, war is a necessary means. War is not only a means towards the ethical good of the separate states, it is a necessary cleansing of the international order. It keeps nations morally healthy, 'as the motion of the winds keeps the sea from stagnation, to which it would succumb by constant stillness, just as would nations by an enduring peace, let alone peace everlasting'.[27]

The idea, therefore, of the European order as conflict, inevitable conflict, between contending nations, and that this conflict is the cause of moral health and not of sickness to the European nations, owes nothing in its origins to Darwinianism and the doctrine of the survival of the fittest. Later men, preeminently the author of *Mein Kampf* but many before him, took Darwin's ideas and used them to propagate an ethical outlook which they framed without Darwin; a characteristic situation of intellectual history, as we now see, though our grandfathers did not see. Hegelians of the nationalist wing propagated the doctrine through Europe and in propagating it made it blunter. Competition between the nations generates or fosters the moral strength of each nation, war is necessary to this competition. War creates the highest moral state of society; courage, brotherhood, selflessness, rejection of personal material gain. The state's right, its highest duty, is to be selfish, and in its quest for its interest it raises the ethical standards of its people. But because it is the highest duty of the state to be selfish, vision of an international moral order is mirage. If there is an international moral order it rises only from power-relations between the most powerful states.

All these ideas were found, not in some extremist pamphleteer, but in a serious and much respected professor of jurisprudence, Adolf Lasson, in a book (observe the date, 1871) entitled *The Principles and Future of International Law (Prinzip und Zukunft des Völkerrechts)*. For Lasson hatred of other peoples is the consecration of one's own people. To strive after everlasting peace is to aim at an immoral goal. 'The dream of a world order over states or between states is an invalid and senseless dream, born of cowardice and sentimentality.' 'A treaty is valid only so long as it is not against the interest of either of the contracting parties.'[28]

These thoughts were not the private possession of a few exceptional or cranky minds. They commanded a wide public, and can be found in pamphlets, newspaper articles, speeches, public meetings. 'This war-mongering literature by Prussian historians', a shrill Marxist historian has written, 'is one of the worst blots of infamous Demagogy.'[29] Nor should it be thought that the attitudes about international politics were exclusively Germanic. The history of Germany between 1792 and 1871 gave them special point and exceptional power there. But the growth of British imperialism during the 1870s affords useful parallels to the power theories of the European

Continent. The word *imperialism* entered the English language about 1858 as a word of criticism, especially to criticize French aggressiveness. Meineke once accused the English of being the most effective kind of Machiavellians because they tried to clothe their naked sword in the self-deceiving hypocrisy of 'pure humanity, conduct and religion'.[30] 'As a rule, this unconscious expedience in political conduct, this political instinct, is lacking in Germans. Bismarck was an important but rare exception.'

We who saw the failure of the League of Nations or the United Nations to take the place of that old international moral order represented by the ideals of Christendom, will not be surprised at, though we may still reject, this new hard-headedness of the nineteenth century; which, however present among thinkers from the age of Napoleon, came only to fruition and to public expression among journalists in the age just before and just after the Franco-Prussian war; and so helps to account for that feeling of a change in atmosphere, from an international moral order to a *Realpolitik*; a change which some like Lecky regarded as improvement, as demolishing the false pretence of international government, and others, like Archbishop Manning, regarded as the harbinger of European suicide.

Strip it to its foundation in the European predicament. Neither the nation-state of Italy, nor the nation-state of Germany, could be created without war; in both cases, more than one war. But a majority of Germans, a majority of Italians, and large numbers of observers outside Germany and Italy, especially in Britain, believed that the creation of these nation-states was right – that is, ethically right as well as politically expedient. And incidentally, but not trivially, the creation of the two nation-states could not be achieved without demolishing two of the pillars upon which old Christendom rested. Germany could not be made without overthrowing the only powerful Catholic government in the world. Italy could not be made without robbing the Pope of his possessions if not his sovereignty.

Old Christian ideas of an international order, of peace on earth, goodwill to all men, looked like self-interest; like a theoretical justification for not changing a European system which was being changed irresistibly.

Politics becoming 'secularized' – true or false? One of Lecky's famous passages was his chapter called *The secularization of politics*.[31] The chapter illustrates the predicament in which students of the nineteenth century find themselves. The contrast in Lecky's mind is the political decision based upon religious grounds – for example, let us go with sword and shield and capture Jerusalem from the infidel – and the political decision based on secular grounds – for example, let us join France in fighting Germany for otherwise Germany will become too powerful and we shall be in worse trouble later.

'No wars the world had ever before seen', wrote Lecky of the crusades, 'were so popular as these, which were at the same time the most disastrous and the most unselfish' (2, 106); and although people who make pencil marks in other people's books are vandals, I could not help being amused that in the Seeley Library copy of Lecky, some offended reader put a note of exclamation against the words 'most unselfish' as applied to the crusades.

Lecky remembered how once it was unthinkable for a Christian power to seek alliance with the Turk; and how in the Crimean War the Christian nations of western Europe allied themselves with Mohammedan Turkey to assail Christian Russia. Then Lecky came to a series of powerful and rhetorical paragraphs contrasting Papal Rome of old with Rome of the 1860s; on the one hand the centre and archetype of the political system of Europe, the successor of imperial Rome (2, 130); on the other hand a condition of hopeless decrepitude, prolonging its existence by a few hundred French and Belgian and Irish bayonets. Why did its glory fall?

It fell because it represented the union of politics and theology, and because the intellect of Europe has rendered it an anachronism by pronouncing their divorce. It fell because its constitution was essentially and radically opposed to the spirit of an age in which the secularization of politics is the measure and the condition of all political prosperity.

If this is right, the secularization of politics was simply a political necessity; not due to change in philosophies of life, nor change in social need or outlook, but political necessity based upon inner laws of political development. We make politics secular not because we are against religion but because only so can we engage in political action to the benefit of European society.

What truth? Certainly the constitution of the Papal States was radically opposed to the spirit of the age, as Mr Gladstone and Lord John Russell remarked in violent language which reverberated round Europe. The tension between the politics of morality and the politics of reason was even more painful to the Papacy of the nineteenth century than it is painful to most governments. This tension permanently afflicts political societies and not only Popes.

The Popes, or their servants, sometimes embarked on what they called the 'politics of the gospel'. What are the politics of the gospel? They were defined in 1829 by Cardinal Castiglioni (who was shortly to become Pope Pius VIII), as 'a political programme derived from Holy Scriptures and venerable tradition, the only school of good government, a political programme for this reason as far above human political programmes, as heaven is above the earth'.

When we hear such a definition we may be glad that Pope Pius VIII was not in charge of politics for very long. When in January 1848 the governor of the City of Rome (Monsignor Morandi) resigned, he is said to have given as reason for resignation that Pope Pius IX followed the gospel in his policy and to follow a gospel policy was very difficult.[32]

This change in European feeling about international politics, men put at various dates. Gerhard Ritter placed it about the time of the fall of Bismarck. Some, who regretted what they conceived as a new and 'secular' struggle for power in international relations, blamed Bismarck as the statesman who rejected the older conventions in European diplomacy. The only thing we may say with certainty is that in the 1860s and 1870s other men as intelligent as Lecky sensed a change in the political atmosphere, and that some like Lecky believed it an improvement in mental attitudes to politics. They held that, since we are bound by the nature of human society to play the politics of power, we shall do better to play the politics of power unashamedly.

But we need to beware of this talk of *Realpolitik*, if historical explanation is wanted. Many people continued (and in hindsight we shall not think them always mistaken) to think the Bible a more reliable guide to the principle of social organization and political conduct than all the expedients of politicians or political economists. Historians have sometimes lamented the decline in European political conduct when nationalism, and popular fervour, took over in the nineteenth century from the aristocratic manoeuvres of European diplomacy in the eighteenth century. In English history we call this, though the term misleads, the rise of the nonconformist conscience and its influence upon politics. It was wider than the nonconformists. It was the new power of middle- and lower-middle-class morality and education; and it had consequences for what governments could do or could not do in their foreign relations and their internal policies. In face of the Armenian troubles, or Bulgarian massacres of the late 1870s, or Neapolitan prisons in 1850, Gladstone became a revivalist of popular emotion, and moral convictions like these could force the hands of the foreign secretaries of Europe.

In parts of the nineteenth century Europe was governed by far less *raison d'état* than Europe of the eighteenth century; and policies which made nonsense in *reason* were pursued because they were obviously the *moral* policies to pursue. When Lecky talked about politics based on theology giving place to politics based on secular balances of power he used the word *theology* in a narrow and Pickwickian sense.

Christendom, and still more Europe, lived on. International law grew in reputation and effectiveness, though in fits and starts. It was no fading relic of the Enlightenment. The quest for the European system became ever more urgent after 1860, partly because men realized the new destructiveness of modern war, and partly because wars were henceforth battles between peoples and no longer between mercenaries. Christian influences, often pacifist in character, were strong in the various movements towards international guarantees of peace. The Red Cross organization at Geneva was founded in 1864. The first proposals for a confederation of states, later to be embodied in the League of Nations and later still in the United Nations, dated from the 1870s. Men had a new sense of moral responsibility in the direction of state policy. Contrary to popular impression Bismarck never lost sight of the moral ends of state policy, though like other statesmen he sometimes identified temporary expediency with the law of God.

He was not the first to deceive himself. If ever a man starts talking about the secularization of politics in modern times he will find, whispering behind his ear, the ghost of Machiavelli.

5

Anticlericalism appeared in countries where Catholics were powerful; and therefore at first sight it might have a connexion with the tradition of Protestant resistance to Rome.

A social theorist concerned in recent years with secularization, propounded the interesting thesis that Protestantism was a direct cause of the process of secularization.[33]

His argument was that Protestantism 'appears as a radical truncation, a reduction to "essentials" at the expense of a vast wealth of religious contents. . .an immense shrinkage in the scope of the sacred in reality, as compared with its Catholic adversary. The sacramental apparatus is reduced to a minimum and, even then, divested of its more numinous qualities. . .' 'Protestantism cut the umbilical cord between heaven and earth. . .' The argument is that the Reformation rested the sacred upon the Bible alone, instead of a breadth of sacramental universe. Then it only needed historical criticism in the eighteenth and nineteenth centuries to shake the sacredness of the Bible, and we had arrived at the 'disenchantment of the world'.[31] 'A sky empty of angels becomes open to the intervention of the astronomer and, eventually, of the astronaut.' He claimed that this interpretation of the nexus between Protestantism and secularization is probably accepted by most scholars. But then we find that this secularization-process has its roots in the Old Testament. We hear of 'the secularizing motifs of Old Testament religion'. The Protestant Reformation may be understood as 'a powerful re-emergence of precisely those secularizing forces that had been "contained" by Catholicism'. 'If the drama of the modern era is the decline of religion, then Protestantism can aptly be described as its dress rehearsal.'

It is not easy to get a purchase on such a theory, or know quite how to begin to try it. One wonders whether it would not be better to reverse the epigram of the sky, and say that 'a sky open to the astronomer starts to empty of angels', if one did not, in saying it, feel that one linked hands with Russian publicists who, to help simple people, explained how the astronaut explored the skies and found no God.

This idea is not quite new. A school of German thinking looked backward to Pietism in the eighteenth century; as symbol and cause of a withdrawal by churches into their sacred enclosures, leaving the world to go its way. Instead of the world starting to do without God and then churches retiring behind their convent walls to find God in their own way undisturbed, churches retired behind their walls and abandoned the world to get along as best it might.

Return to the Syllabus of 1864. For political reasons more than intellectual reasons, the leaders of the most powerful and numerous of all churches identified themselves with reaction in politics and extreme conservatism in theology. I do not think that it will do to underestimate the consequences in European opinion, canalized in the Church and State struggle in France, the Kulturkampf in Germany. The Church erected a wall against the world. But it seemed, at the time, erroneously as posterity sees, less like withdrawal behind the convent wall than as an attempt to dominate. However the Reformation weakened papal power, the nineteenth century recreated a Pope who could make the mighty afraid – even Gladstone, prime minister of the most influential country, even Bismarck, chancellor of the greatest military power the world had seen, even the Swiss government which was believed to be afraid of no one. So there is some element of truth in the proposition that, in those political circumstances, Protestantism led towards secularization. Some of the leading French anticlericals were neither atheist nor agnostic but Protestant. Bismarck conducted his Kulturkampf – which had a secularizing effect in all the German churches and not only the Catholic – in the name of evangelical freedom.

But as for the influence of the Old Testament; or the sky empty of angels; or retirement from the world by Pietists – these are difficult for the historian to test.

PART II
THE INTELLECTUAL PROBLEM

6

VOLTAIRE IN THE NINETEENTH CENTURY

In the first part I surveyed the social issues of the middle and last years of the nineteenth century, and the nature of popular secularization. We saw how social investigation proved a large amount of social motive rather than intellectual; that when, for example, members of the German Social Democratic party favoured what was known as materialism, they cared not for the academic arguments for materialistic philosophies of life. We saw how investigation veered away from the kind of history not too uncommon until 1900, where secularization was identified with advancing knowledge, and started to concentrate on the nature of popular movements and the way in which ideas make their impact upon or among them, the pre-conditions in society which make old ideas obsolete and new ideas magnetic.

Whereas the Whig Protestant historian saw the falling away in churches as a sign of more information, and thought that the young need only to go to better schools to jettison ancient necromancies of illiterate parents, sociologists turned their attention to elements which constitute human society, and instantly ran into the force of religion, as an instrument of social consensus, family or community habit, public and civic rites, and even social control. Then Marxist historians, who proved that our heads are not so distant from our bellies as Whigs seemed to think, diverted attention further from the history of ideas as ideas, to force us to alter our perspective of the way in which social ideas change.

We saw that some attitudes to the themes almost suggested that ideas do not matter. Since no more than a handful of people could understand the philosophy of Kant, Kant (on this view) could be disregarded. Since we are aware how men are moved more by stomachs than logic, since we have seen how inarticulate and how near the subconscious are the motives which drive men, not merely to courses of action, but to the framing of ideas, since we have learnt how a society adopts theories less by reason of their ultimate truth than by reason of their practical effects, the older histories of ideas have come to look more and more eccentric, as though they wore crinolines and bustles in an age of jeans and mini-skirts.

The History of Freedom of Thought – an ancient world the title of that book conjures. Stalinists and Nazis destroyed its illusions.

Still, real men asked real questions. The peculiar difficulty of the intellectual history of the later nineteenth century (as with all intellectual history) is the dissection of the real questions from the arguments of legend or of 'stance' which surrounded them. But real questions existed. The eighteenth century started to ask them. For a time the nineteenth century swept them under cover, either as false because they led to Robespierre, or as too dangerous to discuss because they led to Robespierre. If a question is real enough, it cannot be swept under forever. The age of reason had not lived up to its name. But in it some men, a minority of men, sought for reason and asked questions about reason. The Enlightenment did not bring light in the way in which its intellectual leaders intended. But it sought for light, and in seeking it changed the intellectual conditions of European knowledge.

The Enlightenment, by that name, was not a thing that any English speaker knew during the earlier nineteenth century. It is a modern word. When English speakers first began to need a word to describe the climate of opinion in the age of the Encyclopaedia, they used the German word *Aufklärung*, evidence enough that the notion had not yet reached the popular histories for schools. For three-quarters of the nineteenth century they did not think of the age as an enlightened age. Most of them thought of it with opprobrium as the age which ended in a nemesis of guillotine and terror. Thomas Carlyle, contemplating with disgust the friendship or the irritations between Frederick the Great and Voltaire, held up Voltaire as the very type of the fraudulence and bankruptcy of the eighteenth century.

Common sense is superficial, can be shallow, misses the depths, is prosy, underestimates what it finds difficult to follow, exaggerates the value of clarity, suspects philosophers who think hard, sits too comfortably for poetic language, regards self-sacrifice as imprudence or fanaticism, walks unhappily with faith. But common sense is still sense, and asks blunt questions, and blunt questions are awkward. The Enlightenment, even if not by that name, stood for much that the nineteenth century despised. But it was linked forever with three attitudes towards religion; more than three no doubt, but three which would survive in some form, at times hardly recognizable, but with a continuity evident to our perspective: deism, nature as a machine, and the quest for absolute freedom of opinion, religious or irreligious.

Who by 1859 read the deistic writers? No one. They were deader than the minor logicians of the medieval schools. Who looked at nature as a machine? No one; if men used comparisons of this sort, they thought of a plant, a growth, not an intricate piece of machinery. Freedom of thought? – men still fought Giant Pope and his Syllabus, but the axiom was being incorporated into the constitutions of the new national and parliamentary states. Men thought the Enlightenment a corpse, a cul-de-sac of ideas, a destructive age overthrowing the intellectual as well as the physical landmarks by which human society may live as a civilized body.

Nobody read deists. But deism asked the question of God in the world. And since the question happened to matter, and in the light of more and more evidence happened to perplex, men were going to ask it, whether or not they read deists. The world as a machine was out of favour, and men thought Addison's hymn about *The spacious firmament on high* to be deplorable. But this question was really about design in the universe, and no problem was going to trouble thoughtful people more during the third quarter of the nineteenth century. Men achieved freedom of thought – but was the scientist then to be told that he was irreligious because he reached conclusions about the world on evidence purely physical? For reasons partly political, partly intellectual, and partly by the natural reaction of a generation against its fathers, the old arguments were dropped into a dustbin and disappeared from view. But since they concerned real questions, they could not stay there.

Sometimes a man is emancipated by the death of his father, and his mind begins at last to move, losing its anchor in tradition and heredity. More often the opposite happens. It appears to be a rule, liable no doubt to many exceptions, that we react against our parents' points of view while they are alive, and when they die we realize what a debt we owe, and how much continuity exists between our viewpoint and theirs. This mingled sadness and happiness of heredity touches the progress not only of individuals but of society. The Edwardians and Georgians used the word Victorian almost as a term of abuse, not far from stuffy or puritanical, sometimes not far from worse words like canting. Elizabethans, grandchildren of Victorians, came to admire, even to revere, the

Victorian age. This law of individuals and of society becomes most clear, and most disturbing, when the old age collapses in calamity; when some wide gulf of war or revolution divides the former age from the latter. Then revulsion from the past swings harder; and the swing back, when it comes, runs curiously to excess. A year after the battle of Waterloo France had no use for Napoleons. Forty years after, a Napoleon was again Emperor of France.

Scotsmen affect humorously to regard Dr Samuel Johnson as a typical Englishman. His views upon the French critics of his age lost nothing in bluntness.

'Rousseau, Sir,' said Dr Johnson to Boswell 'is a very bad man. . . I should like to have him work in the plantations.' 'Sir,' asked Boswell, 'do you think him as bad a man as Voltaire?' Johnson: 'Why, Sir, it is difficult to settle the proportion of iniquity between them.'

But in many respects, Samuel Johnson was untypical. Cultivated men of reading were not so dogmatic. Boswell thought this verdict by Johnson to be violent. He read Rousseau 'with great pleasure, and even edification'; enjoyed his company, and could not allow that he deserved Johnson's severity. He even confessed that he admired the Savoyard Vicar's faith for its reverent hesitation before mystery, its state of mind 'to be viewed with pity rather than with anger'. We do not find the same defence of Voltaire. Still, Boswell classed him with Shakespeare among the more celebrated of writers and Johnson agreed with this verdict on his fame. Johnson confessed him readable but attacked him on a charge of falsifying history to make it dramatic. Boswell compared the moral aim of Voltaire's *Candide* (which Johnson thought the most powerful production by its author), to that of Johnson's *Rasselas*, in favour of Johnson; for Voltaire, he thought, 'meant only by a wanton profaneness to obtain a sportive victory over religion, and to discredit the belief of a superintending Providence.'[1]

The Philosophical Dictionary of Voltaire had at least three English translations during the eighteenth century (1765, 1767, 1796) and three more in the first half of the nineteenth (1807, 1827 six volumes translated by J. G. Gorton, 1843 with a memoir of the author). There were two English translations of Voltaire's 'complete' works during the eighteenth century (25 volumes by Dr Tobias Smollett – no less – and T. Francklin, 1761–5, new edition in 38 volumes, 1778–81; and an edition in 14 parts, translated by the Reverend D. Williams,[2] H. Downman, W. Campbell and others, 1779–81).

Other men talked often with respect. It is sufficient to remember Lord Byron's praising Voltaire and Rousseau in *Childe Harold's Pilgrimage*.[3]

But after 1815 the British paid little attention to Voltaire or Rousseau; translated little; read little; studied little, and were repelled when they studied, regarding them as authors of revolution, tyranny and atheism. They knew almost nothing about them, and what they knew was odious.

In 1861 the *Confessions* of Rousseau received its first English translation since the eighteenth century; *Emile* about the same date. Other little signs show interest reviving during the 1860s.

The biographies show the same pattern. There was an English translation of a French Life of Voltaire in 1787. In 1821 Frank Hall Standish, who mostly lived not in England but in Spain or France, published a little Life of Voltaire, bald, plain and sympathetic, but omitting anything that the author calls 'speculative opinion'. Then the ex-Lord Chancellor, Henry Brougham, occupied his years of leisure and sharp abilities in writing *Men of Letters in the time of George III* (1845) and included apologetic little essays on Voltaire and Rousseau as the first two chapters of the first volume. Voltaire, wrote Brougham, was connected in the minds of all with infidelity, and whoever writes his life 'labours under a great load of prejudice' and 'can hardly expect to gain for his subject even common justice at the hands of the general reader'. The world will slowly forget his sneer and his offensive manner, and remember that to Voltaire, more than to anyone since Luther, we owe the spirit of free enquiry.[4] Brougham likewise urged men to a truer judgement on Rousseau, at least by being charitable to a man so diseased in body and in mind. But Lord Brougham was like his old prime minister Lord Melbourne, a man of the eighteenth century surviving into the early Victorian age, feeling odd there, and looking odd.

The next Life was characteristic of early Victorian attitudes to the leaders of the Enlightenment; an English translation (1854) of a French Life of 1851, by F. L. Bungener, *Voltaire and his Times*. Those times were bad, and Voltaire bad among them. Revolution was his child. He was the *perfection of mediocrity*, with wit but little soul, with neither conviction nor seriousness of purpose, yet a man at bottom more serious than Rousseau. The best we can say of him is that his shafts hit the mark. 'We have made no effort to dissimulate', confessed Bungener, 'that we have been writing with an eye to the present day.'

In 1853 the Principal of King's College, London, classed Voltaire with Judas Iscariot as supreme representatives of impenitence and unbelief.[5] Only twelve years later the historian Lecky classed Voltaire with Luther as men who modified profoundly the opinions of mankind.

The 1860s therefore saw a swing in historical attitudes to the eighteenth century. We need to remember Bungener before we understand what John Morley achieved.

Consider now the encyclopaedias, which summarize up-to-date information and (usually) moderate attitudes. As works of reference they must not be too eccentric, too progressive or too retarded. The encyclopaedia of Diderot was based on the first *Chambers's Encyclopaedia*. But Diderot, and a small number of his colleagues, gave it a rather different slant and a vastly different reputation. From 1789, for obvious reasons, the editors of encyclopaedias preferred to distance themselves from Diderot. The supplement to the third edition of the *Encyclopaedia Britannica* avowed its intention, not merely of being different from Diderot, but of being against Diderot. 'The French Encyclopédie', wrote the editors in their dedication to the King (1801), 'has been accused, and justly accused, of having disseminated far and wide the seeds of anarchy and atheism. If the *Encyclopaedia Britannica* shall in any degree counteract the tendency of that pestiferous work, even these two volumes will not be wholly unworthy of your Majesty's patronage.' The preface was removed for the fourth edition of 1810.

During the French Revolution, therefore, and the age of Napoleon, English writers naturally wished to stand as far as possible from the eminent minds specially associated with the Enlightenment though it was not yet called nor yet conceived of as Enlightenment. On the contrary, Protestant authors themselves thought of the Reformation as liberty of the mind, and taught how pure religion stood upon the side of civilization and of progress. Because Christianity is the religion of Europe, this part of the globe has become a republic of letters and of scientific invention, being sometimes compared to ancient Greece ('and it is to be hoped that Russia will not become another Macedon').[6] Voltaire had a sense of light versus darkness, of reason versus the churches, of rationality versus obscurantism. His Protestant critics had no such feeling. They had the sensation of Protestant light versus Catholic darkness, but saw Christian thought in its pure form as the vehicle of progress for the human mind.

'The established religion of France', said the author of the article *France*, 'had for some time past been gradually undermined. It had been solemnly assailed by philosophers in various elaborate performances; and men of wit, among whom Voltaire took the lead, had attacked with the dangerous weapon of ridicule. The Roman Catholic religion is much exposed in this respect . . .' 'The Reformation', writes the author of the article *Europe* in the seventh edition of 1842, 'had a material effect in accelerating the progress of society. . .Those countries in which it took no root seem to have had their progress arrested.'

Articles were being transmitted from edition to edition when they were obsolete. Some surprising sentences, dating from articles written during the eighteenth century, survived into the edition of 1842.

When we turn to encyclopaedia articles on Voltaire and Rousseau, we find them steadily more critical instead of less. The 1859–60 edition, the eighth, of the *Encyclopaedia Britannica*, began to introduce modern historical sympathies into its articles. But Voltaire is worse than ever. Here is an unusual extract from the 1860 article on Voltaire in that eighth edition:

'Much superfluous terror for the fate of Christianity was once occasioned by the writings of Voltaire and that host of sceptical writers of whom he was the coryphaeus. It is sufficient to ask, at this distance of time, whether their works or the Bible be nearer oblivion – whether they or it be most read? Is Christianity less powerful than when they commenced their crusade against it? Have they succeeded in diminishing the world's veneration for the book they hated?. . .Nothing of the kind. . .' They shook down 'some ruinous turrets', exploded 'some pernicious superstitions and abuses. . .', 'and it would have been well if they had destroyed more; but as to Christianity itself. . .'[7]

The next twelve years saw rapid change. When Samuel Taylor Coleridge was a schoolboy at Christ's Hospital he read Voltaire's *Philosophical Dictionary*, 'and sported infidel' (though not, he said afterwards, with the heart). His headmaster sent for him and roared 'So, sirrah, you are an infidel are you? then I'll flog your infidelity out of you,' and gave him his severest flogging; and Coleridge was afterwards known 'often' to say that it was the only just flogging which he received.[8] Intellectual history is certainly a puzzling subject. At some point headmasters ceased to think it appropriate to flog boys, not for reading unsound books, but for verging towards atheism; and at some other point it became impossible to find a boy who would regard the flogging as justice. Coleridge was odd enough, even when a schoolboy. But this concerns more than one man's quaintness.

Turn on the decades: Benjamin Jowett, Master of Balliol, used to run reading parties at an inn at Tummel Bridge in Scotland. In the autumn of 1870 (the date is not certain) he made this remark to his company: 'Voltaire had done more good than all the Fathers of the Church put together.'[9] Jowett liked dramatic aphorisms in conversation; was never historical about the Fathers (or about much else); and his biographer accuses him, in this particular utterance, of being somewhat perverse. I use the saying, not as a measured utterance to his listening pupils, any more than the headmaster's roar at young Coleridge was a measured utterance. It registers a remarkable intellectual change over the decades.

In 1872 a fairly reliable judge, Leslie Stephen, wrote that to divines Voltaire was nothing but a grotesque figure, with horns and hoofs, set up as a mark for their artillery.[10]

A decade later, in 1882, two professional historians conducted a curious debate on the moral status of Voltaire. It was the age when historians thought it proper to weigh historical personages in their scales of justice, and no historians more than Lord Acton and his erstwhile master Professor Döllinger of Munich. As Catholics both men might be expected to condemn Voltaire absolutely, and Döllinger so condemned him. Acton protested. He had an interest, at that moment, in lowering the scales which contained Luther whom, it seemed to him, Döllinger unduly raised. Acton blamed the French for making Voltaire popular. Still, that was not all that could be said. 'In Voltaire there is much that is contemptible, and vicious, but nothing, as far as I know, criminal. He tried hard to save men's lives and to diminish suffering.'[11] The English had evidently adopted a more balanced attitude.

In Britain John Morley had most to do with the change; I mean, in the way of doing what an outward expositor can do. In the early 1870s Morley put the French Enlightenment on the British intellectual map from which it vanished about the year 1789. That does not mean that to him only was due that secret change in climate which is so hard for the historian to record. Jowett (probably) made his remark at Tummel Bridge before Morley published his *Voltaire*. Minds were made ready to receive; and so they received Morley, and read him with pleasure, and suddenly recaptured what they owed to the Enlightenment.

To show how this was not due only to Morley, we turn to the

dictionary again. We saw that the words *secularization, clericalism* and their kin became common usage in English about 1864–5. It is striking that the first quotation of the English word *Enlightenment*, to mean the *Aufklärung*, given by the *Oxford English Dictionary*, dates from the year 1865, in J. H. Stirling's book seeking to interest Britain in Hegel, and entitled *The Secret of Hegel* (i, xxvii): 'Deism, Atheism, Pantheism, and all manner of *isms* dear to Enlightenment, but hateful to Prejudice'. The word here is pejorative. It is used in a context with more than a tang of pretentious and shallow thinking. The word did not rapidly gain a neutral, still less a favourable, sound. The first use of the phrase, the Age of Enlightenment, offered us by the dictionary, is not until 1889 in Edward Caird's study of the philosophy of Kant (i, 69).

So Morley must have helped the change, did not only record the change. He had a consciousness of reviving what was under a cloud. Leaving Oxford under the influence of positivism, and half-casually intending a career in journalism, he identified himself publicly, during the years from 1865, not only with liberal criticism of religion but with anti-religion. Like other positivists, he believed in those years that the destruction of the supernatural was necessary to the progress of the human race. He could be as fierce as any French intellectual.

But this was not all that he believed. If it had been all, his influence would have been far less, he would have advocated his antisupernatural doctrines with the pungency and the absence of lasting influence of a Viscount Amberley. In a surprising way Morley respected religion, understood it, even at times revered it. A man who loved words and rhetoric and sweeping generalizations, he was also a compulsive moralist. If he had been a clergyman (as once was half-intended) he would have preached, not perhaps like a Massillon or a Bossuet, but at least like a Tillotson of the later nineteenth century. His understanding for religion, and his powerful moralism, combined with style and eloquence to put Rousseau (naturally, that was not too difficult) and Voltaire and finally even Diderot on the intellectual map of later Victorian England. He expounded them in a way acceptable to a reading public which refused mere sneers at religion, superficial satire, harsh one-sided aggression, and wanted to have their minds set in a longer perspective of European thought.

He felt himself a renovator. The stream of intellectual enlightenment had been dammed for a time, even for forty years. He held the reaction against the eighteenth century to be part due to philistinism, part due to sterile and vapouring transcendentalism,[12] and identified Thomas Carlyle as the arch-philistine and arch-transcendentalist. But now, he believed, the movement which the encyclopaedists started was under way again. 'The philosophical parenthesis is at an end.' 'Europe again sees the old enemies face to face; the Church, and a social philosophy slowly labouring to build the foundations in positive science.'

To misjudge Morley is easy because he mellowed. His political experiences in the education fight, and then in Ireland, made him prefer Christian allies to non-Christian allies. No doubt he owed his post as Chief Secretary in Ireland to his irreligion. He could view the contending politico-religious parties with an equal detachment, and could never be suspect of partisanship on grounds of religion. This is an interesting example of the way in which modern democratic constitutions created situations where a man known to be non-religious could be politically useful – one part of that contemporary process which made the atheist, as well as the agnostic, socially acceptable. He never lost that detachment. But he ceased altogether to want to *écraser l'infâme*,[13] and therefore we might misread his attitude of the late 1860s and early 1870s and think it more mellow than it was in truth.

Though a critic of preachers, this almost-preacher could not expound the Enlightenment to the British without giving a message for the times. And the message is the old message of the eighteenth century: man, after all, is good. Away with doctrines of our evil human nature. Man is good, the world desirable, evil in the world comes of bad education and bad institutions. *Now*, in the Enlightenment, men ceased to see one another as guilty, cowering under divine curse. They stood 'erect in consciousness of manhood'. Rousseau's *Emile* changed the European theory of education, from the notion that it consisted in rooting out tares to the notion that its work was to tend shoots. 'We may look back to the old system of endless catechisms, apoththegms, moral fables, and the rest of the paraphernalia of moral didactics, with the same horror with which we regard the gags, strait-waistcoats, chains, and dark cells of poor mad people before the intervention of Pinel.'[14]

Human nature is good. This, said Morley, is the key that secularizes the world.[15] This is the principle which fights puritanism in society, formalism in art, absolutism in government, obscurantism in thought. Welcome for the world, freedom in art, government by the people for the people, light of science and rationality to drive away the darkness of superstition.

Morley made the philosophers of the Enlightenment live again. But their ideas were alive already without him, and without reference to the historical personages whose minds he recreated.

Naturally there were subtle differences. The Enlightenment was aristocratic, of the salon. *Atheism not before the maids.* Morley was a democrat of his age. At the same time that he was engaged in his studies of the Enlightenment, he published a little book against *not before the maids*: called, *On Compromise*, 1874. The educated no longer believe in hell. But they still want the uneducated to believe in hell. 'Husbands who think the common theology baseless and unmeaning, are found to prefer that their wives shall not question their theology nor neglect its rites' (57). David Hume had advised a young man to remain a clergyman, 'for civil employment for men of letters can scarcely be found'. 'The ecclesiastical profession only adds a little more to an innocent dissimulation, or rather simulation, without which it is impossible to pass through the world.'[16] Every line of Morley's long and passionate pamphlet is devoted to destroying these half-measures. It is the moral earnestness of the religious nineteenth century, unable to be content with the smiling flexibilities of their grandfathers. The pamphlet was widely read. It had a German translation with long notes (*Überzeugungstreue*, loyalty to one's convictions) and even reached translations into Urdu and Gujerati.

Let us not think Morley prematurely mellow.

Here is an advertisement for the *Encyclopaedia Britannica* of 1898, and the language would sound strange to the editors of the edition of 1860:

The wonderful story of the nineteenth century is told by the men who made its greatness; the history of modern progress in the arts, sciences and industries has the glow that only a soldier can give to the tale of a campaign; for the men who fought against ignorance, and brought Enlightenment to their generation, themselves tell how the light was spread.[17]

In framing advertisements man is not upon oath. But old axioms were being restated, natural goodness, progress of humanity, methods of education, and on top of them a positivistic attitude against mystery, especially religious mystery. When Morley writes of Voltaire, you hear the sigh of gods hurrying away into the bushes, and listen to the excess of eloquence in which the religion of humanity claimed men for its own, turning despair into a new faith:

How shall the universe ever cease to be a sovereign wonder of overwhelming power and superhuman fixedness of law? And a man will be already in no mean paradise, if at the hour of sunset a good hope can fall upon him like harmonies of music, that the earth shall still be fair, and the happiness of every feeling creature still receive a constant augmentation, and each good cause yet find worthy defenders, when the memory of his own poor name and personality has long been blotted out of the brief recollection of men for ever.[18]

2

In France, it was different. Voltaire and Rousseau were not only writers who made a difference to intellectual Europe. They were possessions of literature. They recovered their name earlier than in Britain. But not many years earlier; and as their names were caught up in the political campaigns which divided France they carried with them throughout the century an even more controversial tang.

Napoleon is said to have hired hacks to write busily in the desire to lower Voltaire's reputation.[19] Joseph de Maistre, who can hardly be regarded as typical of anything but an extreme and temporary phase of European reaction, nevertheless offered a famous condemnation: 'To admire Voltaire is the sign of a corrupt heart, and if anybody is drawn to his works, then be very sure that God does not love such an one.'[20]

Conversely, the conversion of the Frenchman to Voltaire could be a religious conversion. A Catholic in reaction like Lamennais condemned the philosophers absolutely. As he failed in his radical Catholicism and moved outwards to radical socialism, his attitude towards the eighteenth century altered abruptly. The historian Michelet, son of a caustic Voltairean, started his adult life, after the battle of Waterloo, by classing Voltaire as the type of all minds who kill life by pretending to analyse it. He began his career as a historian by penning the most romantic of portraits of the Middle Ages, an idealized study of crusades, a reverent (though misleading) portrait of St Thomas Aquinas, a Puginesque glorying in the religious nature of earlier Gothic art and architecture.

In 1839 his wife died and he was never the same. In 1842, 1843, 1844 Michelet and his group of creative friends – Victor Hugo, Lamartine, Quinet – detached themselves from traditional Christianity. Churches became in his mind the enemies of liberty; Christian ethic a narrowness; celibacy an unnatural vice; confession an intrusion into family privacy and confidence; Jesuits the enemy of sound morality – all stated in fierce, unacademic, partisan lecturing at the Collège de France, with a touch of high messianism, the coming of the kingdom of the Spirit to supersede at last the forms and dogmas and hierarchies and church structures of the centuries. His father died on 18 November 1846; and Michelet's meditation at the Père-Lachaise cemetery completed his break with the Middle Ages, repudiated his own immediate past, and revealed to him that he accepted the heritage of Voltaire. 'I came out of the eighteenth century', he soliloquized in his journal. 'I left the eighteenth century for a time. Then I returned there for ever; to find there always my own father, that is to say, the true France of Voltaire and Rousseau.'[21] When the next year (1847) he published the two volumes of his story of the French Revolution, he saw the philosophers of the eighteenth century as the doctors of a new and higher religion, theorists of the new world of justice and equality and liberty. He started to rewrite his old sentences on the Middle Ages, to eject enthusiasm and omit praise. 'What ever was I doing?' he asked himself soon after he returned from his father's grave. 'What was I doing when I idealized the Middle Ages, and hid reality? I have been working against myself. I have been working against the progress of the world. At all costs I must live long enough to weaken the calamitously partisan view of history which I have been fostering, without even knowing that I was fostering it.'[22] By 1863 in the preface to the fifteenth volume of the *Histoire de France* he uttered one of the strangest cries of passion ever uttered by a historian – 'The past, that is the enemy – the barbaric Middle Ages – and its representative Spain ... the Spain that burnt the books of Voltaire and Montesquieu. The future, that is the friend; progress and the new spirit, 1789 distantly appearing above the horizon.' By 1863 Voltaire's work had been consecrated.

This onslaught upon Christianity owed its force, it will be seen, not at all to the science of the nineteenth century. Its basis was ethical; its instrument the ethical criticisms of the eighteenth century. It attacked Christian Churches not in the name of knowledge but in the name of justice and freedom. It had the sense of light versus darkness to be found in Voltaire, but the contrast was not quite the same. This was less juxtaposition of superstition versus reason. It was a contrast of unnatural ethics versus God-given ways of life. It assailed, not the truth of Genesis or the probability of miracle, but the doctrine of the atonement for its lack of justice; the inequity of the doctrine of predestination to death, the diminutions of freedom through the doctrine of grace, the inquisition, the contrast between Christian ideals for humanity and churches' failure to promote those ideals in society. The onslaught was more ethical than scientific; and that was the source from which its passion flowed.

We keep running, suddenly and in unexpected by-ways, into the idea that secularization is a religious process, instead of an irreligious.

Here is another French historian on Voltaire: Edgar Quinet, Michelet's ally and friend, fighting shoulder to shoulder with him in the noisy shouting-matches of the Collège de France during the 1840s, equally emotional, partial and unacademic in his lecturing, but differing in outlook, chiefly because he was Protestant or half Protestant by origin. A few years before Michelet, Quinet harked back to the Enlightenment. Voltaire and Rousseau had not overturned the Church but replaced it. They, the philosophers, were the new papacy which France gave to the world; stripping the essentials of the old religion and reforming it for us; Christianity secularized but still Christianity.'Voltaire is the destroying angel sent by God against his sinful Church'; 'He strikes reviles and overwhelms the infidel Church, with the weapons of the Christian spirit.' 'You seek Christ in the sepulchre of the past; but Christ has left his sepulchre; he has moved on, has changed his place; he is alive, he is incarnate, he descends into the modern world.'[23]

You may say that the ideas of Voltaire died while those of Diderot and Rousseau are alive; that the future lay between Diderot's militant agnosticism on the one hand or Rousseau's undogmatic religious sentiment on the other; and that the only thing that died was Voltaire's deism, the half-religious chilly philosophy of common sense.

That view of the matter has truth; but not all the truth. We shall see why in a cry to God which Voltaire made when he was aged 27:

'I am not a Christian, but that is to love thee the better.'[24]

If he was only an atheist at heart who needed to sound like a deist for public and private expediency, as has often been maintained, this utterance (and others like it) will not be taken seriously. If they are taken seriously they can perhaps be taken too seriously, as in the remarkable biography by the English Catholic Alfred Noyes, where Voltaire appeared as a new Catholic Reformer, not reactionary like the Counter-Reformation, a critic who by furious aggression and boundless sarcasm forced the Catholic Church into modernity. But Christian attitudes to superstition, persecution, tolerance, the Old Testament, Jehovah, fanaticism, and perhaps the world, could never be quite the same. Not long before Voltaire's birth Bossuet said this of the world: 'A Christian is never alive while on earth because he is always mortified, and mortification is an apprenticeship for death, a beginning of death.'[25] After Voltaire that was hard to say. The Enlightenment taught the Christian Churches something about creation.

Voltaire's name was now a symbol in the French political war. When Louis Napoleon took power in 1851 some libraries were forced to bowdlerize their shelves by throwing out the volumes of Voltaire and Rousseau; and this was the time when a reputable scholar, editing unpublished Voltaire papers, thought it right to warn the reader that his author caused 1789 and the terror of 1793, so grievously did his writings harm the Catholic faith and French society.[26] Garibaldi made a speech (10 February 1867) commending a public monument to Voltaire, and one wonders how much Garibaldi knew about Voltaire.[27] Sainte-Beuve, who was less abrasive than Voltaire, became a gentle admirer at this time, and declared that France was not civilized unless a statue of Voltaire was erected in the Place de la Concorde.[28]

In 1878 came the centenary, and by then the name evoked rabid opinion on both sides, and both sides made themselves ridiculous. By an unfortunate coincidence the day of the commemoration was Ascension Day. For weeks beforehand Bishop Dupanloup of Orléans filled his newspaper *Défense* with extracts of impiety, and unsuccessfully tried to persuade the minister to prosecute Victor Hugo for printing other extracts. Renan, Victor Hugo, Littré and others organized a festivity in which the government refused to take part; and in the Gaiety theatre Victor Hugo made a speech on Voltaire's *smile*,[29] while an open-air assembly of 6,000 stood round a ten-foot-high statue of Voltaire draped in red and lowered their flags in processional salute to the tune of revolutionary music. 'No inconsiderable portion' of the French people, commented an English observer sadly, 'exalted the memory of the most inveterate enemy of Christianity and its founder.'[30] Those were the days of the fiercest politics in the French Third Republic. They show how the name of a man became a symbol among many who never read a word of his writings. Probably – from the point of view of our general theme as distinct from the internal divisions of France of which the main division was religious – the symbol was a French symbol, and only faintly a symbol for either the Germans or the British.

3

The construction of the new classical church of St Geneviève in Paris was vowed by Louis XV if he recovered from his illness. He recovered and then found the money by the use of state lotteries. Soufflot the architect lived in the full glare of the Enlightenment, and needed nothing Gothic or mysterious. He was a man of his century and wanted daylight and rationality, and paid small regard either to the history of France or to the customs of Catholic worship. The legend of St Geneviève was not important to him. But the plans ran into difficulty. The construction met trouble with foundations and was not complete when the Revolution broke out. The church was not yet consecrated when the National Assembly of 4 April 1791 decided that it be called Panthéon and dedicated to those who deserved well of their country; Mirabeau the first. Voltaire's remains were translated thither by a theoretically solemn but actually carnival-like procession on 10 July of the same year; Rousseau's remains on 11 October 1794. The architect de Quincy was ordered to obliterate religious ornaments from the church. He removed the furniture and the bell-tower, and replaced the glittering cross and adoring angels over the portico with a France bestowing a crown of virtue, while Liberty with lions crushed despotism; and an inscription, 'To our great men the Fatherland does homage.' He removed the cross on the dome (it was only a temporary cross until they carved a statue of St Geneviève) and put a huge statue of the goddess Fame, nine metres high, blowing an enormous trumpet.

In 1806 Napoleon, who thought established churches were like vaccination to protect the people from sorcery and fanaticism, re-established Catholic worship and the name of St Geneviève and added (1812) a golden cross upon the dome. But the church was not reopened till 1822. The portico had its third sculpture, a shining cross with rays, and lost the inscription 'To our great men. . .'.

In 1830, another revolution. St Geneviève was out again, so were altars and candlesticks and confessional-boxes. The portico got its fourth decoration, the Fatherland distributing crowns offered to it by Liberty while History stands by recording – crowns to soldiers on the right, and on the left to civilians, including Voltaire and Rousseau, but also including Archbishop Fénelon. The inscription

'To our great men . . .' came back, and the cross on the dome was replaced by a flag.

In 1851–2 Louis Napoleon transformed the Panthéon into the Church of St Geneviève, gave it national status, removed the inscription 'To our great men . . .' and put a cross (only a wooden cross) on the dome.

During the Commune of 1871 Communards sawed off the arms of the wooden cross and hung a red flag from the upright pole.

In July 1873 the cross returned – this time a heavy stone cross four metres high.

Victor Hugo died on 22 May 1885. St Geneviève went out again, and Victor Hugo was buried in the revived Panthéon, and all the altars and confessional-boxes disappeared; but on the dome the cross was left, and stands there to this day. It is a great monument of French classical art, killed icy and naked by the troubles of French history.[31]

About the time that Hugo died, it was rumoured that the bodies of Voltaire and Rousseau were not there. An eye-witness was produced that in 1814 royalists, unable to suffer these bones in a sacred place, stole into the church by night, opened the sarcophaguses, tumbled the bones in a common sack, and drove them in a hackney cab to a piece of waste land where they were thrown into a hole. Not until 1864 when the heart of Voltaire came to the nation in its silver vase, was the theft discovered. The story was circumstantial, and appeared in biography after biography.[32] At last in 1897 the minister of public instruction appointed a government committee to investigate it. The committee opened the tombs and held that the remains within were the remains of Voltaire and Rousseau. What was true was that in 1822, when St Geneviève was reconsecrated, the bodies of Voltaire and Rousseau were pushed out into an underground passage in order not to lie in the precinct which the Archbishop of Paris hallowed. The July monarchy restored them to their old resting place.

Here is a symbol of all our troubled intellectual history. The old world started it, a church built in fulfilment of a vow which might have been taken in the Middle Ages, but was fulfilled by modern financial jugglery. Then it became a sign of de-Christianizing revolution, national virtues instead of old virtues, La France instead of St Geneviève; and because it became a sign, it was buffeted to and fro in accordance with the see-saw of party politics, holy and secular, holy and secular, until at last, like so much of western

Europe, it lay almost secularized, but with the not so old stone cross still there to make a memory and a blessing, the past of Europe still speaking to the present, and keeping guard over men once thought to be the vilest enemies of the cross, but now seen to have fought for freedoms and for truths that were necessary to the human spirit.

The roguish Voltaire[33] predicted his own tomb at Ferney. It was to be constructed in a special way, half of it being inside the church and half outside. They would not be able to put him in the sanctuary – still, they could not throw him out altogether. He often did things in jest, but seldom in jest only.

7

SCIENCE AND RELIGION

Science versus Religion – the antithesis conjures two hypostatized entities of the later nineteenth century: Huxley St George slaying Samuel smoothest of dragons; a mysterious undefined ghost called Science against a mysterious indefinable ghost called Religion; until by 1900 schoolboys decided not to have faith because Science, whatever that was, disproved Religion, whatever that was.

The twentieth century strips legends, and among the legends started stripping this. The healthy action of historical investigation, like any other scientific enquiry, refused to be content with inherited ideas received uncritically, and asked how far those axioms were invented, how far they depended on a real antithesis of minds, how far they were devised or made rhetorical by propaganda, and how far they expressed deeper currents of antagonism than the intellectual.

Without in any way subscribing to the doctrine that the famous Conflict was a myth created by special conditions of the nineteenth century, we find it easy at this range to discern an element of the legendary. Pause for a moment to consider the author who published in English the first of all the books called by the symbolic title: John William Draper, who in 1874 published at New York the book called *History of the Conflict between Religion and Science*. If you read it now, you might not think it important. I mention therefore that it was translated into French, German, Italian, Spanish, Polish, Russian, Portuguese, and Serbian, and got into the Index of prohibited books (4 September 1876).

Here the antithesis stands fierce in the opening pages. The Pope, he says, has loudly declared that the Church will accept no reconciliation with modern civilization. This antagonism between Religion and Science (the two words have capital letters) is the continuation of a struggle which began when Christianity first attained political power. A revelation from God is absolute. It can brook no change, no modification, no improvement. But knowledge is always growing, always modifying opinion, always in movement.

Faith is stationary, science progressive. Therefore motionless faith and moving knowledge are continuously at war. Hence we looked backward down the centuries to see this war in progress. But then it turns out that Draper almost exempts Protestantism from the charge.[1] It has never, since the restoration of science, arrayed itself in opposition to the advancement of knowledge. On the contrary, it has always met it with welcome. It has observed a reverential attitude to truth, from whatever quarter it might come. However, some Protestants have lately behaved badly to scientists.

So we find at the outset that, after this parade of antipathy between faith and knowledge, the author is not going to deal with his subject. He is going to attack the Roman Church for its conservatism. Before the end he tells us (284) that Catholicism was a vast system of delusion and imposture. So far from getting a philosophical or historical treatment of the most important theme of the day, we find on our hands the tract of a Protestant controversialist. We awake, and remember that the writer was the son of a Methodist preacher. The Syllabus of 1864 gave him plenty of material. When has Science steeped its hands in blood to repress ideas? But in the Vatican – and Draper gave it a note of exclamation.

But this was far from all. The book contains a paean of praise to science, a hymn, its mighty achievements, a catalogue not exhaustive, telescopes, balloons, diving bells, thermometer, barometer, schools, newspapers, hospitals, canals, sanitation, census reports, cotton-gin, medicines, manures, tractors, railways, telegraph, calculus, air pump, batteries, magnets, photographs, maps, sewing-machines, rifles, and warships[2] – (I select from a much longer list) – all beneficent discoveries of science, but not just science *simpliciter*, of science in contrast, and the contrast is with Catholicism. Draper never stopped to ask himself why anyone who invented a camera or possessed a barometer might be led to think his faith in the God of the Christians shaky. Perhaps he was only saying that the material good of life comes from practical thinking and not from contemplating eternity. But this was not the atmosphere with which he surrounded what he said. He almost seemed to assume, without knowing himself to assume, that *because* Martha washed tea-cups more effectively than Mary, Mary's activity was meaningless.

Legend at work here: or, a measure of illusion. The conflict was hypostatized, Science and Religion were blown up into balloon duellists, Science containing all knowledge, Religion containing no knowledge, and the two set side by side, with know-nothing using sabre to keep know-all from his place. Once it had been hypostatized, it became possible to read back the antipathy throughout history, and see the ding-dong of duel through centuries, Science invented by the Macedonian campaigns of Alexander the Great, Christianity suppressing the schools of Alexandria which were schools of Science, Church putting earth at the centre of the universe and Galileo proving it was not, Church still talking of 'incessant divine intervention' and Science talking of the 'operation of primordial and unchangeable law' (xv).

British scientists were not pleased with these roamings through history. Draper came to the British Association meeting at Oxford in 1860. He was main speaker at the only famous debate at a British Association meeting; and he went on and on, droning away, while the audience longed to hear Bishop Wilberforce, who was rumoured to be about to demolish the theory of Darwin, and to hear how Hooker or Huxley would answer the prelate. Orators who take up time which others want may not get fair judgment on their matter. But the British scientists were not pleased with the attitudes which appeared in Draper's speech, for some were the same attitudes later to appear in his book on *Conflict*. They thought him a donkey and a bore. They said so privately. They called his 'stuff' flatulent. Quasi-philosophical sweeps of theoretical history have often repelled scientist equally with historian. Huxley already saw the element of legend in what was proposed.

But it was not all legend. A popular mind, even when that mind is middle class (we have seen how remote all this was from the interests of working-class secularism) has a need to inflate if it is to understand. It seizes upon the salient point; the point which is easy to identify; the point which is graphic, can be pictured; the point which a newspaper can make readable. In seizing upon the salient point it distorts, casts the environment into shadow, forgets nuances and qualifications, and inflates. Some scientists say the world is millions of years old, some clergymen say it was created in 4004 B.C. – the scientists represent a Gog dubbed Science and the clergymen represent a Magog dubbed Religion, we must label and isolate, because only so do we understand; and we overlook that what are really being opposed are knowledge in the seventeenth century versus knowledge in the nineteenth century.

It is not legend. We have seized upon a salient point. It is a point, and it is salient. A conflict was hypostatized, necessarily, out of a number of conflicts. And even if they had lower-case *C*s instead of capitals, they were momentous in the history of the European mind.

You will have noticed that Darwin and the *Origin of Species* were not relevant to Draper's sense of conflict. Though he wrote in the full spate of argument over Darwin, amid the decades when everyone (when I say *everyone* I use it in its conventional meaning of quarter-of-the-middle-class) debated the conflict between Science and Religion, though he published one of his books four years after Darwin's *Origin* and the other three years after Darwin's *Descent of Man*, though he focussed crudely and yet powerfully (the more powerfully because the more crudely) pressing anxiety over obscurantism versus new learning, he could have written both his books equally well or ill, he need have changed hardly a word, if Darwin had been drowned in the Cam as an undergraduate. Men afterwards looked back at Darwin and found in him the symbol of the conflict, its centre, perhaps even source. We know of a Harrow schoolboy of the early 1880s who heard that 'Darwin had disproved the Bible' and rearranged his faith accordingly. *Darwin has disproved the Bible* – in the mouth of an intelligent schoolboy of fourteen years old. This is bringing us near the heart of the problem over secularization. When we come down to the axioms which intelligent schoolboys of fourteen years learn from less intelligent schoolboys of fifteen years, we come near to the point where the cloudy apprehensions of what is known as intellectual history, so hard to test at any point, can be shown to begin to affect the attitudes of a whole society.

We have sharply to distinguish, it seems, between the theory of a philosopher and the axioms of a society. Bishop Berkeley reasons with conviction, and is convincing in his argument, that all the world exists only in the human mind. And nobody believes him, because men like Samuel Johnson stub their toes against walls and live happy under an illusion that the bishop needs no further refutation. D'Holbach tells the eighteenth century that all the world is matter, that nothing is which is not matter. The theory has no influence because nobody believes him. The common sense of the human race finds it as obvious that everything is not matter as it is obvious that everything is not in the mind. If we start to suppose that materialistic theories of the universe had secularizing force, we find no evidence that this happened because philosophers argued for materialism and persuaded more and more people who think and then the more and more people who think affected the unconscious

attitudes of those who never think or, at least, never think philo-
sophically.

2

During the 1850s German and French scientists conducted a controversy known, more to our grandfathers than to ourselves, as the
materialistic controversy. It was specially associated with the names
of Vogt, Moleschott and Büchner. These were not men of the
Enlightenment like d'Holbach three generations before. They were
men of the laboratory, and especially of the medical laboratory.
They were much more like anatomists who dissect the human body
and say that they find no soul therein and therefore there is no soul.
But they were not simple anatomists. Usually they were trained as
physiologists or zoologists. Comparative anatomy had advanced far
since the time, half a century before, when it offered the strongest
arguments for design in the universe. What was coming out of it
now was kinship; and therefore cousinships; and therefore families,
and so descent. Every scientist prominent as a fighter in the materialistic controversy of the fifties was an anatomist, a physiologist or a
zoologist.

Lamarck died in 1829, believing himself to have demonstrated
with certainty how one species could change into another, and with
probability that life was generated from lifeless matter. He had
proved nothing of the kind. But the development of medical and
biological science in the thirty years after his death brought the
relationships of species ever more into the argument, and with them
the animal nature of man. *Man descended from apes*: at first it was
like Bishop Berkeley's theory of ideas or d'Holbach's theory of
materialism, no man of sense could believe it unless his mind was
unbalanced by night hours of academic speculation. This is not
surprising, since it happened to be untrue. But it was a symbol or
slogan of what was true. Man was proved to have a relationship with
animals such as few men had hitherto realized. In Britain Robert
Chambers put the theory onto the table of many middle-class
drawing-rooms (*Vestiges of Creation*, 1844).

Karl Vogt came from Giessen, lost his place in Germany through
the revolutionary troubles of 1848 and settled in Geneva as professor of geology, hater of clergymen and fierce advocate of a
materialistic philosophy. He found Robert Chambers an admirable
tool. He translated *Vestiges* into German as *Natürliche Schöpfungsgeschichte*, second edition Brunswick 1858. The moment Darwin's

165

Origin appeared, Vogt knew that he had an instrument, not only for his science (for Darwin forced him to change his theory of the origin of man) but for his philosophical purpose. He toured Europe lecturing on Darwin. He was a wonderful orator, with a perfect mixture of humour and satire. In Munich the lecturer even suffered physical assault. His sayings were quoted again and again; the most famous, 'Thoughts come out of the brain as gall from the liver, or urine from the kidneys.'³ He had far more power of popular exposition than Darwin, more power even than Huxley. In Britain Huxley was the man who put Darwin into the consciousness of the popular mind. Yet Huxley always remained limited in popular appeal by a measure of academic restraint. Vogt was more influential in Europe than Huxley in Britain. But he did not lack English readers. He collected several of his travelling lectures and published them (Giessen 1863) as *Vorlesungen über den Menschen*. In the following year 1864 the Anthropological Society of London published an English translation of the work under the title: *Lectures on Man: his place in Creation and the history of the Earth*.

It was also published in French as *Leçons sur l'Homme*, and in France found most enthusiasm. The English translator asked Vogt's leave to miss out passages offensive to English readers and Vogt consented. On reflexion the translator found that he could not omit all such passages without radically altering the book, and so he merely omitted three paragraphs, but printed them in small type in an appendix. The reader of Vogt feels incongruity between the level-headed exposition of his scientific theories (even when later science proved those theories wild) and the sudden ejaculatory onslaughts. Geneva in the 1860s had no reputation for conservatism in religion. But Vogt evidently felt the power of religious conservatism in opposing scientific advance. Genesis Chapter 1 and Noah's universal flood must be demolished, though in most of middle-class northern Europe they were demolished or adapted or allegorized thirty years before. So far from thinking, like the next generation, that Noah's ark was a harmless legend, Vogt felt passionately that it was an obstacle to scientific enquiry. In the usually sober *Lectures on Man* he even brought in the argument about Cain and where he found a wife. And after all his reasonable arguments, he ended the book with a portrait of all orthodox Paris preaching against him and declaring that materialism and Darwinism assailed morality and the social foundations of human life. 'They feel surprised, that people with such views can be good citizens, honest men, good husbands and fathers.' Vogt must be the only scientist ever to have ended a serious work of scientific enquiry with a defiant wave of the fist against yapping dogs and the words, *Let them bark, till they can bark no more.*

This feeling of aggressive defence needs further consideration. Huxley had more than a touch of it, Tyndall a touch, Darwin no sign. Pasteur could be roused to emotional utterance if people, knowing him a Christian, made innuendoes that he used or misused his science to help prove religion. Vogt was roused as any philosophical atheist would be roused if told that he was therefore immoral. The indignation rose because science seemed not to be able to advance without social disadvantage to groups of scientists. Some moralists said, biological science breeds atheism and overturns the moral basis of society, scientists link hands with teachers of immorality. They seized upon Vogt, who by denying free will, and asserting that thoughts are only response to a physical condition, removed all moral responsibility.

Of course, many moralists were aware of the real state of affairs; and most scientists were aware of the real state of affairs – that the advances of science could hardly touch God. Huxley knew it – no enquiry in the realm of the physical could produce results in the realm of the spiritual. Still, the advance of science touched the Bible, and for most of western Europe God's sacredness in society could not be dissociated in idea from the sacredness of the Bible.

A few scientists can be found for whom the physical enquiry seemed to lead to direct contradiction of God and his existence. Scientists engaged in the 'materialist' controversy might be expected to pursue this line of thinking. This was the real importance of Karl Vogt. Above all other men he claimed to infer from his physical investigations the demolition of religion, of God, of a realm of spirit. Unlike other men he was not willing to keep these inferences out of his books on science, even textbooks (or especially textbooks) designed for general reading, like his textbook on geology.[4]

Vogt was the most explosive personality among the scientists of the nineteenth century. This was partly because of his extreme statements of materialism, and ability to frame quotations which ran across Europe; partly because he happened also to be a prominent advocate of social revolution and of the belief that revolution is the only road to human progress. His political pamphleteering, like his religious opinion, was not kept out of his books on animals – the best evidence of his political opinions is found in his *Investigations into animal societies,* published at Frankfurt in 1851 when he had lately been driven from his country as a revolutionary. Twenty years before he died Bishop Dupanloup of Orléans, speaking in the French Chamber of Deputies, called Vogt the *arch-revolutionary* and made him responsible for the doctrines which begot the Commune.[5]

Vogt was a rare though not unique case: of a scientist who afforded both sides almost all that they needed to dramatize the battle between Religion and Science. He held that his science disproved religion, the existence (let alone the immortality) of the soul, of God or gods. He taught an amoral doctrine of the will and revolutionary doctrines of the state, and therefore afforded conservatives everything they needed to associate his science, and by reflexion to associate Darwinism, with the ills traditionally ascribed to atheism.

Yet he was a true investigator and no mere publicist. He did not receive the scientific reputation which his pure science deserved. For one who kept warning his hearers to caution in their conclusions, he was immeasurably confident in his own conclusions. Despite his great abilities, real experimental learning and unequalled power of presentation, he did not find ample recognition among the scientists.[6] Twenty-five years later he was remembered only for sayings of biting humour. That was probably true of all the publicists of scientific philosophy, except possibly (not certainly) Huxley who himself despised Draper. Working scientists wanted quietly to continue their experiments and were seldom pleased when verbal battles ensued over speculations derived from their researches. They reacted only when dogma stood in the way of their enquiries. The most eminent publicists were not usually regarded as the most reliable judges of scientific evidence. If a man went round Europe, preaching rather than lecturing that man is an ape, he was inclined to bend prehistoric evidence to suit his conclusions; for the evidence was still so insufficient as to be easily bendable. In 1867 Karl Vogt published an extraordinary book, the *Microcephali*, with wild exaggeration of the evidence from skulls and behaviour of idiots, assuming that the behaviour of idiots was reversion to an earlier stage of man's evolutionary process; and gaining henceforth for himself the doubtful sobriquet of Affenvogt. Learned men called him 'characteristically hasty'. But then Vogt was a famous jester. And scientists were not sure whether in such a matter, as one of them wrote, pleasantries are not superfluous.[7]

What effect does such a man have in shifting the intellectual axioms of his age? It is no good a writer, however famous, however learned, telling us, with all the proofs of the world, that we have not free will, because we shall never believe him, for a similar reason to that by which Dr Samuel Johnson confronted Bishop Berkeley. It is no good a man telling us that we have no moral responsibility, because we are certain to the contrary. But here was a good scientist and an exceptional communicator. He was famous, his fame depending on a single phrase which rings through Europe, that thought comes from the brain like urine from the kidneys – a dogma which as dogma men would never accept, but which as advertisement gathered audiences and then became a symbol of a standpoint. This good scientist and remarkable teacher declared that his science not only proves positive things about man and his origin, but negative things about man and his religion.

What it did was to popularize Darwinism. In the long run the force did not depend on Vogt, either on his science or on his lecturing ability, but on the material which he used – and in the long run the soundest part of the material lay in the work of Darwin.

Jakob Moleschott was the son of a Dutch free-thinking father, and became lecturer in physiology at Heidelberg from 1847. There he began to read Feuerbach and D. F. Strauss, each of whom had great effect upon his mind. The scientific materialists of western Europe in that age often derived their underlying axioms from Feuerbach or Strauss or both; and the more closely the origin of their axioms are studied the more influence of Feuerbach we find. Unlike Vogt, Moleschott was serene; his autobiography of old age breathes a gentle spirit without bitterness and without the need to defend.[8] But like Vogt, he came before the public in 1850 as the maker of a famous phrase – *no thought without phosphorus;*[9] and it was in his review of this book that Feuerbach could not resist the epigram, somewhat to Moleschott's vexation, 'Man is what he eats', *Der Mensch ist, was er isst.* Feuerbach was provocative. 'It used to be said, *In the beginning God.* Now it is said, *In the beginning the belly.* The old world put the body on the head, the new puts the head on the body. The old world made spirit parent of matter, the new makes matter parent of spirit.' All this made the mild Moleschott a public figure. The publicity was increased a hundred-fold when in 1852 he published at Mainz *Der Kreislauf des Lebens,* wherein a digression of a few pages advocated cremation on the plea that human bodies should be used to fertilize and ought not to be wasted in tombs and graves. This book had a decisive effect upon his career, making it impossible for him to find a chair in Germany and driving him first to Zurich and then to Italy to seek institutes to pursue his researches. In Catholic Italy he inevitably became prominent on the side of the Risorgimento against the Pope. In some north Italian universities groups of Catholic students were formed as defences against the teaching of Moleschott. But he was little more than a name and a slogan and the memory of a phrase. He pursued his researches until his death in 1893, and hardly evangelized for the cause like Vogt.

The years 1863, 1864, 1865, 1866, 1867 – these were the years when the discussion of Science and Religion changed its character. This was because of Darwin; paradoxically, for we have seen from the case of Draper that because of Darwin men who wrote on conflict between Science and Religion did not feel a need to alter what they wrote. Draper changed hardly a word because of Darwin. Vogt was famous in the materialist controversy of the 1850s and carried on the same controversy in the 1860s – but with a wider public, with a revolution of his own scientific ideas, but not with any revolution of his ideas on the relation between science and religion. Darwin was not so much cause as occasion. He coincided with the years when the full implications of new knowledge, in crude form and apprehended simply, reached the middle classes of western Europe and America.

Here is a similar case of a publicist, even more celebrated in the lay world, and less equipped scientifically, far less regarded by working scientists: Ludwig Büchner, another doctor of medicine and also from Giessen, another active politician, who became a lecturer in medicine at the university of Tübingen. In 1855 he joined the controversy over materialism by seizing a phrase of Moleschott and publishing *Kraft und Stoff*, Force and Matter. In consequence of this book he was forced out of his lectureship and reverted to being a general practitioner and then a free-lance writer; founding in 1881 the German League of Freethinkers. The book went through twenty-one German editions by 1904, was translated into fifteen languages, was anxiously or violently reviewed in every country including Britain, and still went on selling. He was neither scientist nor philosopher. Life and men have emerged planless, haphazard, accidents of nature. He used Darwin, after the *Origin* was published, to support this hostility to purpose in the universe. Matter 'thinks', the intellectual forces of men are simply offspring of matter.

If a single book represents the popular, as distinct from the real (though of course the popular crudely reflected the real) oppositions between Science and Religion in Europe of the middle nineteenth century, that book is Büchner's *Force and Matter*. He was a popularizer of modern science; not particularly of Darwin because the original edition was published four years before Darwin issued *The Origin of Species*, but afterwards including and using Darwin. The axiom was physical. Force means matter and matter force. Therefore 'spiritual' force is nonsense. Creation is impossible because matter must be eternal and can only change, cannot be added to. Creation equals force and therefore cannot have existed before matter. No edge can be imagined to space, and therefore space is infinite. Mind and spirit being dependent on matter, pure spirit is impossible. Everything in the organic world is made of various combinations of a cell which has arisen out of living matter which generated it and which we call protoplasm. Everything is heading for ultimate destruction of our world and our race. 'With the most absolute truth and with the greatest scientific accuracy can we say at this day: there is nothing miraculous in the world' (4th edition, Eng. trans., 95). The universe has no purpose. It is a blind, unalterable necessity of the laws of matter. Priests are deceivers or ambitious. Religious men are fanatics. No educated man can possibly disagree with these conclusions. Only 'the ignorant layman' can believe in a personal god.

Büchner found by experience that the reading of his book made for sadness among its readers. Men and women lamented that he left them no hope. Büchner consoled them. To be under relentless law begets feelings of humility, or repose, self-contentment and self-respect. Any idea of a power beyond degrades man by making him a plaything, the slave of a despot. To accept this theory, or rather this knowledge, is to have the stability that comes from resting on a certainty. 'Not as the humble and submissive slave of a supernatural master, nor as the helpless toy in the hands of heavenly powers, but as a proud and free son of Nature, understanding her laws and knowing how to tutor them to his own use, does the creature of modern civilization, the Freethinker, appear;. . .the incarnation of the mightiest effort of Nature. . .' (4th edition, Eng. trans., 254).

Nothing represents better that temporary phase of popular philosophy which combined the contradiction of lowering man to the dust by showing him to be nothing but another animal, while lifting him to the skies and singing his greatness as ruler of the world.

How influential is a popular book? Bishop Robinson wrote *Honest to God* and is said to have sold millions of copies. Does it follow that the book changed so many people's minds? Is it possible that not everyone who bought the book read it, and not everyone who read the book understood it, and perhaps not even the author understood fully every word of what he had written? Perhaps a popular book, upon a theme among the most profound and difficult known to man, is rather a symbol, the focus of the inarticulate longings of a decade, than an instructress like a book of elementary physics and, if so, its influence might be seen in its focussing and not in its instruction; articulating an attitude towards life which some people wanted to articulate and could not articulate for themselves or did not like to articulate for themselves. What can we safely deduce of intellectual history from the knowledge that Büchner's book ran through twenty-one German editions by 1904?

A shrewd critic tells us this of Büchner:[10] 'The great and lasting consequence of Büchner's work rests primarily upon the fact that it was the expression of popular superficial thought influenced by the successes of the natural sciences.' *Great and lasting consequence*, that is what we should like to be able to test: how great? and how lasting? Very few people in the world believe what Büchner proposed, or ever did. Popular thought was influenced by the successes of the natural sciences – but that gets us not far, no one since Draper is going to propose that the invention of the railway or of the thermometer caused anyone to believe less in the Pope's authority.

These books which form men's interest are evidence because they focus men's interest. They tell us, not what people thought, but what they wanted to read about, and what they wanted to be able to say that they had read about. They tell us more about the theme under discussion, than the prevailing intellectual attitudes to that theme. Büchner told his brother Alex that he had written a book of philosophical essays, and asked him for advice about a publisher. Vogt and Moleschott found men willing to publish them, so it could not be impossible.

'What is the title?' said Alex.

'*Force and Matter*,' cried Ludwig.

'*Force and Matter*!' cried Alex, jumping out of his seat. 'Why, the title alone is worth money. Any publisher will buy the book without looking at it.'[11]

If any of us were to offer the publisher of this university the typescript of a book called *Force and Matter*, the publisher might look at us with respect, or he might look at us with astonishment, but I doubt whether he would jump out of his seat and even more whether he would accept the book without reading it. Therefore we can tell something about the climate of opinion from these popular books; partly from their sale, partly from their reviews and partly from their citations in other books or from the pamphlets written to demolish them. But we more easily learn about the theme under discussion than the attitudes to it, and we find it still very difficult to learn how or whether such a book changed anyone's mind; except in those rare cases where an autobiographer looks back and sees such a book as a landmark in the history of his own mind. Most of the books men read are not in this category, any more than most of the sermons men hear. If they do not fall dead-born, they pass into some mysterious background and live hidden for a time and then are forgotten totally. But it does not follow that they had no influence because men remember no conscious influence.

This is important, not only for posterity but for contemporaries. Büchner advocated materialism. His book sold hundreds of thousands of copies. Therefore contemporaries imagined that he had hundreds of thousands of disciples, perhaps even a hierarchy, a cult, an organization. People wrote pamphlets on this axiom. Büchner himself used to smile wryly. He used to look round for disciples and found none.[12]

Readers of T. H. Huxley's *Essays* will remember how at one point[13] he expressed his contemptuous disbelief in Büchner's ideas and his utter rejection of materialism. Frenchmen were surprised to see Büchner and Vogt. They thought atheism peculiarly French, and Germany--the home of idealism and mysticism. Accustomed to deride Germans for imagining matter not to exist, they were astonished to find Germans who maintained that mind did not exist. They had supposed German atheism to consist only of supper parties of Frederick the Great, where most of the diners were French. It seemed contrary to the German habit of mind, the German way of life. French positivism was far more agnostic, and often far more reverent, than the materialists. Positivist utterances could be as interesting as when Littré and Robin used a dictionary to define *soul* as: 'anatomically, the sum of functions of the neck and spinal column; physiologically, the sum of functions of the power of perception in the brain'.[14] Still, the French were surprised at German materialism, and the surprise is a little piece of historical evidence about the nature of the influence.

Here we tread in a mist through that mysterious land which divides an intellectual advance from its popular consequences; in the time which separates the moment when Charles Darwin sent his manuscript to the publisher, from the moment a quarter of a century later when a schoolboy says that 'Darwin has disproved the Bible.' 1,500 copies of *The Origin* were sold on the day of publication. 1,500 copies does not go far in reckoning the movement of axioms in a whole society, especially when we know that some of the first buyers welcomed the book as a most Christian contribution, a further unfolding of the wonders in God's works. Then came the scientific arguments, Owen and Huxley; then the students or publicists on the Continent strengthening their anti-religious attitudes with the aid of the new tool, like Vogt or Büchner, and new men joining the debate and becoming enthusiasts for the propagation of Darwinian doctrine, like Asa Gray in Harvard, or Filippo de Filippi at Turin;[15] with the discussion centring ever more on what Darwin had not yet examined, the descent of man, that is, man's kinship with apes; and then philosophers or theologians enter the fray to ask questions about soul, or conscience, or art, or ideals, or moral basis of society; and as debates, or clashes, spread outward, the question of what Darwin wrote, or how Darwin theorized, has ceased to be important because the debate has travelled beyond the point where the exact nature of Darwinian theory matters to the larger argument now being conducted. *Darwin has disproved the Bible* – as a historical statement nothing could be more legendary. The Bible was proved not to be all historical before ever Darwin wrote. Darwin never touched the subject. But Darwin finally made it probable, not that the history of Genesis was legend (which was probable already if not certain), but that the moral apprehensions founded upon that history had to be restated if they were to survive.

Not many men would read *The Origin*, or understand it if they read it. The secularizing force was not Darwin the author of the book, or of several books. It was Darwin the symbol, Darwin the name which stood for a process, the name which was hurled from one side to the other in the polemics of secularist platforms or journals, an imaginary Darwin, a vague Darwin, without the comfortable homely substantial outlines of the real naturalist of a Kentish village, but however imaginary and however vague still bearing a direct relationship to a scientific achievement, which few quite understood, the truth of which many doubted, but which everyone, without knowing quite what it was, knew to be a scientific achievement of the first magnitude.

Does that mysterious entity Science say, man is no more than an ape? Not at all. Does the entity Science say, down with Religion? Nowhere. These are terms too large for profitable use in a serious debate between informed men. But the debate now being conducted in Europe was influencing many more people than the informed. Science proved – so between 1870 and 1885 many non-scientists recognized – that, even though man was not an ape, he had evolved in some such way as apes evolved. And the book which, more than any other book in Europe, was God's book, said that he did not.

The entity Science did not say, down with Religion. But a few scientists said that Science said, down with Religion; and those scientists, a Vogt, a Büchner (for the public regarded Büchner as a scientist) among the most readable and the most read. They were more read precisely because they said that Science said, down with Religion. Religion is a commoner interest of most of the human race than is Physics or Biology. The great public was far more interested in Science-versus-Religion than in Science.

Men like Büchner brought before the middle classes the idea that there was an alternative explanation to the world, different from that which they inherited. What they said was not enough to persuade that man is only an animal, or that everything is matter, or that all priests are rabid, or that all religion is vain, or that free-thinkers are the noblest examples of humanity.

What they said was enough to persuade that the Bible is not what it was thought, that we cannot therefore be so confident over the precise expressions of religion. It was enough to raise the question whether we need to think of a creator, and therefore whether the world can in any sense be thought of as ordered by a providence. It was enough to persuade that miracles are in doubt – but by the time Büchner wrote, miracles were already in doubt. It was enough, also, to breed popular interest in the problem. Even Mr Punch found it good to be witty about *The Missing Link*. In 1883 the West-minster Aquarium advertised an exhibition of the Missing Link, a Laotian girl called Krao with a hairy body and large cheek pouches.[16]

3

Consider the spread of Darwinianism in Germany. There it was to take deepest root, and bring its most potent consequences, including its nastiest.

Darwin already had a little reputation among German scientists before he published *The Origin of Species*. The journal of *The*

Voyage of the Beagle had not escaped them, and they knew the author of that journal as one who contributed to the geology of South America and enquired into the coral reefs in the Indian Ocean. As such he appeared in the textbooks. But certainly no German could have predicted that the naturalist aboard the Beagle could publish a revolutionary book.

The influence of *The Origin* in Germany was not at first great.

It was quickly and well translated into German, by Heinrich George Bronn, an excellent palaeontologist at Heidelberg; one of the sanest of the evolutionary school of scientists during the 1850s, though he had as yet no theory to account for animal development. Bronn was the first to recognize the importance of Darwin's book. Yet he rejected Darwin's theory, not only as unproven and unprovable but as wrong. He therefore added explanatory notes which weakened Darwin, and omitted the controversial sentence of *The Origin* that 'light would be thrown on the origins of man'. Still, Bronn's translation was very good, and Bronn's reputation high, and therefore the book began to work its way.

Most German scientists were not at first impressed by a scientist like Darwin who claimed to range over several different fields of study, confused different areas of research, threw out suggestions without a big organization or parade of supporting evidence, and then hesitated on philosophical implications from the mingle-mangle. Darwin broke every rule that German scientific professors were accustomed to enforce upon their pupils. Some of them pooh-poohed the book. It fitted neither their evidence nor their preconceptions, and they saw no reason to take it seriously. Exact scientists rejected it as philosophical. Philosophers rejected it as unphilosophical. The young Haeckel, who read it at Berlin as early as May of 1860 and was deeply moved by it, was grieved to find hardly anyone to agree with him.[17]

In 1862 Haeckel (aged 28) started the campaign to convert Germany to Darwinism, and Darwinism in a form which Darwin must reach but had not yet expressed – natural process from inorganic to organic, natural process from animal to man. At once he found enthusiasm and excitement in his audiences. We need not trace the campaign from the Scientific Congress at Stettin in 1863, the *General Morphology* of 1866 (the first study of morphology based upon wholly evolutionary principles) – written in blood and overwork to protect himself from melancholy after his young wife's death of blood-poisoning – a difficult enough work which found few readers:

the *Natürliche Schöpfungsgeschichte* of 1868, afterwards translated into English as *The Natural History of Creation*, which filled in the entire picture of the evolutionary process from matter to man. Darwin, who published *The Descent of Man* in 1871, said in it that he would probably not have written the book if he had known Haeckel's book.[18] The German academics were not yet impressed. At the end of the sixties they made a move to eject him from his chair at Jena, and once Haeckel offered to resign, but was told crisply 'You will do less harm here than elsewhere, so you had better stay.'[19] *The Natural History of Creation* was a quasi-popular book, and put Haeckel on the map beyond the academic circles which still distrusted him, for it ran to nine editions and twelve translations by 1899. The German periodical *Kosmos* became the chief propagator of Darwinian ideas in Germany. By the end of the century Haeckel drew crowds wherever he went in Europe, partly because of his controversial activities, partly because of his publications, especially *Anthropogenie*, 1874, the English translation of the fifth edition as *The Evolution of Man* 1879; and above all, *Die Welträtsel*, 1899, translated into English as *The Riddle of the Universe*, 1900. The German popular edition sold 100,000 copies in a year. The English popular edition sold 100,000 copies. By 1900 Haeckel's name had become a symbol, like the name of Darwin, for countless crowds who never read a word of him. A good historical judge has held Haeckel's reputation of 1899, and the publication of *The Riddle of the Universe*, to be the apogee of the scientific materialism of the nineteenth century. On an Alpine railway Haeckel met some nuns who told him that they had learned evolution from Professor Haeckel's books. If another German professor mentioned the name of Haeckel in his lectures, the class would divide, students make noisy demonstrations for and against. In England a preacher said that Haeckel was an atrophied soul, and in Glasgow another preacher denounced him (erroneously) for his licentious life.

Though a much better scientist than Draper or Büchner, he descended from science into his metaphysics, and then became, like Draper, a purveyor of historical and ethical and religious generalizations. It is no longer easy to read him. But his name is among the most important I could mention because like the name of Darwin it became a sacrament, or flag. Science is always at war with Religion. Religious men are always blind, usually stupid, and often corrupt. Science has solved or is solving all the riddles of the universe; we know now and men cover their eyes if they do not see that we know. We have occupied every corner of space and left no room for God.

Haeckel went on to various things that most human beings could never bring themselves to believe. All things are fixed in mechanical causality. The physical world, the movement of men's minds, the history of peoples, are held in the grip of an iron necessity. 'We now know', he wrote, 'that. . .the soul [is] a sum of plasma-movements in the ganglion-cells.' He talked of the meaning of substance or the philosophy of monism, and in Germany of the early twentieth century the monists numbered some 6,000 people, with more hangers-on. That is not significant. Men seem to need names in which to incapsulate the tendencies of their age, and usually incapsulate them in the names of publicists. Darwin was no publicist, he was a gentle and unassuming experimentalist. But unusually for such a personality, he became a figurehead or symbol of a vast movement of European opinion, in part because two exceptionally able publicists, Huxley in England and Haeckel in Germany (Haeckel much the cruder of the two in his philosophies) identified his name with everything for which they stood.

Names of living scientists were not the only mottoes or catchwords by which a general bourgeois public could follow what was happening in the mighty argument. Certain words served the function. Some words served for a time and then faded away. No one cares anything today about the word *biogenesis*, but in the 1870s it was a red-hot word of controversy. The word *evolution* itself was extremely important in this function, and remained so, though for most people its meaning was never more than hazy. In the middle 1870s the word *protoplasm* served the function, in the 1880s the phrase *The Missing Link*. The names of dead men could be symbolic, as happened for a time, for different reasons, with the names of Galileo and Voltaire. The chief of these was Giordano Bruno, an authentic martyr of science, though no line of enquiry which he pursued was profitable, burnt by the Inquisition in 1600 at the Campo de' Fiori in Rome. When on 9 June 1889 a statue of him was unveiled in the Campo de' Fiori it seemed like a European moment, all the feelings for scientific freedom and all the feelings against religious obscurantism expressed through a mighty demonstration. 30,000 people marched through the streets of Rome to hear a speech by the official articlerical orator among the republicans of the left, Giovanni Bovio, who said that the Pope suffered more from the celebration of that day than by all the loss of the Papal states. In the next year Landseck published a book with a title which speaks, *Bruno, der Märtyrer der neuen Weltanschauung*, Bruno the martyr of the new world-outlook.

A peculiar aspect of public opinion was its self-contradiction. The general public was overwhelmingly in favour of religion, *considered vaguely*, rather than against it. And yet if an utterance or circumstance unfavourable to religion were reported, it was taken up, spread everywhere, talked about. If an utterance or circumstance favourable to religion were reported, it was little remarked. No doubt this was only the law of publicity, that destruction interests and construction bores. But, if a scholar said that all the gospels were forged in the fourth century, it got wide publicity; the refutation got little. Near the end of the century a Catholic professor of theology in Münster (Bautz) made himself absurd by implying that volcanoes are one proof of the existence of purgatory. All the newspapers had it, men laughed, Professor Bautz disappeared for ever into night, bearing the nickname *professor of hell*. Almost simultaneously Haeckel, borrowing information from an exceptionally discreditable English pamphlet and declaring it to be the work of a learned and acute theologian, wrote in *The Riddle of the Universe* that at the Council of Nicaea in 327 (sic) the four gospels were selected out of a heap of apocryphal and forged documents. The error was equally absurd academically. But it was a less interesting error, was made by a man who really understood science, and had not the touch of comedy possessed by volcanoes. No ignoramus would believe the doctrine of volcanoes. Some ignorant men would believe a fourth-century forging of gospels.[20] This points to the way in which a general scientific knowledge was more widespread than historical knowledge. A little knowledge of the physical earth gained in schools would demolish Professor Bautz. To know the historical follies of Professor Haeckel one must be expert. It is also interesting how a scientist of academic stature lost standards when he became an evangelist. As a scientist Haeckel had care, diligence, accuracy and reverence. As an evangelist for anti-Christian scientific religion, he was careless, inaccurate, and irreverent as any hack writer hired to be unfair for the sake of a cause and willing, if necessary, to be scurrilous. The philosopher Friedrich Paulsen said that he read *The Riddle of the Universe* with a burning sense of shame that it could have been published by a scholar in the land of scholarship. But the contents, learned or ignorant, were less important than the slogan. Science has disproved Religion – that was what was being asserted with dogmatism. The way in which such disproof could occur, or the dogmas professed by monists who asserted it, were not intelligible to the general public. 'Science' itself was not intelligible to the general public. The only thing intelligible was: 'scientists', who have a mighty reputation for their advances in knowledge, tell us that the parsons teach falsehood and that no God is. They identified Haeckel with 'Science', and knew Haeckel to be contemptuous of 'theologians'. They could not be aware that in much of what he said about religion Haeckel spoke as theologian and not as scientist.

But the general reader had the strong common sense of Dr Samuel Johnson. He could not be put upon by dogmas that did not carry conviction, any more than he could be put upon about volcanoes and purgatory. Haeckel's leading English disciple uttered this aphorism: 'The death of the animal is like the death of the motor car.'[21] The doctrine that all is matter, and that there is no ultimate distinction between living matter and dead matter ran into barriers of incredulity. No doctrines whatever would persuade ordinary people that the death of an animal was like the death of a motor car. They did not need to be philosophers to understand that the word *death* was being used in two different senses.

Religious men had this advantage, in the conflict of the years round 1900. The wave of agnosticism which unsettled their foundations was wholly impartial as it rolled up the beach. If a middle-class reader found it difficult now to commit himself so absolutely to any meaning of the word 'creation'; he found it equally difficult to commit himself to the corresponding dogma proposed by Haeckel or Büchner.

These were middle-class states of mind, intellectual problems of bourgeois society. But always a wider public was near. The orator Giovanni Bovio was elected chairman of the Working Men's Congress in Naples ten days after his speech at the statue of Giordano Bruno. While Haeckel fought to spread Darwinism in Germany, Social Democratic lecturers or journalists were already spreading Darwinism for reasons which had almost no connexion with Haeckel's reasons. In 1883 Marx's son-in-law, E. B. Aveling, was lecturing on the Ape-Man. The Social Democratic journal *Volkstaat* urged its readers to study Haeckel and Büchner as early as 1874; and three years before, one of its columnists argued that Darwin and Marx, working scientifically in different fields, produced results akin and complementary, and that Darwin was the *sanctioning* by science of Socialism.[22]

The materialists were acceptable in two different publics and for two different reasons, one social and one intellectual; yet the groups, as well as the reasons, were not divided by a line but merged into one another, and it was this merging which made the secularizing force of the conflict between science and religion. So many people identified religion with opposition to the aspirations of the worker that materialism could become a gospel for no philosophical reason, and probably became a gospel only among men for whom philosophy did not count. Haeckel disliked socialism and loathed mobs. But he found himself wildly cheered by a vast crowd of working-men in the Social Democratic Party.[23]

In Russia the materialists could become household gods for the revolutionary of the left. In every peasant's room was a small shrine on which stood holy pictures. In Dostoyevsky's *The Possessed*, Lieutenant Erkel threw down the Christian images in his landlady's room and smashed one of them with a hatchet. Then he put better gods, and on three stands like lecterns he placed copies of books by Vogt, Moleschott and Büchner; and he lit three church candles, and stood a candle in front of each book.[24]

This proletarian aspect marked the difference between atheism in the Enlightenment and atheism in the third quarter of the nineteenth century. The atheist of the eighteenth century no longer risked death, but he could suffer more than Büchner, who would not risk more than loss of lectureship and ostracism by tradesmen. The earlier atheist thought harder, because his problem was harder, he contemplated a generation where God was a living symbol and therefore alive even to him who said that he was dead. The later atheist thought God a dead word, a vacuum. He was therefore less agnostic, and more dogmatic. To the ultimate difficulties which occupied sensitive heads for centuries Büchner was indifferent. He and his contemporaries suffer a little now because they despised their enemies. They were so sure that theologians were obscurantists or absurd (sometimes they had good excuse) that they neglected hard thought about the problems which concerned theologians. Finding the question too easy to solve, they fail to give posterity the sensation of refinement in the mind. And this touches another important distinction between the atheist of the Enlightenment and his successor a century later. The later were more evangelistic, because they aimed at a mass instead of a salon. For the same reason they could be cruder and grosser (as with the comparison of thought with urine), because they wanted controversial popularity more than quiet persuasiveness.

4

Let us try to put ourselves back; a difficult feat when we were born within the twentieth century and never for one instant of our lives supposed Adam and Eve to be more historical personages than Perseus and the Gorgon. Let us suppose ourselves back, to have been born about 1840, of a church-going family but not especially pious, an educated family but not especially scientific. We learn at mother's knee that the seven days of Genesis Chapter 1 are not to be taken literally, and Noah's flood too for it would not have covered the whole earth. We should think already of the earth as very old, much much older than 4004 B.C., for already we should have children's picture-books about dinosaurs and pterodactyls. We should probably have thought Adam and Eve to be as historical as Caesar and Calpurnia. We should feel no tug between school-learning and religious practice.

Draper said that we already felt one tug – from the size of the universe. Draper believed that ever since Galileo the conflict was sore. All the Hebrew scriptures were based upon the earth as the centre of universe, and all the universe as built for man. This is the problem of size, and the question of purpose which size brings with it. Did man learn from astronomy and realize his unspeakable insignificance?[25]

Draper imagined that men must be more and more troubled because Copernicus once thought the sun to be five million miles away and Encke now thought it ninety-five million miles away; but to most men, probably all men in feeling, five million miles and ninety-five million miles are the same distance, a long way away. Man was no more 'insignificant' ninety-five million miles from the sun than he was when divided from Jehovah by the clouds on the summit of Mount Sinai. It is not physical measurement that troubles, it is the question about purpose which follows the study of physical measurement. If you look for Victorian minds troubled about purpose, they are easy to find. If you look for Victorian minds troubled about size, they are hard to find. Some people attributed the growth of irreligion to the proof by science that the world was very large. In Disraeli's novel[26] Lothair said:

'It is science that by demonstrating the insignificance of the globe and the vast scale of creation has led to this infidelity.' 'Science', replied the Syrian, 'may prove the insignificance of this globe in the scale of creation, but it can never prove the insignificance of man.'

The question of purpose is implicit. But the novel *Lothair* is of 1870, and evolution, not size, already raised the doubt of purpose.

To find a real person, instead of a character in a novel like Lothair, is more difficult. Perhaps Tennyson was the eminent Victorian who came nearest to trouble over size. He worried himself over vastness, chains of mountains, grains of sand, and puny men living under their brief day, 'insects of an hour'. 'The lavish profusion in the natural world', he once wrote 'appals me, from the growths of the tropical forest to the capacity of man to multiply, the torrent of babies'.[27] This sense of size was usually brought into a relationship, at least implied, with evolution. Not always. Somewhere in him was a feeling of perturbation for faith about immense physical forces. If one so sensitive felt it, others less able to express themselves must have felt it. On present evidence it was not a feeling so widespread as to contribute to our theme.

The same appears to be nearly as true, though not so absolutely true, when we meet the effect of evolution. Its effect was to throw into doubt all external evidence for a sense of design and purpose in the world. Not however for everyone. For some (Darwin in his first studies, Charles Kingsley, Asa Gray, Haeckel) evolution looked to make the world more purposeful by bringing more phenomena under the reign of law. But when we look round among ordinary Europeans of the 1860s and 1870s, we find it curiously hard to discover men who confess to disturbances because they recognize that the argument to God from the design of the natural world is weaker than before. Once perhaps they looked out, as William Paley looked out upon the marvellous design of the human eye and its miraculous ability to frame a portrait of Hampstead Heath in a miniature orb the size of a sixpence, upon the intricate pattern of beetle's wing or sea-anemone, and inferred thence a Designer. Henceforth they were more likely to begin with their religious experience, their sense of God derived from conscience, and looking out upon external nature to see its beauties and patterns sufficiently confirming their personal insights. Evolution hurried on the change that was already happening and had been happening since the end of the eighteenth century, since the earliest Romantics passed from a reasonable philosophy of religion based upon investigation of the physical world, to the direct experience of God which must be tested against investigation of the physical world.

This was a change for the theologian. Was it a religious change for our hypothetical young man born in 1840? That is, was evolution only demolishing crude outworks of the Christian Enlightenment which would no longer do, and tucking Paley's archidiaconal vestures into the old-clothes box? Had men always in truth found God by their feelings and conscience and arguments about him were always superficial, but they had not realized that the arguments were superficial and now evolution showed how superficial they were and stripped a veil from the reality of religion? It is not easy thus to divide human personality between feelings and argument. Nature red in tooth and claw, to the philosopher of religion, was only the ancient problem of pain in a new form. But this new form made men stumble up stairs in the dark. Educated Europeans in the third quarter of the nineteenth century still looked towards the altar of God, for all that evolution could say. But they stumbled. This change was not just a change for the theologian. It was a change in the religious understanding or attitude of religious men.

So indefinable a change may be described, provisionally, as an extension of the area of intellectual agnosticism within the realm of religion, even for religious men, especially for religious men.

The forties was the time of doubts, in the plural and with a small d; turmoils of Arthur Hugh Clough or John Sterling or young James Anthony Froude. In the sixties Britain and France and Germany entered the age of Doubt, in the singular and with a capital D.

Christians easily reconciled themselves to the general idea of evolution unless they were held from that recognition by dilapidated authorities in their church.[28] When you remember what a revolution this was in men's thinking, and how theoretical much of the construction was and remained, it is extraordinary that it took Europe only about forty years to accept it.

Not all that was associated with the word evolution was equally easy to accept. The law of natural selection was a little less comfortable, if an absolute law, than some quasi-Mendelian theory of mutations, and men were glad as Darwinian theory moved rapidly away from natural selection as the total explanation of every observation. But the points that mattered were the beginning and end of evolution: the passage from inorganic matter to living matter, the passage associated with such words, symbol-words, as *protoplasm*, or *spontaneous generation*; and the passage from highest mammal to man, the passage associated with such symbol-words as *missing link* or *gorilla* or *Neanderthal.* Of course these 'gaps' in the evolutionary series were not especially gaps for religious men but were matters of heavy debate among scientists. One of the most amusing controversies of the nineteenth century may be found in the public experiments in Paris, during the early 1860s, between Louis Pasteur and his scientific assailants on the matter of spontaneous generation, whether insects or microbes arose from decaying matter.[29] At the other end the very secularized and able scientist Rudolf Virchow shocked Haeckel, and a lot of other people, by declaring that a man could as easily be descended from a sheep or an elephant as from an ape.

From our point of view these controversies are important, not for their intrinsic effect upon religious minds which no doubt was little enough, but in two consequences. First, they kept the argument over creation and evolution before the public mind for four decades and more; and secondly they seemed (to some) to be the last places of a special intervention by a creating, acting, living God; the last corner for miracle in the physical world; necessary to defend, or at least to hope for, so that living acting creating power might be apprehended.

Science could not disprove a single miracle said to have happened, still less could science prove *miracles do not happen.* But the successes of science made ever more powerful the old agnosticism of Hume and the Enlightenment, that on the face of it witnesses are probably wrong. The conflict became unnecessarily rabid, partly because of legend, the hypostatizing of a background of conflict; partly because more metaphysical and less scientific scientists claimed that the reign of law reached into every area of life, into morality, personality, and free will, and these exaggerations concealed for a time the force of the underlying objection; and partly because many religious men feared the weakening of faith, loss in spiritual insight and moral goodness, if they allowed agnosticism to penetrate so far into the keep of religious truth. There could be no treaty in this argument until less scientific scientists jettisoned their overweening claims to be philosophers for all the world, and until religious men were ready to accept that widening of the area of agnosticism which was characteristic of the age of Victorian Doubt.

The argument was not really about the animal nature of man, because hardly anyone ever believed that man was 'nothing but an animal', the very use of language insisted on the things which man could do and which no animal could do. Yet: Charles Gore, a man of rock-like faith and a learned theologian, once said that he always returned an agnostic from a visit to the aquarium at the London Zoo because he could not comprehend how God can fit those curious beasts into his moral order. He was once observed wagging his finger at the chimpanzee and rebuking him for turning him into an atheist so long as he contemplated him.[30] More common among educated men of religion was query about the idea of the Fall of Man. Draper had said, If early Genesis is not true, man did not fall. From time to time we find this difficulty reappearing among religious men. Christianity represented man as perfect by nature and fallen from his high estate, evolution now showed him vile and savage and rising up 'towards perfection or quasi-perfection'. Scientists who were Christians were not always pleased with preachers of sermons on the Fall, nor with old hymns which enshrined old language. But the Fall was the easiest of all doctrines to restate. The Victorians were no blinder than the twentieth century. If anyone thinks that Victorians believed man to be a naturally good soul ruined only by education and political institutions, he has read little enough in the nineteenth century. They did not need the coming of World War to make them doubt the moral progress of man.

5

In 1899 Haeckel claimed to notice a difference between generally educated people and professional scientists in Germany.[31] The middle class as a whole still thought religion important and to contain truth. The professional scientists as a whole thought it unimportant and that it would in time vanish away.

Let us not accept this observation uncritically. Men move in their own circles, and meet men who agree with them, and get letters from men who support them, and are convinced that their opinions are obviously right, and therefore expect agreement from multitudes who think quite differently. When the observation is tested in Britain, it will be found to be false. So far as we have been able to test it in Britain, scientists were much like the rest of the professional middle class in these matters. Some of them were devout, a lot of them approved of religion but hardly practised it, some of them were passively neutral or mildly against it, and a few were actively hostile. So far as can at present be seen, British scientists were not as a class more agnostic than British businessmen.

If this is confirmed, it does not suggest that the scientific method, as such, helped to secularize minds.

If we turn to France or Germany, such tests as are possible do not produce quite the same results. More scientists were contemptuous. More scientists were outspoken. Haeckel's orations would hardly have been possible in Britain even though my university gave him an honorary degree (1898) and gained the unjustified reputation with one historian of being the 'hub' of materialistic science and philosophy.[32] At the moment, in view of the British evidence, and until further analysis is available, I attribute this observation (if it is a reliable observation) to two different causes: first, the ferocity of French anticlericalism in the 1880s and 1890s and the entanglement of the entire debate with politics; and secondly, the more developed agnosticism of the German Protestant middle class as a whole towards the end of the nineteenth century, due in part to a similar, though less inextricable, entanglement of religion with politics, and in part to the history of German philosophy and higher education since the Enlightenment. Charles Darwin once said,[33] 'Science has nothing to do with Christ, except in so far as the habit of scientific research makes a man cautious in admitting evidence.' He went on to imply that this caution led him not to believe that any revelation had been given. This was a way of saying that a training in science makes a man test everything, and accept nothing until it is tested. According to this theory the habit of the mind which engages in empirical testing of the physical, will spill over into the attitude of the mind towards the ethical; and this is hard to believe. 'Scientific method' is simply the way we all find out things and test them. The truth behind Darwin's proposition appears to be better stated in this form: more and more knowledge shows up larger and larger areas of ignorance. The more we know the more we know we do not know. Therefore the vast increase of knowledge in the nineteenth century must issue in extending the areas where the human mind could see doubt and ignorance. But, if the proposition is stated in this form, it means that the wider area of the unknown was due to the results of science, not to the method of science.

6

In reading the literature of the nineteenth century we keep meeting the difficulties of adjustment, not to recognition that the Bible was fallible as history, but to recognition that picture language was picture language. In the twentieth century we are so familiar with the notion of parable and picture that it never occurred to us, probably not even as children, to think of God 'our Father' as an old and kindly gentleman, nor to think of heaven as a place not far beyond the clouds. The idea of spirit and of absence of the physical came simultaneously or almost simultaneously with the idea of God. The charge that religious men have anthropomorphic ideas is no charge, of course they do, the kingdom of heaven is like a merchant seeking goodly pearls, parables are the stuff of religious language. But if you read for a time in the apologetics, or the Science-versus-Religion controversy, or the criticism of religious literature, you see how our great-grandfathers had a difficult adjustment. Educated men or women knew, as well as we, that God was not an old man with a pair of compasses and that heaven was not a garden. Still, the charge that they were anthropomorphic worried them, more than it was to worry their grandchildren. God walked in the garden in the evening of the day. Did he rest on the seventh day? Could you any longer think of him as like a watchmaker, taking intense pleasure in the structure and harmony of the mechanism which he designed? Pictures were always pictures, impressions, glimpses, distant from reality, everyone who thought about it knew it. But now they were forced to realize that pictures were indeed pictures, and to remind themselves of vast distances between the picture and the reality which it shadowed forth. They felt, perhaps, as though they had less clear ideas of what God was like than they thought before. This was disturbing. We can discern how disturbing.

8

HISTORY AND THE SECULAR

They tell us that history is in danger from the social and political sciences, because social sciences tackle the need of today and history directs the mind to irrelevant yesterday. They need not be so gloomy. No human being is satisfied if he knows nothing of his father or mother. And no human society is content unless it knows how it came to be, and why it adopted the shape and the institutions which it finds. The European mind demands imperiously the perspective which history alone can give. *Nescire autem quid antequam natus sis acciderit, id est semper esse puerum*, Cicero *Orator*, 120 – that is, you cannot even grow up without history.

This demand, however, does not appear to derive its necessity from the constitution of man's mind. Renan once wondered whether it was a passing mood of the romantic age.[1] Men of eastern philosophies and religions paid small heed to it, neglecting it as a kaleidoscope of trivial little lights which pale before the sight of eternal being and truth. Historical consciousness arose, first among Greek storytellers and their Roman successors; and then within the heritage of Christendom, so that church history was the seed of general history. *Why is the Church of Rome corrupt?* or *What is the continuity in Catholicism?* or *Where was your Church before Luther?* or *Where was your face before you washed it?* – these were the questions of the sixteenth and seventeenth centuries round which gathered the formidable historical enquirers in the age of the Renaissance and after. Rosweyde, and the Bollandists, and Mabillon, and Tillemont were the parents of Gibbon. Ecclesiastical history sired history. Then the Enlightenment interested men in the secular past. Writers like Hume sometimes undervalued the power of religion among the mass of men in the past, to concentrate their attention upon politics and the mighty. But modern historical consciousness arose within Christendom. The question therefore meets us whether history was one of the children which Christendom begot and which slowly began to change its father.

All science is prosaic. History can be poetic, dramatic, larger than legend, because it represents real human beings and human beings when real are more interesting than human beings when fabricated. But history is also 'scientific', in the sense of analysis, and stripping of documents, and statistical enquiry, and techniques of dating, and use of spade or computer. Its business is not legend but accounting for legend, not the beauty of the story but what happened (if anything happened) that lay under the story.

Religion and poetry are bedfellows. Religion and the saga share a house happily. The transcendent worlds of C. S. Lewis, the Hobbit-lands of Tolkien, the Greek heroes of Charles Kingsley were more a part of their authors' religious minds than of their fiction-making minds, or of their historical minds. *Verily I say unto you unless ye receive the kingdom of God as a little child ye shall in no case enter therein.* The religious vision is a vision of something only to be approached through shadow, but a vision where light shines upon the childlike heart. Does it matter whether Noah's flood covered the earth, or Jesus fed five thousand men with a few loaves and fishes, or St George rescued a maiden from the dragon, or Luther nailed ninety-five theses to the church door, or Jenny Geddes threw a stool at the preacher? To the religious mind qua religious mind the historical question hardly matters, or matters only in special circumstances and for special reasons. The historical mind qua historical mind needs to know, or at least to guess. *What happened?* is his vocation.

Human society knows many occasions where *what happened* is less momentous than *what is believed to have happened.* If the enquirer spends his time deciding whether a maiden stood bound for a dragon to eat, or whether a George rode to the rescue, he may miss the myth that bears truth for the moral being and the spirit.

Historians of the later Enlightenment made themselves ridiculous by explaining wonder, by unquenchable prosiness, by 'rationalizing' the 'sandwiches' of five thousand or the walking upon water; reaching peak in the 'scientific' corrections of earlier hymns, as with the editor who was shocked by the hymn of Gerhardt *Now all the woods are sleeping* and, to correspond with truth, amended it to the line *Now half the woods are sleeping.* Pre-romantic history could be very correct in its obedience to the canons of historical truth. And by being so correct it came near to misunderstanding something that was important in its subject; as though the only thing that mattered about the plays of Shakespeare was proving that Lord Bacon did not write them, or that the Dark Lady's name was Emilia.

But Christianity is not only religion. It is historical religion. It appealed to something which could be dated, *while Quirinius was governor of Syria,* and *under Pontius Pilate.* But the events which were so dated came clothed in garments that were not so historical; of poetry and saga, of a nation's hymnody, of legends about the making of the world, and of the patriarchs, prophets and martyrs, a treasure-house of a people's faith. Other religions could say, treasure-house matters, history matters not. But Christianity could hardly go that road. Its founding events could be dated. To be religious events they must be of meaning in eternity. To be events of history they must be moments of time. In one sense, the great question of the nineteenth century was the question whether historians, by probing the moments of time associated with religion, could affect its meaning.

2

In illustrating this new advance in knowledge and method, we stand in the same difficulty as we stood when we looked at the natural scientists in the last chapter, though with history the difficulty is less evident and more subtle. If a scientist attacked religion he might do so because he was a scientist, or because he was a man. Scientific enquiry might be important in his attitude to religion or it might not. The same question stands before the historians. Gibbon described the fall of the Roman empire as the triumph of barbarism and religion. Did his attitude derive in part from his personal history, his upbringing, his world of the eighteenth century, or did it derive in part from his inspection of the evidence, contempt arising from a sight of the theological passions of the fourth century or the intrigues of Byzantine bishops? And if it was in any manner the second of these, did his contempt arise, not only from inspecting the evidence, but from an inability in his deist environment even to understand what Athanasius or Arius argued about?

We are in worse case here than with scientists. For the scientist cannot manipulate his information when his personal attitudes push him to emphasize some of the information more than the rest. The historian (if he is a historian and not a pettifogging attorney) wishes not at all to manipulate his information. But the nature of the information being different from the nature of the information provided in laboratories, and the tests of the reliability of the information being still more deficient, his personal attitude may touch emphasis, presentation, and so convictions of truth. History can even be such that a change in private attitude can change the presentation of historical truth. Writing the history of the Dark Ages, Michelet sang a paean of praise for the celibacy of the clergy. Thirty years later his history bitterly assailed the damaging effects of celibacy upon society, and texts of new editions of the older history were amended. We know enough of the private life of Michelet to see a direct connexion between the family and the personal circumstances of his two successive wives and the change in attitude to historical evidence. To be a historian you need, first evidence, and second evidence. But you also need imagination; not imagination which dreams dreams, or feigns fantasies, but imagination which can clothe the dry statistic in the document, and turn it from flatness into life. And as the people rise out of the crinkly piece of record and take on vesture, you need to beware that the vesture is their own, and not the vesture which your affection, or your hate, or your tidiness, or your zeal, thinks they ought to be wearing.

If we ask, then, how or whether history made a new and secularizing force, we must not rush too fast across the threshold of that question. There are three questions, not one. Did history 'secularize' merely by increasing knowledge, as science 'secularized' by increasing knowledge? or did history simply flow from the pens of historians who took different points of view and some of them (Ranke, Stubbs, Acton) 'antisecularized' and some of them (Renan, Burckhardt) 'secularized', not by reason of their enquiries but by reason of their attitudes? Or, thirdly, was it neither new knowledge nor new attitude, but a new kind of consciousness called the historical consciousness, and distinguishable from the amassing of new information – rather as 'scientific method' or 'scientific consciousness' might be alleged to have become the habit of mind in persons who knew no science? More knowledge? or new attitudes? or a growing consciousness of history? Evidently it is the third of these which, from our point of view of mass secularization, would be much the most important if it could be charted. For most men and women have hardly the time to assemble or assimilate new information, except in elementary forms – *Genesis Chapter 1 is not true because men are descended from apes*. But the sense of depth, of movement, of process, of evolution, of a world in ceaseless change, this does not need assimilating like new information because it becomes part of the constitution of mind, and of the window through which mind looks out at contemporary events or structures.

I must mention in passing the new conception of 'the secularization of history'. This means, to free historical understanding from theological bias or axioms. The phrase was used by certain principled philosophers of history about 1900. It marked the growing neutrality demanded of a scientific historian, so that (for example) it could be proudly said at that time that the best life of John Calvin was written by a Roman Catholic whereas the best life of the founder of the Jesuits was written by a Protestant. This phrase could be used in more emotive contexts. The celebrated utterance of this kind was a lecture given by Richard Fester to the Berlin historical congress of 1908 under the very title *The Secularization of history*.[2] 'Even the church historian has long ago become a secular historian.' 'The best history of Christianity will probably be written by a Buddhist or a Moslem.' Fester did not mean only, neutrality, detachment, freedom from bias, in religion as in all realms of enquiry. He meant the abandonment of a world-picture. The historian works within a general notion of the development of the world. This notion used to be framed by the inheritance of a Biblical picture of the earth; and now we work at scientific history within a positivist framework, or positivist non-framework, to the benefit of historical science. But Fester was still fighting battles that probably needed fighting no longer, he kept using war metaphors, talk of the 'victory' of the natural sciences; with one excellent simile: 'The drawbridge of the schoolman's castle has such frayed and rotten ropes that no one can pull it up.' Here the word started within the conflict between religion and science, and then, in the age when men talked of history as a comparable science, Fester elevated the word into a feature of historical process. What is interesting is Fester's lack of self-perception. What he was celebrating was the coming of detachment, or at least of more detachment than before. But his language was not at all detached. It was an emotional hymn of praise. And this was in the very age when sociologists like Weber and Troeltsch were at last freeing the word *secularization* from the overtones of its recent origin, and using it as an unimpassioned word to describe a historical *thing* which required the attention of students of society.

The nineteenth century *organized* history for the first time. Just as the age saw the creation of the profession of journalist and the profession of schoolmaster, so it detached history from the wealthy litterateur, the country parson, the religious congregation, the German faculty which was a Lutheran version of a religious congregation, or the royal historian charged with a national interest, and gave the historian regular training and social position; created archives like the Public Record Office, commissions like the Royal Commission on Historical Manuscripts, journals like the *English Historical Review*; and incidentally raised up a public interested in the results of research.

Historical research can hardly be 'secularizing' by its nature.

I have seen it argued that all study – in Biblical words, *overmuch study* – is a dissipation of attention to reality. Just as the man who spends every moment collecting money has no time for wife and children, so the man who spends every moment collecting information has no time for ideas; and among collectors of information the historian, though only *primus inter pares*, is certainly first. Much historical work is prosy and practical, and has been compared by an adverse critic to modest utilities like mending fuses with a screwdriver.

When we come to historical synthesis, we find that cold collection of information is not enough; and correspondingly that the personal outlook of the historian enters the result.

There is no history which is not *secular*. If it is not *secular* it is not history; or, to put it thus, no statement that a fact of the past is 'sacred' can exempt it from the ordinary process of historical enquiry. That does not mean that the facts are so objective that anyone, if he knows them, will produce the same history as anyone else. A twentieth-century historian of the French Revolution (if by an impossibility we could imagine one starting on the original evidence without using his predecessors) could not produce the same results as a nineteenth-century student of the original sources who had no predecessors to use. He grew in a different world and had to explain himself to a different world.

So when Richard Fester was pleased at the 'secularization' of history, because the facts are there, and men are impartial, and a Catholic had written the best life of Calvin while a Protestant had written the best life of Ignatius Loyola, he underrated the 'stance' without which historians cannot write, or overestimated the dead neutrality possible only to men who by their deadness could not write history. Understanding is in part sympathy.

Ernest Renan had a famous dictum to the effect that only a man who had been religious and was so no longer could write the history of religion. The historian must have been religious for otherwise he could not understand what he was writing about. And he must have ceased to be religious, for otherwise, he could not write about it with impartiality. (The dictum is disprovable by instances.)

Whether or not the second clause had truth, the first clause was amply illustrated by the history of history in the nineteenth century. These were men engaged on the study of the European past. In that past, religion was of the first importance to society. They could no longer treat a religious past with the cool superciliousness of a Gibbon or a Voltaire. They needed to feel it as well as analyse it. I asked in the last chapter whether the study of natural science, the use of the scientific method itself, fostered agnosticism in the mind of the student. We must now ask the same question of the use of modern historical method since Ranke.

Charles Kingsley, regius professor at Cambridge from 1860 to 1869, was a very religious man. He believed that history provided moral instruction; that wickedness received its just deserts; that history was a vast hidden conflict between God and the powers of evil. Did it disqualify him from writing history that he thought thus of the past? It is not easy to see how it could so disqualify him. It can hardly be denied by the most 'scientific' of historians, that history has sometimes offered moral examples; that wickedness has sometimes (though not often enough) received its just reward; that one view of historical progress among far less religious contemporaries like Lecky or successors like Bury, who believed ardently in progress, saw it as unceasing conflict between the powers of light and the powers of darkness. Perhaps Kingsley was not rash to think this about history, only rash to say that he thought it. And if he was rash to speak aloud, he was accompanied, though at a decorous distance, by no less than Stubbs and Acton, each of whom, in his inaugural lecture on history, took religious views of the purpose of history. And no one has yet denied to Stubbs or to Acton the name of historian.

So when men asserted that you could hardly call Kingsley a historian, they must have meant, not that he was too religious a thinker, or that his lectures approximated a little too closely to sermons, but only that he did not understand the past enough to be able to make reliable judgments about it; and secondly, that if lectures resemble sermons, that must mean an intentional intrusion of that personal element in expounding the past which a true historian seeks always to discipline. E. A. Freeman, whose violent reviewing did as much to lower the reputation of Kingsley as it afterwards lowered the reputation of Froude, was a religious man himself; a member of the same denomination as Kingsley; but taking surprisingly different views of the nature of religious truth.

But Renan said that you must have stopped being religious to write impartially; only an ex-Marxist should write the history of the Bolshevik Revolution; only an ex-Jacobin the biography of Robespierre. The historical process is in some respects, though by no means all, a very practical progress. You get down to documents, texts, artefacts, evidence. To mend the fuse the electrician has no call to say that God made the metal for this purpose. If he does say that, it does not make him any less skilled as a fuse-mender. Kingsley could say that history shows how wicked men are punished; provided he did not manipulate evidence to show how they were punished, provided he did not infer from punishment that the sufferer was wicked, and provided he refused to close his eyes to the multitude of villains flourishing like a forest of green bay trees. Kingsley did not manipulate evidence. But sometimes we wonder whether he altogether fulfilled the other two provisos. When villainy flourished, its perpetrators looked a little less villainous.

It has been said: 'There can be a Christian interpretation of history but not a Christian chemistry.'[3]

Why? Because you are one stage further from the hard facts, and you cannot get at the facts without getting their interpretation simultaneously? Therefore since an interpretation is indispensable, a Christian interpretation is legitimate? But what is a Christian interpretation of history? How does it differ from other interpretations? That the early stories of St Francis of Assisi cannot be explained unless he was a good man, and therefore history proves him to be a good man? You cannot reach this verdict only from the evidence. You must have a prior idea of goodness already in your mind, formed from the moral axioms of the nineteenth century, and those moral axioms are dominated by Christianity. Not that qua historian you disapprove moral axioms of 1200 compared with moral axioms of 1870. Understanding of different moral axioms is part of the historical act of sympathy. Nevertheless, your understanding of St Francis and his influence is touched by the way in which your conscience works; and whether or not you are a Christian, your conscience is led onward by Christian ideas. So much we may allow to the notion of a Christian interpretation of history. Wherever the historian – not acting as the conscience of posterity, not as a magistrate delivering verdicts on the past to edify the present, but simply as a historian because he wants to understand the past – needs to enter the realm of moral judgment, the nature of his own moral stance begins to matter.

Those who say that historians never enter the realm of moral judgment live in dreams. Man being what he is, moral judgment is inseparable from any other form of judgment about people and their effect upon their world. It should play little or no part in historical synthesis. But it can never be wholly absent from the historian's stance. You can exclude moral judgment only by restricting yourself to a heap of facts – that is, by not writing history.

But further: Would a 'Christian interpretation' allow miracles as a possible explanation of events and a 'secular interpretation' would not? Is it being asserted (e.g.) that a man who has experienced miracle in his own life knows that it happens, and therefore is more likely to believe witnesses to be reliable when they give evidence that miracle happened in the past? Whereas a man who shares the common intellectual axiom of the nineteenth century that *miracles do not happen* cannot believe witnesses for miracle however apparently reliable they sound? In this sense a 'Christian interpretation' would mean less reluctance to credit witnesses when they report extraordinary or unique events if the events are congruous with an already formed moral pattern. But the evidence of medieval and monastic historians, who experienced miracle in their own lives and therefore expected it in what they recorded of the past, tends to prove that this kind of 'Christian interpretation' (if it is one) is less satisfactory as an attempt to interpret the past than those who take the view that miracle is improbable and therefore not to be looked for as an explanation satisfying to the historian. The Christian historian of the later nineteenth century understood this as well as the anticlerical historian. In this sense all history was 'secular' by 1870.

3

History seeks to find out 'what really happened'.

But it must start from a mind, which is set in history. The historian selects evidence and cannot help selecting as his eyes see. His eyes see what they see partly because the evidence is there to see. And partly also because he is a man of his time, a Victorian or an anticlerical, a Whig or a Tory. The rule that selection of facts is always someone's selection of facts is not affected by the number of facts available. It applies to the history of antiquity as rigidly as to the history of the twentieth century.

Consider in this light the work of Michelet.

Michelet was a genius; one of the most powerful ever to have written historical narrative. His genius was passion for throwing himself into the past. As no other writer, he lived and felt the events which he tried to describe. He had imagination, fine feelings, willingness to digress and throw in his opinions, sense of drama; no famous historian ever wrote more personal history or used more apostrophes, vocatives, superlatives, rhetorical questions and notes of exclamation; and he had acquired from Vico the aim of turning history from the chronicle of great men or famous happenings to the history of the common people, and finding principles which lay under the evolution of their small life. Heir to the French Revolution, he was consciously the historian of the people, of governed instead of governors. 'The people', he wrote in the *History of the Revolution*,

> were usually better than the leaders. The deeper I have dug, the more surely I have satisfied myself that the best was underneath, buried in obscurity. And I have realized that it is quite wrong to take these brilliant and powerful orators, who expressed the thought of the masses, for the sole actors in the drama. They were given the impulse by others much more than they gave it themselves. The leading actor is the people. To put it back in its proper rôle, I have been obliged to reduce to their proportions the ambitious marionettes whose strings it manipulated and in whom hitherto we have looked for and thought to see the secret play of history.[4]

In 1846 he wrote a book called *The People*, a direct and magnificent apologia for democracy. Shortly afterwards he started a plan of a series called *The Golden Legend*, to be a hagiography of popular rebellions against tyranny. It was too vast for execution, and failed when the Emperor Louis Napoleon deprived him of his professorship, but not before he had written handbooks to help Polish and Romanian rebels. He has been called a 'democratic Bossuet' because he interpreted history by a revolutionary faith as Bossuet interpreted history by his faith in God.[5] But he was not the first of modern social historians. Though he wrote of the crowd, the crowd was to him a collection of free individuals, each of whom he would describe if he could. He had almost no sense of social movement, of a general will.

This passion for the people, love of the dramatic, genius for the vivid, could make him very misleading. The famous instance is his account of the fall of the Bastille. He was writing it when he heard the news of his father's death, and in an earlier chapter I mentioned how that death affected his mind. The Bastille fell when the common people of Paris rose spontaneously and heroically against an impregnable fortress, to end tyranny and win their freedom – the most gripping passage in the works of the most gripping of historians – where almost every detail is erroneous, almost every fact misstated; it did not happen like that at all, it was not so dramatic, so romantic, so noble or moreover so spontaneous; ideal, symbol entered into creed, it ought to have happened like that. Examine the narrative and it will not do. Yet totality, legend, stood for a reality of the French Revolution, and became the cherished possession of every republican heart. Historical enquiry turned into national anthem. Sitting in the Champs de Mars, of a late summer, scenting the breath of the god of revolutionary liberty, he would dream about the Revolution, a movement so peaceable and kind and loving, and misunderstood. And yet Michelet, for all the errors and the sentiment, seized on something beyond the facts which was 'true'. Sympathetic allies preferred his mistakes to the precision of more prosaic or more conservative historians. Aulard, whose generation was more prosaic and more scientific but equally anticlerical, once said that Michelet's book was not the most accurate but was nevertheless the noblest history of the French Revolution. Mark Pattison on the other hand, said[6] that he got from Michelet the same intellectual gratification that he got from a superior novel. We resign ourselves for a time to the historian and his characters, but 'we are not the less conscious that they are beings of his own creation, and that the next enchanter who arises will attach the same names, and ascribe the same fortunes, to a quite different set of spiritual creations'. Pattison intended the passage, not to damn Michelet, but to damn history; its 'shifting quicksand', its 'chaos', its 'intellectual anarchy'.

The first question which Michelet asked of the French Revolution was a question which no other historian has ever asked or could think it sensible to ask – is the Revolution Christian or anti-Christian? He started his book with this problem because he believed it to be the ultimate question, logically as well as historically. He thought the religious structure, not to be entangled with the political structure but, to be the same structure.[7] Christianity was the free grace of God, to sinner as to Pharisee. Michelet felt – and *felt* is right, it was so profound a feeling in his breast that we can only account for it by looking for real religious or quasi-religious experience in his youth – Michelet felt that free grace and justice were opposites. This accounts for the first staggering pages. Students of the twentieth century, however sensitive to the moods of the past, find it hard to conceive a generation where an eminent historian and archivist thinks it right to begin a book on the French Revolution by denouncing the Christian doctrine of atonement, not just to relieve private feelings but because he fancied it the essence of the understanding of what happened. 'Nothing can endure against justice.' 'Then', he asks his readers, 'how can you think the question whether Christianity will last only a subsidiary question?' Christianity and the Revolution agree about fraternity. Christianity found it when it was restricted to dining-clubs in ancient city-states and spread it to all the Christian world. The Revolution, *daughter of Christianity*, took the lesson and spread it to all the world, every race and every religion. Nothing else is in common. The Revolution rose against the men who planned the massacre of St Bartholomew's day.

Michelet started his career as historian by one of the most romantic portraits of the Middle Ages ever penned by a historian. He wrote in the age of Sir Walter Scott. Two or three decades later he came to be the fiercest historical critic of Christianity, openly regarding historical enquiry as a weapon in the overthrow of churches and of Christianity. But this was not such a process that we could rightly apply the word irreligious. No man was ever more tormented about religion, continued to be tormented. This is not a man who sees religion to be irrelevant to the true needs and growth of society. On the contrary, he believed religion to dominate history, religious instincts to penetrate every corner of life, churches (however lamentable) to be powers in society. Catholicism would die, Christianity would die, but men would still be religious. He expected their religion to be patriotism and liberty, God and the fatherland, which is curious when we remember that the phrase God and the fatherland was used to express the contemporary ideas of a very conservative Prussia. Certainly Michelet was a profoundly religious man. He was always thinking about religion, and often wrote about it. For a time his language had a messianic fervour, like the prophecies of some medieval illuminist, convinced of the coming reign of some higher religion than that which we profess. The year 1789 came to be a revelation of the divine spirit. Freedom was the cause of human brotherhood, the Christian God the cause or symptom of despotism. 'Liberty. . .made brotherhood possible. Philosophy found man without rights, or even a nothing, oppressed by a religious and political system founded on tyranny. And she said "Let us make man, create man, let man be, by liberty. And in the moment that man came to be man, he loved." ' He was far from a rationalist, he was man of instinct, intuition, charisma. Biblical language kept intruding. He pictured Liberty being born like a baby, and opening her eyes to the light, and uttering her first words from the cradle – and her first words were the cry *I am!* As he wrote he had, at times a feeling of inspiration from on high, of a light coming down 'from heaven'.[8]

This type of history, in which Michelet was master, impinged upon religion because it helped to identify churches with the political right. In his early years Michelet wrote panegyrically of the medieval Church and was praised by Catholics. But after 1843 he turned against that phase of his past. His history of the Revolution was the story of a black versus white, the white was democracy and rationalism, black being monarchy and Catholicism. An English critic called the book *The Epic of democracy*,[9] and the democracy of which he sang was anti-Catholic.

History is powerful in forming minds because it forms them without the mind being conscious that it is being formed, and the reader thinks himself to be following only a story. The French Revolution continued to divide French society; and therefore the way in which it was understood coloured the nature of the national argument. If a man looked at the Revolution through spectacles offered by Michelet, his belief in democracy took upon itself not only a religious mystique but an anticlerical cast. Young Clemenceau was brought up by his father, a country doctor, on Michelet. The socialist leader Jean Jaurès took, as guides to a socialist history of the Revolution, Karl Marx and Michelet.

As the century wore on, fewer people read the Revolution with his eyes. The young men of the end of the century knew that passion, especially when avowed, is the historian's worst sin. Like all historians he went out of fashion. Style dated, prejudices shrieked, extent of research was far surpassed, overstatements (especially in old age) undermined his authority. Renan once got into trouble with Michelet's widow by talking, in a solemn speech intended to be praise of French historians, of his 'exquisite or sparkling fantasies'.[10] In too many pages, wrote Gooch of the later books, 'we listen to the outpouring of a scurrilous pamphleteer'. The socialists ceased to be moved by that type of mind. Despite Jaurès and his linking of Marx and Michelet, Marx and Michelet were incompatible. But Michelet was so brilliant that no one ever did more to make the French want to understand the history of their country. And he was a historian who offered no choice to the reader in the understanding of evidence.

In England Lecky afforded a parallel, though his mission was Whig intellectual history and not radical history. Lecky's *Rise and Influence of the Spirit of Rationalism in Europe* was published in 1865. For a man of 26 years the performance was prodigious. An Anglo-Irish Protestant, he wrote it on travels across Europe during the tense years of the Risorgimento, identifying the gospel and Garibaldi together with liberty. I need dwell on him only for a moment, because in another form we have met the type before. At bottom his philosophy was almost identical with that of Draper and the *Conflict* theorists. But his range of reading, style, originality of mind and European sympathies raised his work instantly to the status of a classic. This is the noblest of all statements of the meaning of history as intellectual light versus superstitious darkness; a man of the Enlightenment, yet with the insights of romantic historians into the past of religion in society and in morals.

It is not quite clear that this aspect of the matter really concerns our theme: history as propaganda. History is a dangerous discipline because it surrounds self-deception with dulcet odours of antiquity, and anything which has stood there a long time has claims to respect. Young people, and not so young, learn historical attitudes; probably historical attitudes are more important in framing their outlook than historical evidence; and if the historical evidence is wrong, the attitude is imbibed and is still important. In a sense it matters that George rescued a maiden, and who cares if pedants doubt that the maiden existed?

This is dangerous ground, dangerous to intellectual integrity and the cool power of reason. But Christian churches which lived for centuries with forged bulls and charters may not lightly blame other people for using history to make propaganda for a cause.

4

History was about people, people mattered, people were unpredictable, and their choices changed the course of events. In the middle nineteenth century a Carlyle or a Kingsley still wrote history as though it was the history of heroes or leaders, Cromwell or Theodoric the Ostrogoth; and whatever men might afterwards say, whatever statistics they might afterwards collect, the world was never going to stop asking historical questions about men whose choices made a difference, and biographers were never going to stop plying their useful and readable and authentically historical trade. But the nineteenth century came to be aware, as no age before it, that the Reformation would have happened without a Luther to make it happen even if not in the way in which it happened; that society depended on deeper movements of economic structure or inarticulate axioms than could be defined in terms of one man's influence. In the middle of the nineteenth century we find for the first time the phenomenon known as historical determinism.

Historical determinism issued from a discovery and a prestige. The discovery was provided by new collections of statistics in modern censuses. Murder is often the most unpremeditated of men's choices, sudden passion, mad fit, weapon to hand, wild provocation. In the middle nineteenth century new statistics suddenly showed (it was said) that murders are committed 'with as much regularity, and bear as uniform a relation to certain known circumstances, as do the movements of the tides and the rotations of the seasons';[11] and that even the instruments used to commit the crimes bear much the same proportion from year to year. Suicide was to provide the basis of the most famous of all the early enquiries of the new social sciences, in the book by Durkheim. But three decades before Durkheim men observed the statistics. Suicide is the most solitary of acts; dependent on the unique circumstances of an individual, secret emotions, mental stability, frame of mind. Yet statistics showed regularity in the number of suicides. The inference was therefore possible that choices, to all appearance unique and individual, obeyed some hidden law depending not on the individual's freedom but upon the general condition of the society in which he lived.

Determinist history was therefore bound with the origins of the social sciences, and created by the same evidence from statistics. But it was affected by the contemporary growth in the prestige of 'science'; whether science meant, as in France and Germany, the critical and experimental enquiry into any field of study, or whether it meant, as in Britain, natural science. The Newtonian tradition of law in the physical realm was extended into the biological sciences. Law, the reign of law, the quest for natural law to account for differences, the desire for a simple physical explanation of a complex series of observations – these ideas characterized science in the middle nineteenth century. Their successes looked sufficient to persuade some people – always a small minority, but a minority of articulate and able people – that the idea of law could successfully be applied to human behaviour. For a time the prestige of science encouraged deterministic philosophies of behaviour and fostered notions which rested upon a secularized predestination.

The marvellous flowering of historical study during the nineteenth century helped to conceal a paradox which troubled historians throughout its later decades. History owed its new being to the romantic movement; to the recovery of sympathy, and imagination, and intuition, in distinction from the sober reasoning of a classical world. The romantics were individualists. Men were free, and freedom was greatness. Even when a historian had no interest in greatness, and like Michelet saw history as the advancement of the common people by their inward spirit, he still conceived the people as free. They could bring down the Bastille, and change the face of France. History in the age of the romantics was inspired by a renaissance of the imagination. It looked at a course of past events and sought to penetrate beyond the circumstances, 'external' circumstances, 'mere' circumstances, to perceive the underlying movement, the 'life', the energy. Romantic imagination changed the face of philosophy, art, poetry; and history was not left behind. Men approached the past, no longer to sneer at barbarity in comparison with the abstract model of society which reason proposed, but with seriousness, willingness to understand how it was, almost reverence.

Almost simultaneously began the quest for general laws. Natural science brought the world of matter under the reign of law. Historical science must try to bring the world of men under the reign of law. Materialism as a philosophy beckoned its public. Science had new and ever-growing repute. Some taught *that*, although not *how*, man's behaviour could be explained by laws. Individuals do not change the course of history. They only conform. Not free, they only think that they are free. The history of society is determined.

This contest or friction between freedom and law lay beneath the historian's task since the days of Thucydides and made one of its fascinations. But by 1860 the argument was unusually loud because romantic historians sometimes exaggerated the part of one man, hero or devil, and because some social historians, with the aid of census returns and elementary statistics, argued that one man had no freedom and his acts made no difference to the course of social change. This was the paradox which troubled history during the third quarter of the century. It affected the nature of historical enquiry, pulling a man this way or that according to his temperament or experience. In a French historian like Hippolyte Taine law and freedom tugged against each other, and the tug made the special enchantment, and sometimes the complexity, of Taine's work.

Taine received a classical education, grew up a young man of the Enlightenment, who shed his Christianity as soon as he thought for himself. Here was a cool, rational young man, working in his study under the eye of busts of Voltaire and Rousseau which he inherited from his grandfather. In his undergraduate years he discovered German idealist philosophy from Herder to Hegel, and his mind was permanently marked by the experience. Under the stimulus of Hegel he began the quest for general laws in history; and in this endeavour was affected by the notions of 'physiological laws' then being debated in the controversy over materialism.[12] We must try to find laws which produce a civilization. Taine professed ardent faith in science as coming at last to govern the world. He professed simultaneously a historical determinism, and in his younger years expressed his belief roughly, so roughly that he was never afterwards forgiven:

Vice and virtue are products like sugar and vitriol.

History is a geometry of forces.

Our mind is as mathematically constructed as a watch.

Man is a spiritual automaton.

In mature life he abstained from such epigrams, and seems to have thought them too crude. But he never deserted the essence of a determinist doctrine of history. As late as a letter of 29 April 1864 he wrote 'History is a science analogous not to geometry, but to physiology and zoology.' In the public eye he was identified with determinism, and young social historians looked to him as their master.

So he was a man, first of the Enlightenment, and then of the new school of social history. And yet he knew Michelet's work well. He understood what romantics had done for history, and how it was impossible any longer to write history like Voltaire or Hume or Gibbon; how you must picture to yourself the living man behind the document, even – if you could – to his hat and moustache, his wife and home; and behind the outward man the inner, the soul, yearning and fear, aspiration and resentment, condition of society that enfolded him. He saw how a Carlyle had taken a hundred or so of old letters and a few badly reported speeches and thereby penetrated to the soul of Cromwell, and how Sainte-Beuve looked at a group of women enclosed in a nunnery and took the whole world to gaze through a window in the convent wall and penetrate the tensions and the holiness which moved the nuns of Port-Royal. Taine perfectly understood what romantics had done for history. He could do it himself, at least when he wrote of Englishmen or Frenchmen. Never before had a French writer penetrated with such subtlety and power the English view of English literature.

Therefore his principles were not quite compatible with his performance. He wanted to see in human behaviour chains of causation as in physics; and in his descriptions an irrational cheerfulness or lyricism kept breaking in. He talked about the hidden concord of creative forces – these forces are *race, milieu, moment* – that produced a Bossuet or a Goethe; the hidden contrariety of creative forces – that is, *race, milieu, moment* – which produced the drama of Dryden or Wycherley,[13] and then dared to say that these are all the causes, we have exhausted the possibilities when we have mentioned them. So he came at times, like some other positivists, to a materialist version of historical causation. Religion, like everything else, is the product of *race, milieu, moment.* He made it all sound, in principle, very determinist, very materialist. But his performance did not live up to these principles. The word *milieu* is vague enough. A lot of eccentrics practise their individualities beneath the umbrella of the monotonous word environment.

Race means character transmitted by blood, by genes, a totality of psychological and inherited temperament or attitudes. *Milieu* means the totality of circumstances which a people experience, climate, habitat, economic life, inventions. *Moment* is the impetus given by the past to the present, the action upon each generation of the preceding generation. These three mighty forces are always present, and through hundreds of thousands of men and women create the current running through and forming the nature of a society, its mental processes, its morals, its achievements. The effect of these forces we cannot fully chart, only because the work would be infinite. But it is possible to chart in outline.

The critics said that Taine pretended to explain what was inexplicable. They said that Taine attributed the rise of genius to certain impersonal characteristics which were simultaneously producing mediocrity in the same village. They accused him of applying to literature and art a system which obviously failed to fit; that you could talk about general laws producing Michelangelo and you would still have no idea what 'caused' Michelangelo. They attacked him for accounting entirely for Shakespeare by climate and country and race, and so far explaining all the qualities in Shakespeare common to other men born at Stratford-on-Avon during the age of the Reformation and failing to account for everything about Shakespeare which matters, that is, genius.

This was not fair to Taine. He knew as well as a romantic that genius could not be explained by law. He continued to think that the historian's task was the discovery of general law. Shakespeare especially fascinated him because the plays portray characters led by forces greater than themselves which they cannot control, men like Othello or Hamlet or Lear or Macbeth, driven by visions, men as earthy creatures yet of the same stuff as dreams, men 'possessed' or 'inhabited' by mysterious power, man's essence and acts as the issue of elemental powers. Taine's determinist reason was married to a kind of intuitive mysticism. The mind and heart leap towards true apprehension of genius; and then reason comes in to 'explain', to see general laws working upon society to generate genius and genius to respond to society.

Taine's experience of England modified a little his determinism. He learned to admire, even to love, its liberal moderate society, where men were free and responsible without becoming adherents of rival and contending parties. It gave him a little more respect for religion, seeing rite coming second to moral endeavour, evidence more plentiful than in France of Christian minds open to new knowledge and to natural science, conviction of man as a free being because a moral being. For the rest of his life he judged and sometimes condemned his own country on a model of constitution and society mainly derived from idealized understanding of England.

Taine's study of English literature is an exceptional, ungainly, cumbersome, wrong-headed work of brilliance. Read Taine on *Paradise Lost* and you throw the book away and swear never to read another word. Read him on the Christian renaissance of the north and you marvel at the delicate sense of European background, and care nothing about the length, the occasional extravagance, the periods compulsive for all their rolling solemnity. Read him even on Milton and you cannot but learn. The book could not have been written by an Englishman, and thereby gains its freshness and falls into its traps. But it was written by one who loved literature and the English people, and who searched for the individual and his uniqueness, placing him in front of a backcloth of intellectual history, and bringing out the lights and shades in colours that were strong or too strong by reason of the author's habit of mind.

The exceptional nature of the work rises partly out of the rare penetration of Taine's mind. But, even more, it rises out of the mutual incompatibility of the principles with which Taine approached his task. This self-contradiction is what matters to our enquiry, because it is a dazzling instance of the self-contradiction inherent in the intellectual history of the later nineteenth century. Man, what is he? Is he a wonderful creature, conquering the world, subjecting nature, advancing in knowledge, curing disease and crime, liberating his mind from superstition and relics of primitive barbarity, mature, mellow, adult at last in the growth of mankind, servant of faith and of conscience, king of science and society, master of kings? Or is he brute like the brutes, descended from apes, bearing marks of ancestry, irrational, instinctive, covering his needs of belly with veneer of mental gymnastic, still the servant of sex and stomach, cleverer than a gorilla but only therefore more dangerous at the kill because of subtlety and willingness to hunt in packs?

Taine's head gave a different answer from Taine's heart, and had no consciousness that reason and feeling stood at war.

Shakespeare's view of the human race is presented as though Caliban and not Prospero were king. The common man, Jack Cade, man of alehouses and brothels, these are the human race, let them not loose, 'we know not what lusts and furies may brood under a sober guise'.[14] And these 'cannibal moods', are they only of the porters and fools, 'among the scum'? 'Why, the princes are worse.' All his people, however crude or however refined, were slaves of their needs and their circumstances. All of them, good or bad, gross or delicate, he made 'void of will and reason, impassioned machines, vehemently hurled one upon another, who were the representation of whatever is most natural and most abandoned in human nature'. Caliban, Taine came near to saying, is natural man, Shakespeare's, everyone's natural man; Darwin's man is natural man; a deformed savage. If Shakespeare, wrote Taine,[15] had framed a psychology, he would have defined man as a 'nervous machine, governed by a mood, disposed to hallucinations, transported by unbridled passions, essentially unreasoning, a mixture of animal and poet, having no rapture but mind, no sensibility but virtue, imagination for prompter and guide, and led at random, by the most determinate and complex circumstances, to pain, crime, madness and death'.

As he grew into middle age, he allowed a pessimism about the human race to grow in his mind until it began to diminish the quality of his historical work by preventing sympathy. This pessimism was derived from Darwin and the doctrine of natural selection; but then was fostered by the French military rout of 1870 and the melancholy which afflicted all France thereafter; and then the Commune and its murders confirmed him in dismal views of man.

He became gloomy. If Macaulay was optimist among historians, Macaulay's admirer Taine was the saddest. For the mood consorted and contrasted with fine perception of highest quality in literature and art. Taine exalts by magnificent analyses of literary genius, by elevated discussion of the mighty movements of an age, sometimes you almost think he will tell you that man is a wonderful spirit. But then he remembers himself. He reminds himself that this is not at all what man is; that after all man is only a type of orang-utang. He rises up to Shakespeare as the climax of his book in English literature, emotions are touched, reverence is round the corner, he wants to sing a hymn of praise. And then he catches at himself, disturbed at what he said. 'Strictly speaking', he tells us, 'man is idiotic, as the body is sick, by nature; reason and health come to us as a momentary success, a lucky accident.[16] He is gloomy with the inspissated gloom of a man whose instincts do not want gloom, but whose mind nags at him that this is a horrid world, and the human race is contemptible. *Strictly speaking* – that is what nags him. He sees when his eyes are open that many men are not in the least idiotic. But then his principles come tumbling in like a cascade, and blind his eyes, and make him say *strictly speaking*.

So this historian was quite unlike Lecky or Bury – the men whom we may call the science-versus-religion historians. For they were still in the throes of the Whig interpretation of history, with its optimism and expectancy. They still saw light of reason repelling darkness of superstition. Neither Lecky nor Bury could have any deep understanding of western society during the Middle Ages. That is a remarkable thing to say of a man like Bury who introduced Byzantine studies into Britain, but it is true, for no more than Lecky could Bury understand religion in general and Catholicism in particular. Like Bury and Lecky, Taine could not understand the Middle Ages. How did Taine sum up the Middle Ages? He wrote this: 'A thinking society had ceased to think; philosophy was turned into a textbook, and poetry into raving; and mankind, slothful and crouching, made over their conscience and their conduct into the hands of their priests, and were as puppets, capable only of reciting a catechism and chanting a hymn.'[17]

That sounds like Whig history, of progress and enlightenment, like Lecky or Bury. It differs subtly, but fundamentally. *Strictly speaking* has come in. *Mankind, slothful and crouching* – Taine published only four years after Darwin's *Origin*, at the moment when everyone argued about man's descent from apes. *Mankind, slothful and crouching*; this is not Lecky, this is no Whig, this is no believer in progress and the future of reason, this is a pessimist of the first water, because he has lost faith in man. And he lost faith in man, whose intellectual and artistic achievement he was capable of apprehending, because his principles told him that (*strictly speaking*) he ought to lose his faith in man. For a long while, he told Gaston Paris in 1877, he was prevented from marrying by the idea that life was too sad to be passed on to others. 'Debauchery in a Frenchman' as contrasted with an Englishman, and Taine's compliment was not whole-hearted to the French, 'is only half disgusting; with them, if the animal breaks loose, it is without abandoning itself to excess. . . When we scratch the covering of an Englishman's morality, the brute appears in its insolence and its deformity.'[18]

The last twenty-two years of his life he devoted to writing *The Origins of Contemporary France*, which he began in the year of the Commune. This survey of the Revolution is a study in a barbarism of the human race that rises to the surface in the moment that men come under pressure. He picked all the savagery which marked the Revolution. This, he seemed to say, was typical of man.' He studied the pathology of human beings in a great political crisis, and hinted, this shows what a man is. After the Commune he was afraid of democrats and started to read revolutionary history under this fear. Free-thinker that he was, he started writing of the necessity of religion in conserving society:[19]

Religion by its nature is a metaphysical poem married to faith. In this way it is effective and popular; for, except for a tiny elite, the pure idea is but an empty word, and truth, to be felt, must put on a body. There must be rite, legend, ceremony, if it is to talk to the people, women, children, the simple, every man engaged in daily labour, to the human mind itself in which ideas willy-nilly express themselves in pictures. Through visible form it can throw its great weight upon the conscience, be a counter-weight to natural egotism, cool the mad impulse to animal passion, guide the will to self-sacrifice and devotion, direct men to give themselves wholly to the service of truth or of others, make ascetics and martyrs, sisters of charity and missionaries. In every society religion is a precious and natural organ.

Men need it to think of the infinite and live well; if it suddenly failed, they would feel a great sad void in their soul and would hurt each other the more. You would try in vain to snatch it from them. Hands which attempted it would touch no more than the envelope; it will grow again like flesh after a bloody operation. Its roots are too deep to be pulled up.

After such a passage we need reminding that so recently as 1863 Bishop Dupanloup of Orléans warned the young and their parents against reading Taine because of his atheism and his mockery of theology (*Avertissement à la jeunesse et aux pères de famille*, 54–5). The views were not incompatible with those of Comte, especially the later Comte.

This later Taine had no desire to abolish religion. It was determined. The social process created it. Man found in it a theory of the world which gave him security. He feels at home, is no longer anxious, at least for a time. Taine was a liberal-conservative who disliked anticlerical campaigns against Christian monks or nuns. Religion has helped society, perhaps helps it still. Religion gives the community part of its sense of community, aids the nation to corporate conscience, diminishes personal conflicts in society. Religion is an eternal consolation, and an eternal lie. Social process caused it and probably social process will cause it to disappear. Taine was nothing less than anticlerical.

Taine's philosophy was of nature red in tooth and claw, with man as the animal to bite and be bitten. It was the historian's version of a theory of despair. He was quite as sad about science as about men.

5

Historical science cannot but be influenced by the intellectual and social environment of the historian's generation. French intellectuals of the 1870s were surrounded by positivist theory. In historical discipline they therefore contributed to the advance of the subject. They freed the search for true information about the past from the theological stances found in a moral historian like Kingsley, and from the philosophical slant found in every historian who suffered the influence of Hegel. They helped historians towards detachment, pushed them to examine their standpoint or prejudice, wished them to be free of any compulsion to read evidence in the light of preconceived ideas. In this sense the *secularization of history* represented authentic gain. But positivist history was not all gain. Historical investigation requires as lively an imagination as scientific, and positivism stunted the imagination.

How we understand the past matters to how we understand the present. Therefore 'secularized history' ought *a priori* to contribute to secularized attitudes in the readers of history. Though the application of notions of natural science could and did mislead and unbalance, it also disciplined, and stripped off layers of inherited superficiality.

Did history 'secularize' by new knowledge of ancient literature and therefore of the Bible? Was there a growth in historical consciousness, bringing with it consciousness of continuity, of relativity, and of the possible weakness of evidence?

We shall get help towards an answer if we look at the work of Ernest Renan.

He was destined for the priesthood, and at Saint-Sulpice began the study of oriental languages and of the historical foundations of Christianity. He left seminary and Catholic Church in 1845. Several works, especialy the *History of Semitic Languages* in 1855, established his reputation. The *Life of Jesus*, which appeared in 1863, was intended as the first volume of a big work on *The Origins of Christianity*, eventually completed in seven volumes to the death of Marcus Aurelius. He then undertook the *History of Israel*, of which the first volume appeared in 1887 and the last posthumously.

It is odd that French historians should have adopted Renan as master. His subject was remote from the centres of historical interest; his skills lay more in philology than in history narrowly understood; he occasionally produced journalistic articles or not very good plays, a habit out of keeping with the austere traditions of historical schools; old-fashioned, he believed that history was also literature, a faith which the scientific mentality of the later nineteenth century outgrew. Moreover he publicly confessed regret that the bias of his early life drew him into history, and believed, or alleged that he believed, that he would have done more lasting work in the natural sciences. His too clear head saw the evanescent nature of all historical writing, how much of it rests upon guesses, how soon the historical thesis falls obsolete in the light of new evidence. Certainly his faith in history looked as pale as his faith in anything else. So far from thinking that the historian made an indispensable contribution to the way in which society understands itself, he thought that quite soon Europe would lose interest in history.[20] At a time when history turned away from being a history of the great and mighty and tried to understand the people, Renan was a man who believed in genius and the power of genius to change the mediocrity of most men and women. He made no effort to become leader of a school, or director of other men's work, or head of an academic party. He went his own way, solitary, throwing off papers and journalism by the side of his *Origins of Christianity*.

Historical schools became positivist, and confessed Taine and Renan as their masters. Yet, if he was positivist, like Taine, his positivism could hardly bear comparison with that of the founder of positivism, Comte. Comte could never have made a historian because for understanding human beings he possessed only the faculty of rational analysis. Renan, the literary historian, believed in a legitimate use of insight to comprehend and portray men of the past and wanted history to be 'aesthetic' as well as 'scientific'. In feeling he was still a romantic historian. No one disbelieved more strenuously in the writing of prosy and factual history.

By 1876 he was capable of writing that 'the one object in life is the development of the mind';[21] and yet his behaviour, his nostalgia, his sense of tradition, his sensitivity and even his philosophy of life contradicted that sweeping absurdity.

Renan's priestly education, his art, his memory of mother and of Brittany, prevented him from being a positivist historian even in the manner of Taine. He knew too well that intuition is one way to truth and saw better than Taine how historians cannot do without it. He abhorred the notion that history could be like geometry. He knew that human behaviour would be reduced to laws only in certain areas where statistics could be applied, and for the rest that mankind was too complicated, and individual men were too odd, for tidy historical patterns. Auguste Comte rested his faith upon scientific enquiry and testing, followed by reasoning. When Comte came to demand that men express their highest needs in religion, he still fancied that he inferred his needs, and his doctrine, from scientific enquiry. Renan saw the human need for religion and wanted it for himself. His problem was more troublesome to the soul than that of Comte. Comte said that men must have religion, and since the religion which they have will not do he must create a new religion that will do. But Renan had found in Christianity religious feelings or intuitions which he could not dismiss as dreams. The religion which Comte founded had a continuity only at the most superficial level ('Catholicism minus Christianity') with the religion which he left. The religion which Renan wanted but could not find had continuity in its deepest intuitions with the religion which he had left. For a time he tried to think of modern science as a new religion, but he attributed to science qualities which it hardly recognized in itself, like poetry and art. The definition of religion was never precise because it could not be more precisely defined than any other part of a moral understanding in the world. But he often used high terms:

Whether one is pleased or not, the supernatural is disappearing from the world; only people not of this age have faith in it. Does this mean that religion must crash simultaneously? Indeed not. Religion is necessary. The day when it disappears the very heart of humanity will dry up. Religion is as eternal as poetry, as love. It will survive the demolition of all illusions, even the death of the loved object. What am I saying? The object itself is eternal. Man will never be content with a this-worldly destiny. Under some form or other faith will express the transcendent value of life.[22]

The language kept bearing evidence of the continuity between the religion which he had lost and the religion which he wanted. These expressions of Renan could startle even familiar friends. His disciple Gabriel Monod reported an extraordinary utterance at dinner. Someone said, by way of paradox, that modesty is only a social convention, artificial, and that a very modest girl need have no shame at nakedness if she offended none. 'I don't know', said Renan. 'The church teaches that over every girl stands a guardian angel. True modesty consists in the fear of clouding even the eyes of the angels.'[23]

In retrospect, then, we may wonder why such a man should be regarded by scientific historians of the next generation as the leader of French scientific history.

The first reason was that he was a martyr for true scholarship, or at least a confessor. While he was in the Lebanon during 1861, he was recommended to the government for the Hebrew chair at the Collège de France, vacant four years. No one denied that he was suitable to be professor of Hebrew. The emperor confirmed the appointment on 11 January 1862. The Hebrew chair was of language and philology, not of divinity. But Renan was already a marked man. To his inaugural lecture at the Collège de France (21 February 1862) came prepared and rival groups of clericals and anticlericals, and when they heard the contents of the lecture the anticlericals demonstrated with an ovation, and no doubt contributed thereby to government's refusal to allow Renan to give a second lecture. Authority suspended him (27 February) from lecturing, though not (till 1864) from his stipend. But to students the standpoint cannot be dismissed as merely political. Renan taught France what Germany and Britain simultaneously learnt with equal anxiety, that men must be as free to study and debate the origins of Christianity as the origins of any other movement of history. Still, politics mattered also. In Sicily sermons against Renan were punctuated by anti-clerical cries of *Evviva il Renan!*, and we find it hard to imagine that Sicilian anticlericals studied the Bible with the academic impartiality which was Renan's ideal.

The suspension of his lectures by government created, in classical form, passionate debate over academic freedom. Government was not very clerical but it rested for support upon the Catholic Church and could not afford to antagonize Catholics. Catholics believed that Renan corrupted the young with untruths which hurt their moral beings as grievously as their intelligence. Renan asserted the right of scholarship to pursue its ends unhampered by imperial concern over expediency or popular agitation. In that assertion he was backed by the majority of British, German and French academics engaged in higher study and education. The argument must be followed wherever it led, and Renan was martyr to doctrines of expediency and public order. The series of papers in which he collected his side of the case (afterwards printed in the first volume of the complete works) formed a brilliant exposition of the necessity and right of academic freedom in the study of religion against a state of which the politics, but not the constitution, demanded respect for a conservative Christian public.

The inner circumstances of Renan's own loss of Christianity are not easy to penetrate because like most intellectual autobiographers he made incompatible statements at different epochs of his life. But at certain moments he said that history, nothing but the study of history, destroyed his faith.[24]

On why history had done this, he vacillated. He once claimed that history could prove – 'and, to my mind, prove beyond possibility of contradiction' – that Christianity is not (what he called) 'a supernatural fact', and that there were no such things as 'supernatural facts'. What a supernatural fact is and how it may be defined, Renan never explained. By nature and habit of mind historians are often uninterested in philosophy, and sometimes appeal to philosophical axiom without feeling a need to justify the appeal. But he had no doubt, in retrospect, that history took him out of Christianity. Once he asked himself whether metaphysical scruples influenced his mind, whether the idea of the Trinity or the Incarnation caused him to hesitate and he was sure that they had not. He debated within himself whether the ills or crimes of the Church, that of past centuries or those of his own generation, moved him away from the Christian religion, whether the inquisition of Pope Pius V or the Syllabus of Pope Pius IX helped to turn him out of Catholicism, and he was sure that they had not. 'If I had no material reasons for disbelieving the Catholic creed, the atrocities of King Philip II or the faggots of Pope Pius V would not be obstacles to my faith.'[25] What material reasons? In the same passage he mentioned contradiction between the fourth Gospel and the first three. History – that is, historical study of the Biblical texts – satisfied him that the Bible was in parts untrue and no man could be a Christian who thought the Bible in any part to be untrue.

But Protestants, in Germany or England or America, cheerfully confessed the Bible not to contain historical truth in all its parts and yet claimed to be as good Christians as others. Renan knew all about the Germans, his academic advance owed its progress to their researches, he knew that the leaders of the school of Biblical criticism in Tübingen, whom he disapproved as unbalanced and over-sceptical, had no idea whatever that they were not Christians. He once envied Herder because, being Protestant, he ended life as a bishop without a glimmer of awareness that he was almost not a Christian.[26] If you were a Frenchman, or at least if you were a Breton, you must either choose Catholicism or abandon Christianity – and Renan was not only as French as any Frenchman but was also a Breton.

Renan imagined Christ saying to him, 'You must leave me if you would be my disciple.'[27] Everyone nurtured in the Christian tradition, and then thinking his way into the intellectual maze of that age, could feel the power in this paradox of discipleship. Christ laid upon his followers the goal of truth, the duty to pursue truth; and for the first time since the fourth century the pursuit of truth seemed to lead away from Christ. Voltaire had said almost the same, and we hardly believe it sincere because of his relentless gift of irony and flair for publicity. We hardly believe it sincere in Renan because he is so smooth, so graceful, so unimpassioned, and so easy a writer. Probably it was reflexion and had little to do with what happened when he left the Catholic Church in 1845. We have more reason to doubt whether it stirred his heart than whether it was true to his intellect.

Truth led away from the Christ; not away from Jesus. As the road led towards Jesus it ran through mists which were not the same mists as those which wrapped the heads of old-fashioned students of the gospel; yet, it obviously ran towards Jesus, (as it then seemed) on a straighter course because it led away from Christ. History – not necessarily nothing but history, but at least history – seemed to take the God-man or man-God of the Christian centuries and shed all its light upon the man because it could only describe man and by its nature has no light which it can lift to illuminate God; unless it be found that the study of man leads beyond man.

Even in the purest of scholars we must not exaggerate the effect of learning upon the loss of Christianity. Since Renan's expertise lay in Semitic language and the Bible, and since he was a 'pure scholar' if ever there was such a thing, we infer that his study of the gospels, and especially his use of German Biblical criticism, contrasted so violently with what the French Catholic Church taught that he could be in no doubt which must be sacrificed in the cause of truth. But this was not always how Renan pictured his loss of Christianity. All truth, he said, is now 'scientific'. Our age sees the method of natural science as the way to truth. The supernatural is unverifiable, therefore the supernatural is not. On this explanation Renan came to reject Christianity by the same road as Taine — as a philosophical axiom, and not by reason of his study of history. It can hardly be doubted that if his philosophical conclusion had been different, he would have written his history differently and not better. But history was not the only study that led him to accept the positivist axiom; even though he sometimes said that it was.

The boy at school refused to play games during the hours of recreation but would sit on a seat in two or three coats, still at his books. He supposed himself to be a man of the mind, and of nothing but the mind.

The academic profession was coming into existence with truth – that is, the truths of reason – as its sufficient goal and its moral base. But the difficulty was, the highest duty sometimes seemed not to find truth but to criticize what was commonly held for truth. Not so much in the natural sciences where theories could be tested in laboratories, but in philosophy and history and the social sciences, the moral basis could be caricatured as the necessity of doubting. For all his underlying ethic, Renan found it difficult, at least in the last decades of his life, to appear other than a detached uncommitted ironical observer of men and society, so uncommitted and (his critics said) so cynical as to become the arch-dilettante of the nineteenth century. To identify Renan with dilettantism was unjust to a man who in his soul remained a post-Christian thinker and moralist, and was only possible because Renan liked to startle and dared to utter what more prudent contemporaries thought but did not say. But he illustrates a problem which we have met in another context: whether the advance of learning outside the natural sciences, in the intellectual history of the age, was identified so necessarily with the suspension of belief in anything (not merely belief in religion) that lack of commitment began itself to resemble a moral quality; or, to put it thus, that the detachment of mind, without which no historian could hope to come near to impartial treatment of the past, was elevated into a principle which might *look as though* it contained detachment from commitments necessary to the full life of a man whether in politics, society, or ethics. Renan's mind showed how the ethical basis of scholarship in that age engendered vacillation, nostalgia, wish-fulfilment and then suspicion of wish-fulfilment, perpetual questioning of the self and its judgment, at times (if he had worn his heart less frequently upon his sleeve) near to self-torment.

As once he stood under the temples of Paestum and wondered at the frailty of civilization, in 1865 he stood in the Acropolis at Athens and expressed the same wonder, but this time in religious terms. He started to compose a prayer to Athena, goddess of the Parthenon, and published a polished version eleven years later, under the title *Prayer on the Acropolis*. Looking at the Parthenon he was ravished by the perfection of beauty in Greek architecture, and on this experience of beauty knelt in heart before Athena as a sinner returning to her after thinking her nothing. But as he came to her, he saw that she also is a passing goddess, creature of a moment in the stream of human consciousness, and her claims to worship, which are claims to absolute allegiance, are claims too far-reaching for reality. She, goddess of a time and a people, demands his worship though he is out of her time and not of her people. She must learn that Greeks are not the same as mankind, that her fair temple is not a temple of all the earth; and at last be willing to be carried away by the stream of evolution into the nothingness where gods like men are forgotten. But as he prayed before this passing divinity, trying as it seemed to teach her a lesson, he felt, with the modest amount of agony that Renan was capable of feeling, a link with worshippers of Athena, who granted her a total commitment, who believed in her help, and also in truth were deluded. He did not mock the deceived. On the contrary, he felt the suffering of their 'betrayal', the pain of knowing how 'gods die like men and it is not right that they should be eternal'. A student of Renan[28] brilliantly described what Renan was thinking in these terms: 'He is the ex-seminarist, as well as the dark god from the barbarian north, who once again buries his old faith, not in camphor, but in "the purple shroud where the dead gods lie sleeping". He could hardly have given it a more magnificent funeral or more emphatically shown how important he thought it.'

In 1863, the year after the suspension of his lectures, he published *The Life of Jesus* which he almost finished during 1861 in a Maronite hut in the Lebanon while his beloved elder sister, chief preceptor of his young life, died at his side.

The Life of Jesus was a landmark; no landmark in theology, where its influence was negligible or neglected, but in the attitude of the middle class to religion. It was the first time that a biography of the man was written, which excluded the supernatural and at the same time was aimed at the general reader and written by a master of the evidence. It was also the last time that such a biography of the man was written by a scholar, for the progress of enquiry made men see that the historic materials were not sufficient to enable the writing of a biography which excluded the supernatural. Renan saw this; but he was too much the heir of the romantics, too ardent a believer in the virtues of historical imagination and feeling to be deterred by the nature of the evidence. The book was unique, because it appeared at a unique moment of time, late enough for the learned world to begin the quest for the historical Jesus and move towards the idea of biography, early enough for the world not to have seen that the quest could not result in that kind of biography. It happened also that the language of this unique book was written by a master of French prose. It was the most famous book written in France during the nineteenth century, and until about 1900 its author was the most famous of French writers. This cannot only be due to the author's genius. It must also be something to do with the politics, and, the intellectual battles of France. For in Germany and in Britain New Testament scholarship went ahead as though Renan had not written a line.

The effect was more popular than academic; except that the popularity gave sharp impetus to academics.

Renan believed in history by genius and saw in Jesus the greatest genius and inspired transformer of human society. The continuity is obvious between *The Life of Jesus* and the sense of *abandon me to be my disciple*. The world will no longer have the Christ because it receives a picture of him which is incredible. It shows a person moving through primitive stories of wonders and exorcisms. If we could get behind these layers of piety to find the man, we should not only understand him better for ourselves but make him intelligible again to all men. The Christ we have received is a Christ who stands outside history, and anyone who stands outside history is not man. Therefore we must put him back into history. 'His glory does not consist in being relegated out of history; we render him a truer worship in showing that all history is incomprehensible without him.'²⁹ In his own time the world was full of the supernatural, everyone expected marvels, people were astonished at his healings but did not think them impossible for holiness to perform. He was a man of that time. 'The greatest miracle would have been the refusal by Jesus to perform any miracles.' In our time the world is not full of the supernatural, and no one expects marvels, and many think healings impossible even for holiness. Therefore the miracles which first commended his Messiahship to Jews are now a bar to his Messiahship among Gentiles. So Renan came to one of the famous epigrams of his book – 'If ever the worship of Jesus loses its hold upon mankind, it will be precisely on account of those acts which originally inspired belief in him.'³⁰

Renan had no doubt of the substantial reliability of the texts, apart from the interpretation of the miraculous. With the aid of the texts he attempted to paint a portrait of a beautiful and original and self-sacrificial genius of ethical understanding, who by the union between moral person and moral teaching changed the world. 'Philosophy does not suffice for the multitude. They must have sanctity.'³¹

From so great a person stemmed the discipleship of religious men. No need for churches, creeds, dogmas, denunciations which narrowed or codified the freedom of this moral insight. 'However dogmas may change, Jesus will always be the creator of the pure spirit of religion. The Sermon on the Mount will never be surpassed. Whatever revolution takes place will not prevent us attaching ourselves in religion to the grand intellectual and moral line at the head of which shines the name of Jesus. In this sense we are Christians, even when we separate ourselves on almost all points from the Christian tradition which has preceded us.'³² This was Renan's biographical version of the personal cry, *abandon me to be my disciple*.

The stripping of the supernatural Christ and quest for the human Jesus was not achieved without faults of taste. Wishing to paint the portrait of the moral genius who changed men's lives, Renan kept calling him names – superior personage, illustrious being, incomparable man, admirable teacher. This reaches its climax of absurdity when the Sermon on the Mount is described as *charming*, Renan's favourite epithet of praise. He could not mention the parable of the prodigal son without calling it *delightful*. Jesus was smothered in compliments. The effect is that of an elegant court chaplain, swishing his seminarist's cassock rhythmically, bowing and smiling and scraping and rubbing his hands and exclaiming *superior personage* as a king strides up the hall to his throne.

The texts being what they are, a personal portrait reflected the vision of the painter. Renan was the Victorian and romantic version of a cultured and worldly abbé of the eighteenth century, and could not help but select his sources or attitudes in faithfulness to that not contemptible ideal. But during the 1860s there were two Renans still competing within him; the one a pure scholar, élitist, lover of genius, disdainer of the mob, intellectual aristocrat; the other a Breton man of the people, a critic of authority and hierarchy.

The intellectual aristocrat was a rôle which he fitted more easily.

Repeatedly we meet a frank confession of philosophical superiority. The world of men is still a world of brutes, lost in a night of unreason. Reasonable, thinking, learned men are few, will always be few. Yet on those few depends the hope of man's advance. He placed no hope in the people, disliked democracy and when it came was surprised to find that it did little harm. The man of books, scientist/philosopher/historian, holds the key to the future. Every student of ancient Greece and Rome knows the feeling that civilization is frail and easily lost, that the loveliest of architraves can tumble into ruin, the most comfortable of cities can fall to fire and sword, the fairest statues can be toppled and buried. Renan looked at the temples at Paestum, and there had a sense of a little group of good and wise men threatened by the brutes who were ordinary men and women and trembled for civilization.[88] 'How many men are there in Europe', he asked, 'who are really of the nineteenth century?' He intended to be part of the élite which pursued truth and beauty and goodness. Realism saw that this élite would be small. But he wanted it to be a religious sort of élite, where the dedication to art and to scholarship took the place of self-consecration to God. Sometimes he was filled with the sense of human grandeur that men could live well and in accordance with their conscience though they had ceased to believe that this had meaning and purpose in the providence of the world. On his own death-bed he remembered that his death was to be 'one of the finest moral spectacles of our age' and was sorry to be dying at a time of year when so few people were in Paris.[34] He told the people of his birthplace that on his grave ('Oh, if that grave could be in a cloister! – but cloister means Church and the Church will not have me though it is wrong') he wanted the words inscribed, 'I loved the truth.'[35]

But for a time, in his middle years, he came near to trusting the people, or rather, so distrusting the powers which guided the people that only the people was left to trust. In later life, when he lived under popular government and saw democracy in action, the élitist won the competition so comfortably, that his old contempt for mobs rose into cynicism. Then he came to sigh how nearly he was enticed, and to explain it to himself implausibly – 'A priest who has thrown up the Church is under strong temptation to become a democrat . . . for by so doing . . . he merely exchanges one sect for another.'[36]

But *The Life of Jesus* proves in him a less superficial affection for the people. In the 1860s he lived under an imperial government which he had small cause to bless. Part of the power in the biography is contained in the picture of Jesus emancipator. He took his gospel to the poor, made poverty an object of desire, 'sanctified the coat of the poor man'. Renan once compared him to 'a democratic chief, who feels the spirit of the multitude live in him, and recognize him as its natural interpreter'.[37] 'The established powers', he wrote, 'have never entirely recovered' from the crucifixion. 'How can they assume infallibility over the poor when they have Gethsemane on their conscience?'[38] Even when he meditated upon the greatness of an individual and his power over a society, the meditation was in essence revolutionary. He imagined some lone religious teacher like Elijah, coming out of the mountains into modern Paris, presenting himself at the Tuileries, ordering the sentries to stand aside, and telling the emperor of coming revolution. The sentries would bar the gates and refuse to let him in. Therefore we think him remote from our modern world, a giant in an age which could not have been real. 'Profound error! These men were our brothers; they were of our stature, felt and thought as we do. But the breath of God was free in them; with us it is restrained by the iron bonds of a mean society, and condemned to an irremediable mediocrity.'[39]

Faults of taste. Portrait reflecting self-portrait. Biography based upon materials insufficient for biography. History which hardly changed, except by way of stimulus, the course of historical enquiry. But within itself, an epoch-making book. For the first time a historian attempted to see the founder of Christianity with the clear light of historical vision. Traditional Catholicism or Biblical Protestantism could not do it because they were prevented from examining the texts as a historian must examine them. The German critical schools, without which Renan could not have written so successfully, could not do it because philosophy or theology still mattered more to them than history. *The Life of Jesus* by D. F. Strauss nearly thirty years earlier (1835), started a long process of enquiry but only after Renan's date did history take precedence of theology or philosophy. The meditations of piety took Jesus out of history. Renan, not merely as a lone student but as meeting the insistence of that age, put him back into history. In the 1860s many educated men wanted a Christ whom they could understand without simultaneously accepting stories which they could no longer understand. Renan gave them such a Christ. It marked a new stage in the link between history and religion.

6

Faith is not founded on historical research.

Faith is not founded on scientific research.

But research is only a pompous name for rational enquiry.

Faith is not the conclusion of an argument. Could it be shaken by argument, especially by an argument from new evidence? Probably the ultimate act of faith could not. But the way it finds expression, the understanding of its conscious object, could be. Within Christian faith, as understood through the centuries, certainly not constitutive of Christian faith, not the centre of it, but still important within, was a reliance on historical probability; about the nature of a single person.

But within the subconscious or partly conscious areas of feeling and dependence where these ultimate acts of trust take place, no man can dissect the constituent skeleton or, if a man succeeds in dissecting, he finds it a tormenting piece of surgery. Perhaps a man grew up with a portrait of the Christ in his mind, drawn in part from reading the gospels, in part from the beautiful meditations of art and poetry through the centuries. Then someone tried to describe what was called 'the Jesus of history', implying by the very name a contrast between the Christ of meditation and the man of reality. This adjustment of the mind was no different as process from the adjustment of the mind to evolution. But it had this difference;

however speculative early Darwinian theory might be, the natural sciences were a more precise instrument than history. If someone said that the Jesus of history was such and such, how reliable was his evidence likely to be, and what measures was he using to test the historical evidence? Renan's *Life of Jesus* was the best of all efforts at the impossible task of writing a biography; and yet, very quickly, everyone could see how powerful the character of Renan in selecting and presenting the evidence.

So the historians did not mainly unsettle religious men by offering portraits of a man unlike portraits hitherto received. The real unsettlement lay in the proof – not just the probability – that the evidence was less secure than anyone had expected. The Swiss historian Burckhardt read the *Life of Jesus* by David Friedrich Strauss and became convinced that the history of the New Testament could not bear the weight which faith sought to place upon it. The Oxford philosopher Thomas Hill Green read the critical studies of the New Testament documents which came out of the university of Tübingen, and embarked upon a quest to free Christian morality from its base in history. These experiences are often found in Europe of the mid-nineteenth century.

Together with the act of faith was still integrated a view of historical evidence about a person. But it was coming to be accepted that this evidence of history, like most other evidence of history, afforded room for doubt about what happened in detail, and that the documents could be more trusted as general impression of a person than as a selected description of what happened exactly.

It was also coming to be accepted that only two choices were open to religious men. Either to free their faith from all its historical content. Or to insist that, since this was history, it must meet the canons by which all other history was tested.

For a time it looked as though historical advances must touch Protestants more grievously than Catholics. Protestants said that they rested on the Bible, Catholics on the Church. Even for Protestants the Church must rise in importance, within the act of faith; for if the historical content of faith was general impression, the impact of Christ upon people was the deepest reason for historical assurance, and those people who knew him, those who heard from those who knew him, were the first Church.

Historical advance forced Protestants to change their doctrine of authority; that is, of the way in which the historical content of faith was transmitted. And at first it looked as though it need not force Catholics to change their doctrine of authority. But this was soon seen to be illusion. If Catholics retained their existing ideas of transmission unchanged, all they were doing was to employ one method of freeing faith from any historical content. It would have been almost equivalent to declaring: whatever the evidence, you must believe legends provided we tell you to believe. The Pope came near to saying that in 1907. Catholicism was far too deeply rooted in history to be able in the long run to free itself from history in that way. Johann Adam Möhler and John Henry Newman were only the first of a school of thinkers who sought to marry Catholic faith to the acceptance of genuine standards of historical criticism.

Here we have the main force of historical understanding as it made an impact upon religion. I do not mean that Renan, or Strauss, or Ferdinand Christian Baur, or any other individual caused the quest for the historical Jesus. I mean that the development of historical study itself, the entire movement, carried with it the quest for the historical Jesus. And evidence proves that here was a place where historical consciousness penetrated outside the circle of men who studied the past, and into ordinary non-academic minds. This is encouraging to the historian, for it shows (nothing shows so clearly) that a sense of history came through and altered the perspective of men in the street. We cannot chart this process. But we detect fragments of it. Jesus was a man. Christians had faith that he was the Son of God. But they now knew, what perhaps they hardly knew before, that he was a man. How did they know that? Not by Chalcedonian definition that we must not ascribe personality to the human nature as it is universal human nature, *man* and not *a man*. Man and not a man – it would never do, for he was set in history, and was in all points like as we are, and was born and walked and smiled and ate and suffered and died. Theologians always knew this. But men in pews were seldom theologians. In the last years of the nineteenth century the people came to know it.

Had this humanizing of the Christ anything to do with secularization? Or had the sense of process, of continuity, of relativity, induced by the sense of history, anything to do with it? Did ordinary men understand time better and so understand eternity worse? To prove him a man was to prove him a man of his time; and to prove him a man of his time was to prove him sometimes wrong, as in thinking that Moses wrote the book of the Law when he did not, or mistaking who was the high priest when David fled from Saul's murderers, or sharing an attitude to disease not that of nineteenth-century doctors.

It is very likely that some evidence exists. At present it is hard to find. Some people now found it difficult to preach good sermons, especially about the Old Testament; but in these sensations they may have overlooked previous long experience that to preach good sermons had always been difficult. We find that this interest in the human Christ was a help devotionally; as may be seen plainly in the flowering of devotional literature about the imitation of Christ during the last decades of the century. For some religious men of the middle nineteenth century the 'discovery' of the historical Jesus gave a marvellous fresh food for their faith. They had known, or had hardly known, a remote figure of ritual, and now perceived the humanity at last. They felt that they could begin where the apostles began – come to a man because he was such a man, and then slowly find conviction that more was in him than man.

7

History tells of the experience of the human race. So large a portion of that experience is religious that history cannot avoid religion, and if it seeks to avoid it, it will be as poor and superficial history as history which knows nothing of the economic basis of society. To try to see society in the historical perspective is like probing the inner being of a man, that part of him which lies below his utterances and self-justifications. Therefore, though I admit the lack of empirical verification, I guess with Acton that, so far as history may impinge upon our question, it is a way towards sympathetic understanding of religion, and not a way towards contempt for superstition.

The nineteenth century was the age of the great historical revolution in the human intelligence. Every form of intellectual revolution disturbs and shifts landmarks, axioms of a by-gone age. Christianity was the tallest pillar among existing landmarks. The historical revolution shifted the soil all about it, made the pillar look more like a leaning tower of Pisa, and caused men to be anxious lest it topple. But in my judgment the historical revolution was not so upsetting for religion as the scientific revolution; for the very reason that it often brought with it more understanding of the nature of religion.

I had the good fortune to know one of the most remarkable and lovable teachers of our age, Martin Charlesworth, historian of the Roman Empire and one of the editors of the *Cambridge Ancient History*, a man never so well known to the outside world as he deserved to be, because he died (1950) suddenly at the age of 55, on the way back from an expedition to his favourite spot, Hadrian's Wall. During the last three years before the Second World War he recovered a religious faith, inherited from childhood, abandoned in youth as scholarship and enquiry and academic learning took hold of him, and then refound, no doubt restated, in his forties. When he analysed the reasons for this – and he was the first to admit that the essence of the matter lay below the level at which full or adequate reasons could be given – he was inclined to attach importance to the course of his historical enquiries. As he traced the intellectual history of the Roman Empire he ran almost unexpectedly into the religious problem; the acceptance, at first sight an incongruous acceptance, by a traditional classical world, of a Palestinian faith rising out of Judaism. As he traced the social history of the Roman Empire, he began to see continuity between the imperial system and the early medieval states of Christian Europe which succeeded it. He became fascinated by certain examples of this continuity, as from Roman Britain into Celtic lands. And simultaneously with this process of historical enquiry, he, humanist and classical student, came again to profess Christian faith. He felt that his own mind grew in perception in some such way as he found late Rome developing in its perception.

I do not lay stress on so individual a case. There are other views of the fourth and fifth centuries than those which Charlesworth came to hold. We need only mention the name of Gibbon. A man easily lends more importance to the acts of his upper mind, which can be expressed, than upon half-conscious reaction to contemporary experience. We need cite it only as an example of a link, to be found elsewhere, between historical enquiry and the understanding of religion.

Historical synthesis helps men to understand the world; sometimes also to misunderstand. Some of the Whig history of the nineteenth century reflected the light of reason versus superstition, some of it the needs of the people versus the conservatism of possessors. Some history, from Buckle to Fester, spread positivist ideas by historical instances or impressions, with increasing force as history became more 'scientific' towards the end of the century.

So far as the general public acquired a historical sense, they saw how unreliable ordinary evidence can be. That meant, as in Renan's work, that the widening area of agnosticism within religion, or at least recognition of a wide area, which we noticed as characteristic of religious men during the age of conflict between Religion and Science, must have a parallel in a wider agnosticism about what was religious evidence but was also historical evidence; or at least that such evidence must be judged on its merits by the accepted canons of historical judgment, historical discrimination, and historical doubt.

History contributed to a deeper understanding of the part played by religion in society – an understanding which incidentally was indispensable to the new sociologists; and thereby helped to dissipate an important illusion of the 1870s and 1880s and 1890s; that science or philosophy were not only changing religious attitudes but strangling religious instincts.

9

THE MORAL NATURE OF MAN

I

In England of the 1860s the word *secularization* began its metaphorical career in phrases like the *secularization of art* or the *secularization of politics.* In Germany the word *Säkularisation* only began its metaphorical career some twenty years later, and not quite in the same contexts. It began to be used in a moral context; in phrases like the *secularization of morality,* which was intended to describe, the freeing of morality from its basis in theology. It was taken by a German historian of philosophy, Friedrich Jodl, (1889) from French historians of philosophy.

To find a morality detached from religion was nothing new in the world, being as old as philosophy if not older. The individual thinker had a choice of three or four ethical systems, none of which needed religion to stand as systems. Philosophers well knew that their task of constructing a theory of moral obligation was not made easier if they confessed God's rule.

But our problem does not directly concern the existence of a satisfying theory of ethics. We are interested, not in the construction of a system, but the way in which moral axioms take root in a whole society, how they change, and on what foundations ordinary men believe them to stand. At the beginning of the century nearly everyone was persuaded that religion and morality were inseparable; so inseparable that moral education must be religious education, and that no sense of absolute obligation in conscience could be found apart from religion. That moral philosophers taught the contrary made no difference.

Except in the case of a small number of exceptional groups or people, morality never had been separated from religion in the entire history of the human race; and therefore those who undertook to provide a system of morality which should have no links with religion, because they were convinced that the prevailing religion was in ruins, had a task of exceptional difficulty, a task which was perhaps beyond their power if they wished to make their system of morality no mere theory but a system which would touch the conscience of a large number of ordinary men and women. To look for an 'autonomous' morality was nothing extraordinary. Not only philosophers, but Voltaire and Pierre Bayle, wrote of it; Michelet and Victor Hugo also. A century before, Bishop Butler provided Christians with an autonomous theory of ethics which yet fitted the religious view of the world, and three-quarters of a century before, Kant produced a different theory but a theory still marriageable or even married to a religious view of the world, though Kant's idea of religion differed radically from the idea of Bishop Butler. But from our standpoint there is all the difference between a philosophical theory of ethics, which is always likely to be the property of a small group of specially equipped thinkers, and a system of ethics which has the potency to be acceptable in society. In the circumstances of the nineteenth century men who attempted to devise such a system were perhaps embarking on what was then impossible.

In his old age even Mark Pattison, ablest Oxford critic of the century, believed that the link between religion and morality was impossible to deny. Some thinkers refused to admit any necessary connexion between religion and morality, but nevertheless admitted that in the situation of western Europe history had connected them; and on this ground even some non-Christians like Henry Sidgwick, and in his mellow years even John Morley, refused to attack religion because they had no desire to weaken morality.

In 1877 the journal *Nineteenth Century* printed the record of a discussion between Christians and scientists on the subject. It was entitled *The Influence on Morality of a decline in religious belief.*[1] Some of the contributors refused to accept the hint of the title, if it was a hint, that religious belief declined. But whether this was so or not had no relevance to the real question in issue: whether, *if* religion declined or will decline, public and private morality suffers or will suffer. Almost everyone in the argument accepted the proposition that an individual's moral standards need not or would not fade if he lost his religion. Everyone but W. K. Clifford also agreed that the standards of society would fade. Some of them thought they would fade because the decline of religion meant the decline of truth. Others thought that they would fade because in Europe men associated their moral obligation with religious doctrine and practice, and therefore the end of religion must mean release from the sense of moral obligation. This made a difficulty; for the contributors also agreed that you could not go on propagating a creed which you thought untrue, for the sake of preserving good conduct associated with that creed. Not all the contributors who believed decline of religion to mean the decline of morals, believed the creed of reigning religion. And if they had tender consciences, like that of Henry Sidgwick, they then found themselves in a new moral predicament of anxiety.

For they found it self-evident that the moral behaviour of a society was conditioned by two foundations: first, by inherited habit; and second, by an attitude to the universe; or a belief, however hazy, about the way in which the universe is organized, if such a word as *organized* can be used. If Büchner were right, and all was but a series of accidents, moral attitudes were hard to found. But the nineteenth century as a whole did not believe that all was chaos. The general trend of sciences appeared to create more and more organization; not moral organization indeed, but obedience to physical laws which in their totality appeared to be purposive or might be said to be purposive. After 1864, the word *evolution* was not quite a neutral word. It was quite near the word progress. From protoplasm to fish to mammal to ape to man, the world looked to be going one way. Under the axiom that a system of ethics must depend upon a right attitude to the construction of the universe, several of the quests for a non-religious system of ethics attempted to found them upon an idea of evolution.

There are few of us for whom the word *evolution* is either emotionally or morally evocative. Such is our distance from our great-grandfathers that the word is the driest of words, and we squeeze as much warmth from the idea as we can from the idea of taxation. That was not the experience of all men in 1870. A Fellow of Trinity College in Cambridge, W. K. Clifford, read Darwin and was converted away from an Anglo-Catholic faith, and helped to found a group which should practise evolutionary ethics; and for him at least the endeavour was at first as devout as the faith which he had left.

But the lives of several eminent agnostics of the later nineteenth century, led by Leslie Stephen and Henry Sidgwick, show the difficulty and frustration of a quest for a system of 'scientific ethics', or 'evolutionary ethics' which could be meaningful among a people and not the private property of a clique of academics.

The burden sat heavier because nearly everyone, agnostic or not, assumed that the morality which they inherited was absolute and must be preserved, even though the creed linked with it might be dropped. The most militant of French anticlericals, fighting in the

1870s and 1880s for a lay and non-religious education in the schools, wanted a moral education which agreed in every respect (but religious background) with Christian moral education. The churches claimed their ethic to be the foundation of family life. The critics like Michelet did not answer by denying the institution of the family but by assailing the Church for destroying the family through its cult and through the power of the priest in confession. To the end of the century the churches were still being attacked, not for teaching a certain kind of morality, but for being unfaithful to the fundamental moralities which were assumed to be natural to humanity. On the one hand critics were afraid that if religion declined morality declined. On the other hand they identified the morality which would decline with the morality which they inherited in association with religion. This inherited morality was sometimes declared to be 'natural morality', a code of ethics on which all men agreed, and for which they needed no religion as support. Only in the last two decades of the century, with the influence of rebels like Nietzsche, did doubt about this axiom begin to dawn. 'Nobody', wrote Nietzsche,[2]

has doubted that the 'good' man represents a higher value than the 'evil', in terms of promoting and benefiting mankind generally, even taking the long view. But suppose the exact opposite were true. What if the 'good' man represents not merely a retrogression but even a danger, a temptation, a narcotic drug enabling the present to live at the expense of the future?

2

The only non-religious morality that had a chance with most men was what we may call a system in a low key; a little common sense, a little axiom about human nature and its power of doing good, and a little incentive – all quickly intelligible, and rational in easily explicable terms.

The name which symbolized all this was Auguste Comte.

You feel about him, this assailant of all the orthodoxies in the world, that he was an arch-figure of the establishment. He sits upon a throne, serenely lecturing the world on why everyone else is wrong.

It is a relief to remember that he led the most dramatic of student revolutions, at the Paris Polytechnic which served him for a university. But the sense that he is of the establishment is a measure of his stature. Have these vast platitudes only become platitudes because we are the heirs of the science of the nineteenth century and he was its theorist? In the mind of every one of us, even the most devout of us, is tucked away some little secret piece of Comte.

The word *positivism* became a key-word of the nineteenth century and after. The name of Comte became a symbol, like the names of Darwin or Voltaire; a symbol which by 1870 carried a power far beyond the intellectual influence of the lectures which he gave or the books which he published. No philosopher, he was the only French philosopher of that century to make impact in Britain and Germany. His name stood for a very coherent idea, a very plain and intelligible attitude to life – *experimental science the only way to truth*. Apart from all the structures built upon it, his name was powerful in conditioning attitudes to truth. He did not invent positivism. But he was widely believed to have invented it, and was the man who tried to make it the key which opened all doors to the only truths said to matter for life and society. The notion of positivism stood for an attitude destined long to outlive the Comtean positivism of the later nineteenth century. Of this attitude Comte was the hero, even for minds who gained nothing from his books.

During the third quarter of the nineteenth century some men believed that science, that is the natural sciences, could solve all problems, even the problems of men; that man and society could be brought under universal laws like the law of gravitation; that we live under a determined process which no free act can stop or check or change. For two or even three decades the idea was magnetic. Science, queen Science, goddess Science, could do all. By 1890 the act of faith was seen not to fit the experience of men. It faded away; leaving behind it still the immense reputation of science as the quest for all kinds of truth, but leaving also the sadness that science is not fitted to offer truths about the moral being and therefore that perhaps truths about the moral being are not to be obtained. Comte stood for the faith that science could get for us sufficient truths, both for ourselves and for our society.

He was persuaded – it was his deepest conviction, and it went hard against the persuasions of many of his contemporaries – that how you act depends on what you believe. If you want to remake society, you need principles to start from, that is, a creed. Start by trying to reform your institutions and you get nowhere. Start by reforming your philosophy and you transform your institutions. In this he went directly against one of the central beliefs of the Enlightenment, that you can improve men morally by altering their institutions.

Comte stood with the old tradition (Christian but not only Christian) thus far, that good institutions depend on good men, the old saw *quid leges sine moribus?* You and I are responsible. We cannot plead the rottenness of government or the injustice of the economy, we cannot shift our responsibility to a political monster bearing a curious resemblance to the scapegoat without the camp. The moral being is the foundation of society.

That this axiom can be extracted from the belief *experimental science the only road to truth,* is not certain.

He began by repudiating all systems of ethics, even the utilitarian. For they are based upon theology, or philosophy, not upon science, which is observation of man and society. If we are to choose between old-fashioned ethics of theologians and new-fangled systems of philosophers, then choose the old; for religion deals in real people, while philosophy deals in abstractions. Priests know more than philosophers about man's heart and motives. Catholicism has the merit of seeing morality as the first of duties. It is subordinate to nothing. It dominates all life.

Unfortunately this morality was tied to a set of doctrinal assertions which had not succeeded in keeping up with modern knowledge or the scientific method. New principles and new knowledge dissolved the doctrines of Catholicism; and because they dissolved the doctrines, they seemed to dissolve all morality simultaneously. The family is a foundation of morality. But because the family is believed to be founded upon Catholic principles, men who start by attacking Catholicism end by attacking the family. Social morality depends upon agreed standards, upon a consensus which is received as so axiomatic that it hardly ought to be discussed. Our social morality depends on propositions which are very discussible, need to be discussed, and can no longer be axiomatic. Therefore our social morality is on the verge of ruin. It must be so, when what used to be sacred is sacred no longer.

We cannot restore private or public morality by restoring religious doctrines. The doctrines can hardly maintain themselves, still less can they maintain moral principles. Tell a child that he must do good because he will go to hell if he does bad – when he ceases to believe in hell, which he probably will, he will suppose that now he need not do good.

So we must free morality from religion.

Then, on what basis?

We have to admit at once that in these circumstances all morality is 'relative' and nothing is 'absolute'. The moment you talk, as Kant used to talk, of absolute duty, or absolute anything, you are in philosophy which is worse than theology.

Some people say, then no morality. Either morality is absolute or no morality.

Comte believed this to be a false dilemma. It is like saying 'either truth is absolute or it is not truth at all'. Moral standards can be seen to develop down the centuries as knowledge grew. They are modified by new circumstances, new understanding, better information; while they preserve what is good and permanent in what went before.

So we discover 'systematic morality', that is, a system of ethics, by using two instruments: first, history, to see how human societies have behaved and developed, and second, ordinary common sense. The making of a system of ethics is nothing but looking back down history and seeing what principles led to the moral progress of man.

If, by this prosaic low-key common-sense enquiry, we look at men and women including ourselves, we find that they all have unselfish instincts. Observation proves it. Without the existence of these instincts in all of us, society must instantly collapse.

But observation also shows that we all have selfish instincts. Worse, it shows that the selfish are stronger than the unselfish. Our natures are not evenly balanced. They are biased towards the ego. How then are we to discover the balance?

This would be impossible, because the unselfish instincts are in origin feeble, but for two things in the circumstances which surround us: first, family life – we are born into a group of affection, and the group fosters altruistic instinct against ego-instinct; and secondly, if we behave unselfishly, we find it pleasant – it satisfies. 'You get tired of doing. You get tired of thinking. You never get tired of loving.'[3]

These affections can never replace the unselfish instincts. Those are instincts – they cannot be driven out, to lose them would be to cease to be human, you cannot abolish nature, to try to eradicate the ego-instinct is folly. 'If you try to make an angel, you end by making a brute.' Affection cannot abolish selfishness, it can only hold it in check. Affection holds before us an ideal which we know to be unattainable but towards which we can always look.

This is all very precarious. Comte says it is precarious. And it would remain precarious but for the widening of the group-affection into a society-affection. As man advanced, laws and social framework fostered good acts. Though institutions cannot create a moral being, they can help it onward. The external order of society exerts a continual pressure in regulating our egotism.

This was not so far from the theory of ethics in the Scottish common-sense moralists. Comte replaced, in theory, the basis in an 'attitude to the universe' with the notion of an order of society.

The word order was very important to Comte. It was being used with a meaning not far from the meaning of the word *harmony*. Society brings our contradictory warring selfishness into a harmony: and this is not just external force holding incompatibles together, it is healing (partially) wars inside the group and wars inside the family and even wars inside the soul. It generates order in the individual mind, fosters feelings in harmony with the whole race, and thereby encourages the doing of good.

In Comte's mind is a close link between evolution of knowledge and moral progress. As we know more we see relations of things better, we become more benevolent. As we become more intelligent we become more moral. This is what we can control. We cannot control feelings, they are spontaneous; but as we try to become more intelligent, we understand that the intelligence is not a satisfying end in itself, that it needs to bow to the heart, and that the only happiness possible for human nature is founded in self-sacrifice.

These proposals of Comte about ethics laid themselves open to many criticisms and many questions from the moral philosophers. But they were important because they were the nearest to a popular theory of ethics, not religious, that the middle classes of the nineteenth century achieved.

Religion and morality were entangled, so deep in the mind of the human race – deeper than the mind, in the instincts, inherited through countless generations. No evidence suggests that this axiom – morality needs religion for its support and without religion it cannot stand firm – was seriously shaken during the nineteenth century. But a small group of middle-class thinkers, slowly growing into a much wider group, associated the existing religion with stories or ideas which they could not believe, like the brief antiquity of the world or miraculous interventions in physics, or with retrograde or obsolete political systems. If they cared for morality – and most of them cared for it very much – they could not go to philosophical ethics for an alternative, because the philosophers' systems were either above their heads or as difficult to accept as the old religious basis. So, usually without having read a word of Comte, their ethics were often like his: low-key; not absolute; a conviction that we can be unselfish and that unselfish men are happy but that to be unselfish is difficult and can be fostered by family and by society, we must do the best we can for others so far as we may in these complicated circumstances. Par excellence this was the agnostic morality; perhaps it is to this day. And its strength was (and is) the claim that nothing need be accepted, no axiom and no principle, that cannot be verified by observing men and women. No one should underestimate the persuasiveness in a generation where the young had just learnt that the principles of religion and morality which their fathers accepted from their grandfathers were founded, at least in part, on error. This is not to identify such wide groups of the middle class with those who called themselves Positivists. The societies formally organized as Positivist never numbered more than a few hundred people, except perhaps in Latin America.

It has been said that Comte, being a bad scientist and not a very good philosopher, created a philosophy which enabled good scientists to dispense with philosophy.[4] It was an agnostic standpoint, not atheistic. The atheist was still a theologian. He needed an assertion which could not be proved under the axiom *experimental science the only road to truth*. He was 'not really emancipated', as Comte's successor Littré once said.[5]

3

Moral principles could exist, did exist without religion; even when they were the moral principles of the religion. The complicating fact for the late nineteenth century was the claim that you could have morality without Christianity while the morality which you must have was Christian morality. But men were good Christian men morally without possessing Christian faith. The witness of altruistic agnostics, of whom, among the British, Henry Sidgwick is the most celebrated, persuaded more easily than theory.

But was it *better* if the moral principles were backed by religion – a religion – religion that was true? – *better* in the sense that the morality would in this way cease to be the privilege of a coterie of intellectuals and pass into the habits of a society?

Auguste Comte himself had no doubt that they must be backed by religion.

To found a new religion is not a little thing. To found a new religion in the middle nineteenth century, in the generation of Marx and Feuerbach, is a still bigger thing. And to claim to found a religion out of modern science is the biggest thing of all.

Some of his admirers – not least Mill, not least Littré – resented the religion of Comte, and thought it aberration. And the question has been debated ever since whether there were two Comtes or one. Was the founding of a new religion an aberration of the scientific philosopher because suddenly he fell in love with Clotilde de Vaux? Or was the system of 1857, true religion based on science, inherent in the intention of 1825? Littré, far the ablest French expositor of Comte, held that the Comte he wanted and needed was the early Comte and that the religious Comte was decay and madness. George Eliot became a Positivist because of the religious Comte without whom she would not have been drawn to the scientific Comte. It is a long argument. But more and more weight has fallen away from Littré, upon the side of those who contend for unity and naturalness of development in the mind. This is not to say that there was nothing new. The love of Clotilde was passion. Her death evoked agony which spilled over into his self-regard as founder of a religion and touched his sense of authority as high priest. But he had a killing answer to Littré and all who taxed him with treachery to himself. At the end of his life he republished six little works of 1818–26.[6] They declared philosophy of science to be the first task, a clearing of the ground, a necessary preface. Then, when the foundation is laid, we must go forward to the highest part, the building of a positive religion upon the substructure of a positive philosophy.

Morality is founded in the affections. Therefore, in the end, it needs adoration. The mere assent of the mind is not enough. Most men have believed that such an effective devotion depends on perceiving something or someone absolute. For Comte nothing can be absolute. But he found the equal of an absolute in humanity. Men become more than an object of scientific enquiry. 'Humanity' is the object of worship. Man is raised above the animal because he 'shares in humanity', and finds by growing knowledge that he must live for humanity. History will become the sacred science of humanity, bringing humanity an ever clearer knowledge of itself and of its long advance towards the light and towards the good.[7]

Comte did not mean that we can worship each man or each woman. He did not even mean that we can worship any man or any woman, not at least if that person is taken as all that person. Humanity is not the same as all the men and women that have existed and shall exist. It is a poetic description of those parts of each and all of us which help man to advance, which help our well-being, our increase of knowledge, our inheritance of culture. 'Humanity' is a personification of the high potentialities of intelligence and morality in human nature. That is what becomes the object of worship.

One is hardly surprised to find Comte, at the end of his life, making *The Imitation of Christ* his daily reading. Science the only source of knowledge and therefore of morality; but science bringing with it the necessity of religion, partly as the stay of morality, partly as the natural outcome of true morality. Religion necessary – only, alas, it cannot be the religion that we have.

4

We come upon an area of feeling easy to illustrate but very difficult to chart or analyse.

What was so unsatisfying about a common-sense scientific moral system, whether backed or not backed by a religion of humanity? What feelings were aroused which were not simply Church reaction, not simply orthodoxy defending its portcullis, but human feelings, or at least the feelings of more or less educated western Europeans, which are, after all, the feelings not only of more or less educated Europeans, but also of plain men and women?

In the 1880s passed over western Europe one of those movements of mind that history perceives but cannot easily analyse or define. It was something to do with a reviving sense that the world holds mystery and that the prosaic explanations of the age after the romantics will not satisfy. More a breath of spirit than a reasoning of intellect, you find it in the new movements of English and Scottish philosophy as they turned away from Herbert Spencer and John Stuart Mill; in the sudden French feeling, akin at times to inspiration, at the discovery of Henri Bergson, where intuition and imagination came into their kingdom; in French novels reacting against the naturalism of Zola, and historians repudiating the determinism of Taine; among the impressionist painters conquering the eyes and taste of aesthetic men; in the last stages of the life of Richard Wagner, where the opera *Parsifal* was a slow passive brooding on a heaven or kingdom which no man could define. You find the movement in the growth of Christian interest in the old mystics of the Middle Ages or the Counter-Reformation, and in the new access of attention to Blaise Pascal. A few natural scientists went on saying that they could see no more mystery in the world, but this was not what intellectual Europe or unintellectual Europe believed or professed to believe. Hippolyte Taine suddenly felt as though he had lived out his time – 'I infer just one thing – taste has changed. My generation is finished. I'm going away to hide in my hole in Savoy.'[8] Even Emile Zola started writing novels about religion, hostile novels, but he was too big a writer not to portray with sympathy, and he selected his subjects because he knew what his public wanted. The experience of suffering, or the sudden charismatic sense of light or of inspiration, were too potent to be dismissed from the tidy map of the world which confident men had not been able to draw but had boldly predicted as possible shortly. The extremist who was typical of no one and yet (because an extremist) symbolized the entire mood, was Nietzsche, for whom intellectual truth was nothing and moral feeling all, passion for the individual, courage to live and to think dangerously. The noises were confused; a Babel of voices, moral and religious and philosophical, but amidst the din one thing was clear; the generation put aside the serene hopes and optimisms of the mid-Victorians. They seemed to be prising the soul out of the clutches of scientific law, and thereby restoring to it its sense of liberty.

To illustrate this turning, I select two close friends from the last two decades of the century, both eminent as French literary critics: Brunetière and Vogüé.

Ferdinand Brunetière (1849–1906) was the child of a sceptical father and devout Catholic mother, and the inheritance may bear on the inward struggle between reason and heart which afflicted his later years. He aimed to be a journalist and critic of literature. From 1875 he was associated with the *Revue des deux Mondes*, of which he became editor in 1894, the year in which he was elected to the Academy. When Taine and Renan disappeared from the scene, men thought of Brunetière as the dominant figure in the current of French intellectual thought during the 1890s.

As a young man he read Taine and Renan, and something of Strauss, and was carried away by them. He committed to memory sections of both Taine and Renan. He regarded himself as the heir of Taine, allowing far more scope for individual genius than Taine's theory allowed, but understanding literature by seeking to place writers in their historical and social environment. To this end he developed the instrument already used by Taine, the philosophy of evolution derived from Darwin.

The Origin of Species was translated into French in 1862, and again in 1873 and 1876; but this does not include every variety of popular exposition of Darwinism to the French. In Germany, outside pure science and anthropology, the influence of Darwin created new theories of society, of race, and at last of politics. In France the influence of Darwin was chiefly powerful by its impact on literature. It changed the character of the new school of naturalism in the writing of the novel. Through Taine it affected the criticism of literature and touched upon the principles of historical writing. Amateurs carried Darwin in their pockets when they visited the Zoo or the botanical gardens.[9]

Brunetière became a passionate Darwinian. *Evolution* was the key to unlock all the secrets of literary history. He always retained a critical attitude to the detail of Darwin's theory, while of Haeckel he had the lowest opinion. In the same way he sat detached from Comte. But he knew himself a positivist as well as a Darwinian, and applied these principles systematically.

He was one of those who struggles with the principles of morality all his adult life. Moral principles must be saved or man will return to the brute; and if they are to be saved they must be detached from religion. Though a positivist, he was soon dissatisfied with purely positivist answers to the ethical difficulty. It was good so far as it went; but it could on reflexion be seen to be insufficient. By 1881 he recognized that any morality depended on a general attitude to the world, upon some conviction about the nature of man, perhaps also of man's purpose in the world. For a time he tried to find moral basis, in this sense, which had nothing to do with religion or philosophy. But he came to see that 'a general attitude to the world' touched on either religion or philosophy. For six or seven years he considered whether we could detach 'religion' from all the particular religions, and find a social morality which should be religious in its atmosphere without being linked to a particular religion. Eventually he surrendered this last idea as impracticable or even absurd. For a time he befriended the theories of Schopenhauer and the philosophy of pessimism, asking whether it was not possible to found morality upon a rational open-eyed conviction that man is wretched and life miserable. As late as 1892 he praised Pierre Bayle in his *Revue*[10] for having freed morality from religion.

But even in this 1892 article his mind hesitated. The Enlightenment freed morality from religion. But the problem is not solved. It hangs about us now. We still do not know whether we can preserve the moral order when we have lost the religious aspirations which were its end and its crown. We cannot derive a moral order from a social order. To find a moral order we have to find principles which are independent of the social order, and are not equivalent to the axiom, *justice is what profits the state.*

In the autumn of 1894 he visited Italy and Rome. These were the years when Pope Leo XIII tried, rather vainly, to reconcile intransigent French Catholics to democracy, and less vainly to state the principles of a Christian social order. This endeavour of a Pope met the interest of Brunetière in finding some link between religion and social justice. On 27 November 1894 he had a private audience of Pope Leo XIII.

In the way of conversation nothing momentous passed at this audience. Its importance lay only in the impetus which it imparted to the meditations of Brunetière. On his return he published in his *Revue des deux Mondes*[11] an article which caused sensation in France. It was entitled, *After a visit to the Vatican.* It was a meditation upon science and religion.

Scientists no longer claimed (if anyone but Büchner and Haeckel and a handful ever claimed) to solve all the riddles of the universe. These pretensions, however, had just been revived in France by the posthumous publication (1890) of a book which Ernest Renan wrote as a young man in 1848 and which he had refrained from publishing, *L'Avenir de Science*; which, being written in 1848, and by an immature Renan, claimed science as the only saviour of man. But if we look back, wrote Brunetière, we find that these pretensions were an excess.

He asked himself, what was happening, deep down, in contemporary thought? Why did scholars no longer think it necessary to be unChristian to show how scholarly they were? Are we to talk of the 'bankruptcy of science'? The natural sciences promised to rid us of mystery and they did not, we are surrounded by mystery still, where we came from, where we are going, and why. 'If it is true that for a hundred years science has offered to replace religion, then for the moment, indeed for a long time to come, it has lost the game.' Darwinianism gives lessons in how to behave like animals. Somehow we have to live not like animals. Let us then refrain from putting science and religion into conflict, let each reside in its domain of intellectual or emotional life.

Free morality from religion? Is it certain that this is possible? The moral obligation must have an absolute – 'duty is nothing unless it is sublime, life is trivial unless it implies an eternal relation'. One day, perhaps, we might get a non-religious morality. We can be sure that the time is not yet. It does not matter whether morality springs from religion or religion springs from morality, it does not matter whether gods existed without moralities or moralities existed without God, these are questions only for the historian. 'What is certain for us is, that neither religion nor morality has its full meaning unless they interpenetrate each other.'

This article raised storm in Paris. Brunetière was accused of saying what he had not quite said, that science was bankrupt. That a positivist, a Darwinian, a non-Catholic should write like this caused every anticlerical to lament. Brunetière had been less than prudent in his choice of language. It was a lie, said his critics, that science was bankrupt. So far from science promising everything and giving nothing, it promised nothing and gave much. The Union of Republican Youth organized a banquet (5 April 1895) against Brunetière, to defend science and the French Revolution. The speeches were uncompromising on the idea of any reconciliation between science and faith. Nor were Catholic theologians all pleased with Brunetière. They still shrank from the proposition that science has absolute rights in its own sphere. That shrinking was an important constituent in the European intellectual difficulty .

The onslaught had the not unnatural effect of stiffening Brunetière in his stance. He had no intention of becoming a convert. But more and more he accepted the belief that society cannot dispense with religion in its acceptance of moral axioms. Like several other French writers of those years, he who in 1870 had stood so far from Catholicism, slowly moved towards it. It took him five anxious years, 1894–9. Simultaneously he moved to the right in politics, and to a conviction that French history united France with Catholicism. Shortly after the process was ended, he wrote a series of articles which turned (1904) into a curious book, *How to use positivism for the benefit of Catholicism.*

He never ceased to revere Taine. But in September 1903 the anticlerical government raised a statue to Renan at Tréguier in Brittany. Brunetière used the most violent language of his life about Renan ('like a libidinous Silenus') in five letters of protest on moral grounds. The letters marked his final break with the memory of the master whose writings he once tried to memorize.

5

The Vicomte Eugene-Melchior de Vogüé, friend of Brunetière, came of a long line of French aristocrats from the Ardèche, but was himself child of a Scottish mother famous for her beauty. His cousin was French ambassador in Constantinople, and gave him a post there as attaché. He used the chance to study the Near East and especially the traditions of the Greek Orthodox Church. In 1877 he moved to be secretary at the embassy in Russia. There he married a Russian wife in presence of the Tsar, and spent five years studying the Russian language and people. In 1886 he published in Paris a book which placed him in the front rank of literature and opened to him the doors of the French Academy. It was called *Le Roman Russe*. The eleventh edition received an English translation in 1913. It was a study of the contemporary Russian novel, written from the point of view of a western moderate Christian democrat.

As stimulus to literature the book was of the first rank. It met a need of the moment. A Paris jest of the time ran that the Russians were revenging themselves for the burning of Moscow by Napoleon Bonaparte.[12] Men talked of a 'Russian invasion' by novels. Dostoyevsky and Tolstoy were obscure names one month and on everyone's lips the next month. To forge the bond of sympathy between France and Russia was destiny after the rise of Germany to military hegemony in Europe. The effect of Vogüé's book depended not only on its quality but its timing, just as the French began to open their eyes to the Russians. Universities began to found chairs of Russian. The more famous Russian novels were translated into French during the early 1880s, so that it was newly possible for many to read them. But not many did read them, till Vogüé told them why they should. His book was so critical and yet constructive, so personal and yet objective, so penetrating without being astringent, so prosaic and yet so haunting, that even after so many decades you cannot read it without wanting to go back to read the Russian novelists for themselves. If we say that Vogüé 'popularized' Dostoyevsky and Tolstoy, that would be true. But the description is very inadequate both to explain what the book achieved and the way it achieved that effect.

The book was not at all a preaching book. It was a work of critical appreciation. In the realm of literature it was controversial and controverted. The controversy was intended. Vogüé aimed a protest against the dominant sex-and-belly naturalist school of novelists headed by Emile Zola; on the ground that this so-called realism was unreal by omitting some of the most real parts of human life. Whether or not *soul* existed was in doubt. But men had experiences which did not fit mere sex or belly, and were tiring of novels which disregarded all sign of soul in human existence.

Thus, in literature, the book became a sign of the movement of intelligent minds away from materialism.

This marked its strength and its weakness. In the short run it was powerful in literature because it perfectly fitted the mood of the decade. In the long run it was weaker because Vogüé could be accused of idealizing, of suffering from optical illusions about Russians by the bias of his crusade against naturalist novels. In the literary enquiry into Dostoyevsky and Tolstoy, a little more psychology, even a little more scepticism was in the longer run to prove useful. Hardly concealed within the Russian mood was an aching soul of revolution, easily overlooked, but in time working subtly and uncomfortably upon the moderate French conservatives who were first led by Vogüé to idealize Russians.

In the realm of ethics Vogüé's book was symbol for a similar and more lasting change of climate. Its importance in France depended upon the message which Frenchmen thought that they understood by it. Underneath the study of four or five foreign writers and their books, Vogüé seemed to tell the French something about France, if not the Europeans something about Europe.

The Russian predicament, he seemed to suggest, is only the predicament of us all. A government of the old régime, a church of the old régime entangled with it; young men educated by Hegel and then by materialism, looking for and beginning to plot revolution; Slav temperament, resigned, enduring, dumbly conscious of an unknown eternity; a people for whom government was the enemy and for whom the materialism of the revolutionary was bizarre; a people with a religious heart in travail, always seeking an outlet, not finding an outlet in the orthodoxies of the past, but finding a dim perception of truth through its chief characteristic, the acceptance of unavoidable suffering. Dostoyevsky enduring four years of crude imprisonment in Siberia, for no crime by western standards, and under his pillow every night the New Testament given him by the wives of Decembrist revolutionaries – Raskolnikov throwing himself at the foot of the girl whose prostitution keeps her parents from starving, and saying to her, 'It is not before thee I kneel – I prostrate myself before the sufferings of all humanity' – sense of sin weighing upon the conscience more heavily because the nature or extent of the burden is unknown – the *Idiot* losing, by defect of intelligence, the sharp qualities which make original sin, and so for all his idiocy venerated by a world of usurers and liars – the way of religion, Vogüé seemed to tell France, is not by reconstruction of vanished power. In learning to be agnostic about too tidy systems of religion, they learned also to be agnostic about too tidy systems of irreligion. They have refused to discard ways into truth by character and by feeling. Science and history have made us all 'realists'. Our faculty of suspicion for the unreal is stronger than at any time in the story of mankind. But these Russians show how, at certain moments of life (suffering the chief) the real occasion is shot through with a sense of what is not confined to this material world, and to miss this is to be 'unreal'. Vogüé called this 'mystic realism'; an effect achieved in the novels by making men and women more extreme, passionate, committed, strong-willed, odd, and better able to suffer with indifference.

This very religious agnosticism was still agnostic. The extraordinary power of the Russians issued from the profound religious sense which shot through page after page of books by men with sceptical intelligence. In *War and Peace* Prince Andrew Bolkonsky lay on his back, grievously wounded at the battle of Austerlitz, and watched the sky, and wondered whether to pray.

If only I could say *Lord have mercy*...But to whom would I say it? Power whom no one can reach, whom I cannot even define – the Great All? – the Great Nothing? – or, is it the God shut up in this charm given me by Mary?...Nothing is certain, except the nothingness of everything I can conceive, and the majesty of something I cannot understand.

Vogüé contemplated Tolstoy looking coldly down on his own characters and making them dance like marionettes. But behind them he could see more than the human hand which pulled the strings in the novels, but 'something occult and formidable, a shadow of the everpresent infinite – not one of those dogmas, pseudo-definitions of the divine which my nihilism could tear to pieces'. Vogüé described a visit which he paid to St Isaac's Cathedral in St Petersburg. As he went through the doors, he seemed as it were to pass from day to night, into a building so gloomy, and badly lit. Then the doors of the chancel were opened and

a flood of light descends from a great Christ painted in the windows of the apse...It has not the same calm expression given to it by the 'western' to the Son of Man. It is thin, emaciated, fervent, with a wild look in the eyes.

It is the Slavonic Christ, betraying intense human anguish at the loss of a dream unrealized, or that of a God dissatisfied with his divinity. For him all things have not been attained, and the last word has not been spoken. It is, indeed, the face of the god of a people still groping about in darkness, and truthfully represents all their anxieties.[18]

One extraordinary new thing about the Russians was the place of religion in the novel. It was hardly articulated. These novels were distant by all the world from English Victorian novels designed to do good. They were not designed to do good, at least in the same sense of good. They did not preach at all. Religious striving lay inside the texture of the whole book. The authors were like men talking to themselves, answering the doubt which tormented them and then dissatisfied with the answer. They talked to themselves, not in efficiently catalogued western libraries, not within complacent groups of friendly worshippers, but like men alone, amid the limitless space of a steppe with never-ending horizons. They had little time for churches, and one of them, Tolstoy, became for religious reasons the bitterest assailant of churches; as though the true Christian escaped from all organizations which claimed the Christian name and attacked them in the name of Christ. They preferred disorder (Tolstoy preferred anarchy) to order. They rejected not only answers too neat and systems too tidy, but any form of system, as insufficient for the mystery of the world.

A main theme of the Russian voices – and it was heard with intensity by western ears – was the message of contradiction between reason and feeling. These were not ordinary novels, portraying a religious solution to the problem of pain. They proceeded from minds racked in private conflict, and making that conflict public, even trying to reconcile themselves to it by making it public in the novel. The west felt an incongruity, a gulf, between its religious inheritance and its intellectual advance. The Russians portrayed this grief in their own hearts, as a contradiction which was intolerable and yet must be lived with. The *arguments* against God look irrefutable. We cannot live without God. But we cannot live a lie. 'God is necessary', said Kirillov in *The Possessed*. 'So God must exist. But I know he doesn't and can't. Surely you understand that a man with two such ideas cannot go on living.'

Vogüé was the crowning example of a mood to be found all over western Europe during the 1880s and 1890s. That mood was anxious, doubtful of progress, seeing the physical sciences withdraw into the proper field and cease the claim to order all the affairs of men,

concerned over the moral ordering of society, positivists by instinct
and discontented with positivism, part-sure that the churches had
little to offer and part-eager to reconcile the new intelligence with
an ancient inheritance in religious apprehension. It was a different
mood from the mood dominant among French intellectuals in
1871.

It would not do for western Europe, this Russian self-torture.
Were they hunting for the irrational at the expense of reason? – and
whatever else Europe had learnt, it knew that the questions raised
by reason would not go away. Were they questioning, even denying,
that modern civilization was civilized, and were they persuading men
back to the austerities and asceticisms which moderns rejected when
they rejected puritanism, a repudiation of suffering for the sake of
suffering?

But the Russians helped to show western Europe, what it knew
already but had hardly framed, that the positivist system of morality
failed to satisfy at some ultimate point of truth about the human
predicament.

6

The mystery of being existed. Comte affirmed it. He only said that
since we could know nothing about it, we must leave it alone. And
it showed an irksome refusal to be let alone because human beings,
in their inheritance, their mutual relations, their mental attitudes,
and their private agonies, refused to be contained within an affec-
tionate low-key morality of optimism.

No greater contrast could appear between the impact of Comte's
morality and the impact of the Russian novel. Comte was full of
calm acceptance of the world, made better by good men. The Russians were full of a sense of guilt, torment and madness and crucifixion, satanic passion and paradisal innocence, denying God more
for the sake of defying him than for the sake of neglecting him.
Comte was all order, the Russians all disorder. In Comte evil has
a weight of inertia difficult to shift, in Dostoyevsky evil is alive,
driving, possessing. Comte said that humanity was the better part of
humanity. Renan and Strauss said that since men needed religion
and could not have the old religion, they must satisfy their need with
art, with music, with beauty; and religion was therefore of an
élite. The Russians were full of humanity as humanity, madmen,
drunkards, adulterers, condemned to death, for Comte mere animals
('digesting machines'),[14] for Dostoyevsky as precious as any saint.

Marmeladov, drunk in the tavern in *Crime and Punishment*, imagined to the publican all the drunkards being summoned before the judgment seat –

And we shall all come forth without shame and shall stand before him. And he will say to us, 'You are swine; made in the image of the Beast, and bearing his mark – but come to me, you also.' And then the wise men will say, 'Lord, why dost thou receive these men?' And he will say, 'This is why I receive them, O wise men; because not one of them believed himself to be worthy of this.' And he will hold out his hands to us, and we shall fall down before him, . . .and we shall weep. . .and we shall understand all things.

Humanity which is but the better part of humanity, the progressive part, the noble part, the part that will survive to posterity, after all this was not the only humanity that mattered.

10

ON A SENSE OF PROVIDENCE

I have considered two kinds of unsettlement: unsettlement in society, mainly due to new machines, growth of big cities, massive transfer of populations; and unsettlement in minds, rising out of a heap of new knowledge in science and in history, and out of the consequent argument. We saw how easily the two unsettlements merged. Now we pause on a stable element in European society and the European mind. The churches still harnessed the worship and the aspirations of a mass of people, and exercised influence far beyond the edges of their congregations, among many who because of urban habits or rural conflicts sat more lightly to once-accepted customs of church-going.

Naturally, these events made much difference to their internal lives. Bertrand Russell's father tells you that religion is shortly to disappear. Then, if you value your relation to God as source of what is best in you, you feel a little under siege. You close the mind to noise without, and listen to the voice which you hear within. Defenders of Christian orthodoxy looked to their gates, lowered the portcullis, raised the drawbridge and boiled the oil. They had too little consciousness that part of the assault arose out of some of their own principles. And this devotional siege, most powerful in the Ultramontane movement within the Roman Catholic Church, but powerful among Protestants, repelled intelligent men and widened the sense of breach. 'Who among us would be a freethinker', asked Nietzsche with his characteristic excess, 'were it not for the Church?'[1]

Still, religious men knew what they knew. Whatever philosophers might contend, or scientific historians, or anthropologists, or psychologists, religious men and women had God, knew God, obeyed God, felt joy in God, had an experience, an experience of simplicity, surrounded by darkness but still experience. Amid all the perplexing questions they seemed to themselves to do best to have the single eye, or simple regard.

A book is to write on the cult of simplicity in the later nineteenth century. They did not know where they were. Then they felt as though they should return to what they knew to be authentic, the posture of the little child in the gospel. In Catholicism this cult of simplicity begat extraordinary events like the vision at Lourdes. It could be as anti-intellectual as Levin in *Anna Karenina* declaring that all evil comes from the tricks of reason. As an anti-intellectual force it could lead to ecclesiastical disaster, like the suppression of the modernists in 1907 and after, which stamped not only upon errors and wildness but upon the most promising and courageous ways by which Catholics of that generation might aim to meet the intellectual challenges of the age.

To be simple it was not necessary to be anti-intellectual. The Curé d'Ars liked to put on an uneducated accent for the benefit of visitors and was quite proud of having failed the examination before ordination. But he concerned himself not at all with philosophies of the world and just went on with parish work. Thérèse of Lisieux wrote an autobiography so naive in its beauty that she became for a time the centre of the cult of simplicity among some very clever men; but so simple that it was not anti-intellectual, she knew what she knew and described it without conscious art.

This return to the foundation may be seen far outside the borders of Catholicism. For the first time since the Reformation Protestant thinkers concerned themselves with the mystics of the Middle Ages.

> What can I give him
> Poor as I am?
> If I were a shepherd
> I would bring a lamb.
> If I were a wise man
> I would do my part.
> But what I can I give him,
> Give my heart.

Christina Rossetti's poem represents the mood of the childlike, without worrying over intellectual relations or historical scepticism, without trying to write apologies for Christianity or theodicies, loving the three wise men without bothering much whether they happened as St. Matthew said. Why did the reputation of St Francis of Assisi rise so rapidly during the last forty years of the nineteenth century, among Protestants and unbelievers as well as Catholics? Partly because of the new historical consciousness and the resulting interest in the imitation of Christ. Still more because of simplicity. We go back to foundations. We know what we know. Why did the reputation of Joan of Arc rise so rapidly during the last forty years of the nineteenth century? Partly because of French nationalism. But there, too, simplicity. The voices of Domrémy were subjective, nearly everyone agreed they were not 'real' voices. Yet those voices spoke of immediacy in the divine. In an allegedly religious age the English burnt her as a witch; in an allegedly secular age they came to revere her as saint.

In this mood, which was part consciousness of reality in religion, part defensive attitude appropriate (or inappropriate) to an unsettled age, they found, sometimes to their surprise, bridges to the intellectual world that looked so hostile.

2

The reason of the Enlightenment, after jerking its way in the turmoils of revolution, came again into its own, and remade philosophy, and sought to reconstruct society, and to end ancient prejudice and superstition. But its confident mood could not last. Men who expect the impossible run into disillusion. The more they used the reason, the more knowledge they gained; and gaining knowledge was accompanied by its bedfellow, recognition of ignorance. They had thought their confidence due to great learning, and saw now that it sprang from too little learning; that as the questions were solved more questions multiplied. In the reconstruction of thought the old metaphysical questions refused to lie down. In the realm of religion, practice and belief were pertinacious, unexpectedly pertinacious, and showed no sign of vanishing under rational education. In the realm of politics the mighty ideals of liberty and nationalism transformed the states of Europe, their constitutions, societies and frontiers – and still men hungered, and were exploited, and were slaves of unpredictable economic forces, and those ideals of liberty and nationalism were usable, and were used, to clothe the nakedness of power.

'Sad times', Renan represents a philosopher as saying in the park at Versailles in May 1871 – all Frenchmen, not only philosophers, saw May 1871 as sad times – 'is life worth living if we only watch the ruin of everything we have loved? Happy the man who believes like St Augustine in a City of God and can die comforted.' The world, they were sure, was working its purpose out as year succeeds to year, a mysterious purpose, but no mere chain of accidents. *Something* 'unfolds by inner necessity, by unconscious instinct, like the movement of plants towards water or light, or like the blind struggle of an embryo to come out of the womb, or the hidden need which changes the shapes of insects. The world is in travail over *something*.'

Nature propagates species and is careless about individuals. Men live and work and suffer, knowing not why. Something is playing a game at our cost. Nature has a plan to make an unknown end justify these means. To be good is to be deceived. One must be good, but it is not one's interest to be good. To be happy is to be deceived. Seek happiness and you end in disaster, yet you must seek happiness because this is nature's instinct. Said the philosopher in the park at Versailles, I submit. The worst thing of all is to revolt. If everyone grew so educated that they all realized the deceitfulness of goodness and of happiness, life would come to an end. But there will always be men who will sacrifice themselves instinctively, irrationally, for some transcendent reason. There will always be men who believe and who love. It is the duty of wise men, said this wise man, to resign themselves and, while undecided themselves, cooperate in the deceit.

What matter? replied his colleague. 'I saw little tortoises in a ravine in Syria. I knew the ravine was drying out and in two days they would all die. But they did not know it. They were as gay, as alive, as ever.'[2]

Democracy had arrived. Did it depend upon an ethical axiom about the value of each human being? Reason, pure reason, had little use for liberty, equality or fraternity except as temporary slogans or expedients of politicians to gain votes from a crowd. Reason meant Darwin and survival, or Plato and philosopher-kings. What reason could justify pity? In reason, compassion must mean the survival of the least fit. The first fierce reaction against Christian ethics, late in the century, arose from their link with democracy. 'The people have triumphed – slaves, mob, herd, whatever you like to call them – and the Jews caused it. . .Everything is rapidly becoming Judaized, or Christianized, or mob-ized – the word makes no difference.'[3] Physical science did not point to democracy. The moral basis of popular politics appeared to be in glaring contrast with the consequences of scientific progress and evolution.

Renan meditated upon Caliban and Prospero. Caliban had been made Duke of Milan. Prospero knew himself powerless. He ruefully admitted that Caliban in power is more teachable and prudent than anyone could have expected, and if he is tidied and washed will be quite presentable. 'The eternal reason certainly works by means apparently contradictory.' Prospero the wise man resigned himself. The people need illusions. They need religion. They need plenty of amusement. Let them dance and laugh on the bridge at Avignon. To enjoy oneself is a way of being wise. Perhaps, even, if we pursue justice, a little justice will in the end appear in the world. But we shall never get rid of injustice, because it is the fundamental principle by which the universe moves forward.[4]

Renan in old age was melancholy. But literary men may enjoy melancholy and Renan was one of them. Rheumatism was the one blight of his old age. He told a group of young people in 1884 at Tréguier:

I won't tell you how to make your fortunes...But, being near the end of my life, I will tell you something about the art of being happy, because I have succeeded...There is only one recipe: do not look for happiness, but follow a selfless object, knowledge, art, the good of our neighbour, the service of the country...Our happiness is in our power. That is my experience...I've always enjoyed life, I shall not be sad when the end comes, because I've enjoyed it to the full...Life is an excellent thing.[5]

Men were perturbed at this ability in Renan to enjoy philosophical despair. Be good, goodness is all deceit but it is elegant to be good so long as you know you are deceived – the standpoint shocked more serious men. I do not think that any evidence can be found that the attitude could affect ordinary men and women, and therefore it might be said strictly to be not relevant to our subject. To enjoy melancholy is the pride and property of the dilettante, the litterateur, the detached critic, the observer of life and not the participator, the man with a well-lined purse who thinks but need never commit himself. You might say that this brand of pessimism was peculiar to a certain generation of literary critics. Sainte-Beuve, who laid himself open even more than Renan to the charge that he was not serious, practised to perfection in his weekly articles the art of being so uncommitted that it is almost a relief to detect in him traces of a philosophy of pessimism. And yet Renan's delightful insouciance is more attractive to the reader now than the corresponding German earnestness about the illusions of the world as we find it in Schopenhauer or Hartmann. But whether Renan was right or not in thinking hope to be a lie and an illusion, the human race must hope. Hope is a commodity which men and women in the mass cannot do without. Therefore most intellectuals had to be more serious than Renan need pretend to be. Increase happiness, Renan wrote in an attack on the philosophy of pessimism, that is, the sum total of happiness. End the talk of sin, expiation, redemption. Talk of gaiety, tolerance, good humour, resignation. Hopes beyond the grave have begun to vanish. So we must persuade ephemeral beings to regard life as supportable.[6]

Be in tune with the universe – it is the cry of Marcus Aurelius, which Taine and other positivists took to themselves. But if the universe were not in tune? The universe of Isaac Newton turned itself into the universe of Darwin. You might conceive yourself in tune with a benevolent process. It was difficult to be in tune with natural selection. Science and the pantheistic strand in nature sat uncomfortably together in a Darwinian world. Conscience demanded morality, absolute morality. Science, that is the science of the 1870s and 1880s, which some men still conceived as the instrument to settle all the lives of men, conformed to no such demand. 'The antithesis between science and the moral life is probably irreducible', wrote Bourget sadly in December 1882.[7] Be in tune with the universe – and Europe suffered the sensation of discord between the things it longed for and the things that are.

They looked back upon an age, no doubt with the illusion which children suffer if they imagine the time of their parents' youth, when men felt in tune with the universe. This was not all illusion. Some of them, brought up in the Catholic faith, then lost it. Some of them did not mind, to lose it was liberation. But others minded very much. Baudelaire lost his faith; no formal faith, no mere acceptance of another's word, no mere recitation of a creed not understood, he lost a vision, lost an experience which gave every sign of being real. In discarding their faith some men won a new faith – in Science, or Progress, or Humanity, or Liberty. But most could gain no such faith. In jettisoning faith they jettisoned all faith. They inherited the dreams of the romantics, when society would be refashioned in justice. Now the dream was sour, and men were mediocrities, and society refused to be refashioned, and romance died. Anatole France summed up the mood in a sentence: 'We have eaten an apple from the tree of knowledge, and the apple has turned to ashes in our mouths. . .It was sweet to believe, even in hell.'[8]

On 3 June 1845 it was the day of St Clotilde. Auguste Comte sent his beloved Clotilde a letter on the meaning of the Catholic tradition of saints' days. It keeps the memory of good men and women, offers their lives to our admiration, gives each of us a special patron, the man after whom we have a Christian name in baptism, and solemnly invites us to emulation. It fulfils, he wrote, an instinct in our nature, denies death, and joins the succeeding generations in a single society. Positivism has the task of preserving this continuity in mankind. Its temple is wider than the narrow chapel of Rome, for it will remember all who worked for the progress of humanity.[9]

'The worship of the dead', he told Clotilde, 'will become even more popular than under Catholicism.'

'For the philosopher', wrote Diderot, 'posterity is the other world of the religious man.' Nor was Comte's response to the idea of posterity irreligious in content. For it depended, this response, partly on faith in progress, and partly on the sense of God working himself out through the history of humanity, 'realizing himself'; so that men working for the happiness of posterity fulfil the purpose of God for the world.

Can you feel all evolution running through you? You look back, with gratitude to your parents and see how they stemmed from your grandparents, and beyond them the lineage starts to be lost in mist, but your reason knows that the weight of descent is immensely powerful even when your feeling cannot apprehend it; that, as Comte often put it, in humanity the dead are far more numerous than the living. You look forward to your children, and see how they distinguish themselves from you by revolt or by self-development, and wonder what kind of a world it will be when they are old, and whether it will be worse or better, and what problems they will find insoluble. By these acts of mingled reason and feeling you place yourself in the current of a stream of human development, and know a measure of helplessness, and imagine your children's helplessness, and yet are certain that you are not without free will, and hope that you will do what in you lies, for this entity so much greater than yourself.

Clotilde de Vaux was soon to die. Comte sat by her pillow disgusted as the priest, summoned by her family, administered extreme unction. She died on 5 April 1846, and five days later, Comte, founder of the Positivist philosophy, prophet of a scientific world, began daily prayers. Clotilde was dead. But she lived in his heart, the only being in his chequered life to whom he had looked up. 'If Dante could really imagine his Beatrice as the personification of philosophy, it must be easier, and more right, for me to represent my Clotilde as the image of humanity.' Soon he built his Positivist calendar; each year of thirteen months of four weeks, each month under a patron to symbolize one aspect of the progress of man;

Moses for early theocracy, Homer for ancient poetry, St Paul for Catholicism and so on. Every day the new church was to commemorate one great servant of the human race. 31 December is the feast of All Souls, or rather, all the dead. Not to die – that is, to live in the memory, or in the good deeds, of the living. He began, in the dreams of his old age, to plan elaborate funeral rites for the good, take over the Panthéon, plan an altar in the centre with a mother holding a child, no Madonna but a smiling symbol of humanity.[10]

3

An elementary knowledge of primitive religion agreed with the evidence offered willy-nilly by Auguste Comte, that one of the foundations of religion is the memory of the dead; that human beings have need, a hardly avoidable need, to place themselves in a relation to the dead; that they often feel a moral sense of failure if they altogether neglect the dead. The British monuments of the twentieth century which have been uncontroversially national as well as uncontroversially religious have been war memorials of 1902 and 1918 and 1945. Whatever else the human race is going to do without, from old customs of religion, it is not going to do without funerals; which will for always speak not just of another 'place', but (at the lowest) of another set of values, of everything that remains when passions and strife are ended, of a state of being which Christians, but not only Christians, think of as the realm of eternity.

Once the realm of eternity pervaded these lower regions. We must not exaggerate. We must not suffer from the illusion that at any point of time the tiniest flower in the crannied wall spoke to ordinary men about God. We do not read sophisticated pantheism into any past century, for pantheism is by essence sophisticated. But Comte reminds of Queen Clotilde, and humble St Geneviève, and Joan of Arc and the voices of Domrémy. Such voices do not speak only in a world of medieval shepherdesses. In the middle twentieth century T. S. Eliot, than whom none more sophisticated, came melancholy with torment of mind and sleeplessness in the London blitz to the tiny church at Little Gidding, and said his prayers, and something or someone spoke to him, a word felt to come out of deep mystery of being not conceived as earthly. On 31 October 1941 at breakfast time, more than fifty people were burnt to death in a factory fire in Yorkshire, and a few were killed when they jumped from the top storey down to the pavement. That was a long day. I spent all of it seeing burnt skin and the relatives of corpses, the most miserable and most exhausting day of my life. When at last I got home after 11 p.m., dog-tired and empty and wretched, I opened a Bible and found, reluctantly, the lesson for the day. And the words leapt out from the page as though they were illuminated, and swept over the being like a metamorphosis, with relief and refreshment:

The souls of the righteous are in the hand of God; and no torment shall touch them. In the sight of the unwise they seemed to die, and their going from us to be utter destruction. . .Like gold in the fire he put them to the test – and found them acceptable like burnt offering upon the altar.[11]

Such are occasions in men's lives when they get a glimmer of understanding of what happened to Augustine in the garden near Milan, when he heard a voice over the wall, a child's voice perhaps, saying *take and read*; and understood that through the voice divinity spoke to him, telling him to open the Bible and see what he found.

To know when a subjective experience is subjective – is that what is meant by the phrase so common since Weber among sociologists, and so prominent in the argument over secularization, *Entzauberung*, de-magicification, dis-enchantment? Once upon a time the wood was bewitched, and goblins and fair spirits dwelt in the trunks of trees and among the roots. But now the wood is administered by the Forestry Commission, and although romantic men still hear a goblin running in the undergrowth and glimpse beauty behind a bush, they know when a subjective experience is subjective. *Entzauberung*.

It will not do to exaggerate the number of goblins that used to run. You need to beware of the word *Entzauberung* as cautiously as you beware of the word *secularization*. Both describe processes where it is easy to have fanciful pictures of an earlier age, and as easy to have illusions of our own generation. We got rid of imps and demons but we pushed them into the subconscious and called them by different names. We got rid of witches by learning to take no notice of their spells.

Something happened to religious people which affected their attitude to the world; I do not say for better or worse, for gain or for loss; a change in attitude remotely comparable to the change when Greek philosophy became available to the schoolmen, or to the change when the Renaissance altered men's attitudes to humanity. We may have less sense of providence in our lives.

4

In October 1870 the city of Paris lay under siege, bombardment and famine. Preaching at Radcliffe early in October 1870, Bishop Fraser of Manchester – a rational and remarkable bishop – preached a sermon on the dread fate of Paris. A shorthand writer made a summary of what he said.

He referred to the wonderful development in Paris of vice, libertinism, and profligacy. He said: 'splendid and beautiful as Paris was architecturally, social and political immorality had long been eating at its heart, so that it had become a moral plague-spot in Europe.' He desired to avoid sitting in judgment over the unfortunate city, but it was difficult to help seeing that in regard to it the story of Sodom and Gomorrah was being repeated. It mattered little whether the instruments of judgment were fire and brimstone from heaven, or the shot and shell of a hostile army. The effect was the same in both cases.

When this was reported in the newspapers, Bishop Fraser was criticized. He gave a corrected text of his sermon, but the corrected text said very little different from the report.[12]

Here was a direct sense of God's intervention in the daily events of life. We are still in the world which Voltaire accused, when he dealt with the Lisbon earthquake. You cannot now imagine more than one or two odd preachers preaching a sermon on the judgment on the occasion of some air disaster. But in the sixties of the last century, if there were a great train crash, the occasion was at once the subject of sermons, whether to remind men of judgment and of mortality, or to attempt some theodicy of providence and suffering.

Let us try to test a little further how or whether a sense of providence changes.

Natural disasters, like the Lisbon earthquake in Voltaire's time, are events which force men to ask questions about suffering, especially the suffering of the innocent. Western Europe of the later nineteenth century was not accustomed to vast natural disasters. But its nearest events were the calamities of accidents, leading to multiple deaths known otherwise only in war. Let us try a sample test and see what we find. I select shipwrecks: three different shipwrecks of 1870, 1875 and 1912; let us see whether reaction to these calamities bears upon our theme.

On the night of 6–7 September 1870 a cruiser squadron of the

British fleet sailed by Cape Finisterre in a storm. When dawn broke one of the warships, *H.M.S. Captain*, had vanished. Later eighteen survivors got ashore on the Spanish coast near Corunna, and the searching warships found pieces of wreckage. *Captain* was the first of the heavily armed turret-ships, newly invented; still with sails as well as steam, to make her ocean-going, but top-heavy with the first swivelling gun-turrets. Her inventor was aboard when she heeled over in a gust, went on heeling over, capsized and sank. Nearly 600 men drowned.

On the following Sunday the preacher in St Paul's Cathedral, who happened in normal course to be H. P. Liddon, delivered a sermon on providence.[13] God is no subject of the laws which he has made for the world. He has made laws of nature and is revealed by them, but he is master of them. Man is no insignificant toy, the sport of death and of accident. God numbers the hairs of his head; and if objectors say that man is tiny in so vast a universe, let us remember that physical size is nothing, that moral stature is of far more weight, that the ability to conceive God and love him, not like an animal but with an immortal soul, is that which has the quality of grandeur.

So Liddon gave his hearers an elementary theodicy; a movement towards justifying the ways of God to man; leading them to conceive that his guidance is all about us, and though we see no meaning in such a calamity as the sinking of the *Captain*, we know that it is within the providence of eternal purpose.

Just over five years later a ship of German emigrants, the *Deutschland*, left Bremerhaven for New York. The same night, which was the night of 5–6 December 1875, she drove in a snowstorm upon the Kentish Knock just north of the mouth of the Thames, smashing the propeller. During the following day they had great difficulty getting their rockets observed; and when they were observed Harwich had no life-boat. During the following night the ship sank with the loss of 78 out of 213 people aboard. Five of the drowned were Westphalian nuns fleeing from the Kulturkampf in Germany. They clasped hands and drowned together.

Of Catholic commentators: Archbishop Manning, who became a cardinal that year, preached at the funeral of the five nuns in Leytonstone. He made no theodicy. He was simple, and grateful.[14] It is not important that there was no theodicy. If there is any place in the world where the temptation to justify the ways of God to man is misplaced, it is a graveside.

In his college on the border of North Wales Gerard Manley Hopkins was moved by the accounts in *The Times*, especially by the five nuns. He had written no poetry since he became a Jesuit. His rector gave a not delicate hint that he would like someone to write a poem. So came *The Wreck of the Deutschland*, certainly the greatest Catholic poem in the English language on the theme of suffering and sudden death. He offered it to the Jesuit journal *The Month*, which refused to publish it mainly because of what they described as its 'oddnesses'. Robert Bridges eventually published it in 1918, many years after Hopkins' death. It only became famous after 1930, when Charles Williams published another edition.

It is a kind of theodicy. But that is misleading, for there is nothing philosophical about it, nothing plain about providence. The deaths are taken at once into a poem about the meaning of suffering and life in the world to come; a flicker here which is all of mortal life, the ship sailing outward from Bremen towards eternity though no one knew that the destination was eternity, snowflakes falling in the storm transfigured into showers of lilies strewn by angels from heaven, the descent into the waves transformed into the journey of a soul towards purification, the taking of the worst environment and turning it into the best, misery into nobility, meaninglessness into purpose. It is only a cry of faith; and yet behind the cry of faith is a deeply religious kind of theodicy, with its claim to purpose for suffering in the world.

Now the latest of the three shipwrecks: on a starry night of April 1912 *Titanic* hit an iceberg south of Newfoundland on its maiden voyage and of the 2,200 people aboard only 705 were rescued.

We find ourselves in a different atmosphere; not a less religious atmosphere, for the coverage by the press of this disaster was more religious in tone than the coverage of the sinking of the *Captain* nearly forty-two years before – still, a different kind of atmosphere. After horror, the first thought that entered the heads of several commentators was judgment. The pride of man; he believed that science conquered nature, and after all man is puny when confronted with elemental force. The *Titanic* was declared unsinkable – and sank in a few hours. 'Is it megalomania at its worst thus in superlative self-confidence to have surpassed all others?'[15] They almost felt it to have been a sin like the Tower of Babel; a monster effort at material luxury, £780 for the most expensive cabins, and just that week the miners' strike for a wage of 30 shillings a week desolated the country. One cabin for six days equal to ten men's wages for a year. 'Whatever other lesson should be learnt', we read, 'this seems to be written in searing lines on ice-floe and curling wave-crest – "Whosoever exalteth himself shall be abased and he that humbleth himself shall be exalted." '[16] 'Has the world', asked Canon Newbolt in St Paul's Cathedral, 'has the world, the old enemy, intoxicated with its progress, forgotten God?' Men wrote to the newspapers protesting against this opinion of catastrophes.

In 1870 Liddon came near, as far as the limitations of a pulpit permit, to a genuine kind of theodicy, a theology of providence. In 1912 many commentators were just as traditional in their attitudes, in some cases even more traditional. We cannot detect that the theological attitude to natural disasters changed markedly during the decades that concern us. The difference in tone is striking. Use the occasion to denounce science and materialism – that suggests a little pressure which was not so present forty years before. But this could be wholly due to the difference of circumstance, where the great ship which sank seemed the symbol of a capitalist society of luxurious competition. No one could do for *Titanic* what Hopkins did for *Deutschland*. But the reason for that is not difficult to discern – the interest of a lone genius.

The *Titanic* reports do show one thing important to us: a distancing of God from the detail of human disaster; a determination not to hold God responsible for human error in the design of elaborate machinery. The trenches of 1914 to 1918 and the suffering in them insisted terribly on this notion of distance between God and human error.

Was all this a change in the theory of providence as Calvinism continued its steady decline through the nineteenth century? Why did Calvinism steadily decline? Why was Spurgeon the last Calvinist to be eminent among English religious leaders, and he a moderate Calvinist? We cannot diagnose the decline of a sense of providence by saying that Calvinism declined. We should rather explain the decline of Calvinism by the decline of providence than the other way round.

And yet – put the question another way round, and ask this: was it more difficult in 1900 than in 1800, was it a bigger act of faith by 1900 than by 1800, to trust that all the hairs of your head are numbered, and that not a sparrow shall fall to the ground without purpose? For all the shipwrecks and railway accidents, for all of natural selection or Marxist theory, it is not certain that the answer to that question is in the affirmative. It may be so. It is easy to think of reasons why it might be so. In logic, perhaps, it ought to be so. It is not clear that it was so. Did the faith in God's care even of sparrows rest solely upon the authority of a single teacher whose words are recorded in the New Testament, words which by 1900 were regarded as less immediately authoritative than in 1800? Or did it rest upon its intrinsic quality as natural outgrowth of a religious attitude to the world, *the* religious attitude to the world, unshaken by Lisbon earthquake or wreck of the *Deutschland*, because it had roots in human nature; an attitude to which Jesus gave the fairest expression?

H. P. Liddon was a sophisticated Victorian who for all his sophistication pressed himself to believe all the miracles of the Old Testament, even to the sun standing still upon Gibeon. Yet the interesting thing is that religiously they did not matter. They mattered to him theologically, because otherwise the authority of the Old Testament would be diminished, and, if that happened, the authority of the Church would be diminished. But what mattered to him religiously was God in all phenomena, not God in exceptional and strange phenomena. 'God will not', he told his people,

be in our eyes more certainly the ruler of the spheres when at his bidding the stars shall fall from heaven than he is now, when 'the heavens declare the glory of God'...Great catastrophes (he was still thinking of the shipwreck) may, and do, from time to time recall man's earthbound soul to the ordinary processes of growth and decay, of disease and death, he 'worketh hitherto'; nay with us, as with Elijah, it may be that the still small voice manifests his presence, amid the repose of order, rather than in the earthquake and the fire.[17]

Here was the blessing of the natural order. It would be easy to provide many illustrations from Christian thinkers of the later nineteenth century, in all countries and all churches. For Renan to believe in the supernatural was like believing in ghosts. For Maurice to believe in the supernatural was seeing the natural in the perspective of eternity. The question is, whether the exceptional quality ascribed to events or things in the dawn of humanity was the only way to perception of the sacred? Was this movement from unusual to usual a deprivation, so that if all the world is supernatural nothing is supernatural and everything is dis-enchanted? Or was it an insight, like seeing that because Sunday is a holy day all days are holy days, or that because an altar is a holy table for a holy meal all tables and all meals are holy?

5

The word *secularization* began as an emotive word, not far in its origins from the word *anticlericalism*. Sometimes it meant a freeing of the sciences, of learning, of the arts, from their theological origins or theological bias. Sometimes it meant the declining influence of churches, or of religion, in modern society. Then the sociologists, heirs of Comte, aided by certain historians and anthropologists, did a service by showing how deep-seated religion is in humanity and in the consensus which makes up society. They therefore made the word unemotional; a word used to describe a process, whatever that process was, in the changing relationship between religion and modern society, a process arising in part out of the industrial revolution and the new conditions of urban and mechanical life, in part out of the vast growth in new knowledge of various kinds. Modern sociologists (and others) have not always kept the word to this unemotional plane. Sometimes they have used it as a word of propaganda. This is because this study is like trying to write the history of the Reformation in the year 1650 – everyone is still committed.

This question of emotion in meaning is not trivial. It is easy for religious men to use the word *secularization* like a lamentation of Jeremiah; as a way of harking back, of yearning for a promised land which they once occupied and from which they are expelled. Religious men are not going to get far if they refuse to see some element of a clearer apprehension of the world and its independence. Religion can include many different qualities. It is hard to find among those qualities the quality of retrospective brooding. If the word secularization is going to mean a lament, then we must beg men of religion not to use it.

But there is no need for the word to be used in that sense. It describes an objective process, still obscure in its causes and consequences but a matter of history. I will seek to define it in these terms: 'the relation (whatever that is, which can only be known by historical enquiry) in which modern European civilization and society stands to the Christian elements of its past and the continuing Christian elements of its present'.[18]

No historian can blind himself to the force of continuity. Let us go back to the Panthéon in Paris, still with its cross upon the top, but still with the cold empty spaces of a national laicized memorial, cleared within of religious symbols and usages.

In the centre under the void of the dome, vacant spiritually as well as physically, Auguste Comte, the positivist, the philosopher of science, wanted to put a new goddess where the old altar used to be; a new mother cherishing a new child; Humanity caring. That was sign of a sense that all was not well with emptiness, that the human spirit could not accept vacancy, somewhere was conscience and its ideals and aspirations. But what the later nineteenth century seemed to show was that no new Madonna would serve; that (if you did not want a museum or a car park) the only image which would serve was the former little child, at the breast of the former Madonna; understood in a new way, surrounded now not only by a fresco of St Geneviève but by an unprofaned Voltaire as well as an unprofaned Fénelon. Once the human race has an experience which it has found to be in part authentic, it does not let go.

The historian knows how powerless are revolutions. Men chop off the king's head and remake the constitution and declare that it is the year one; and at the end the historian sees how like new is to old, and how Stalin's political police are but the Tsar's political police with an equal tyranny, secrecy and inefficiency. The historian's vocation is to see continuity, and he therefore meets temptation to underestimate change. We will destroy Asclepios and build a temple of Christian faith. But the sick and maimed still need healing, so St Nicholas will cure the sufferers who once came to lie at Asclepios's feet. We will abolish the cathedral and turn Notre Dame into a temple of reason. We will set the goddess Liberty on the pedestal where once St George cut shackles from a maiden. We will have a Religion of Humanity; and at the end we shall find that there, back on the plinth and blushing because of the glare of modern arc lights, is still the blessed Mother of God, looking down with affection and prophetic pity upon her child that will suffer to free men from an inner bondage.

The historian knows how powerless are revolutions. And therefore he might underestimate change and fail to mention that something irreversible happened to the past; that though the instinct of religion might be as powerful as ever, and men use hallowed words to express it, yet they begin to understand those words in a new way, often a radically different way. Umbrella terms, however doubtful, are useful. I do not think it an abuse of such a term to call this radical process, still in part so obscure to the enquirer, still in part undefined and possibly in part undefinable, by the name of secularization; on the one condition (and it is an absolute condition) that the word is used, neither as the lament of nostalgia for past years, nor as propaganda to induce history to move in one direction rather than another, but simply as a description of something that happened to European society in the last two hundred years. And what happened, and why, must still be matter for much enquiry by students of history and religion and society.

NOTES TO THE TEXT

NOTES TO INTRODUCTION

1. David Martin, *The Religious and the Secular* (1969), 1, 16, 22.
2. Ibid. 31.
3. J. Delumeau, *Entre Luther et Voltaire* (Paris, 1971), 319, 330.
4. Talcott Parsons, *The Structure of Social Action*, 2nd ed. (1961), 427.
5. Daniel Mornet, *Les origines intellectuelles de la révolution française* (Paris, 1933), 25, 53. Mersenne's figure is in a colophon to *Quaestiones in Genesim*, 1st ed. (1623), 669–74; including as 'atheists' Machiavelli, Charron, Fludd, Vanini, i.e. anyone of 'impious' opinions. He removed the colophon in a second edition.
6. Adrien Dansette, *Histoire religieuse de la France contemporaine*, 2nd ed. (Paris, 1965), 281–2.
7. Heinrich Hermelink, *Das Christentum in der Menschheitsgeschichte* (Stuttgart, 1955), II, ix.
8. Vernon Pratt, *Religion and Secularisation* (1970).
9. A. MacIntyre, *Secularization and Moral Change* (1967).
10. *Guardian* (1905), 1065, 1026.
11. Friedrich Engels, *Socialism, Utopian and Scientific*, preface to first English edition, xiv; cited by MacIntyre, op. cit. 9.

NOTES TO CHAPTER TWO

1. Edward Irving, *Babylon* (1826), 1, iii, 246; J. H. Newman, *Apologia pro Vita Sua*, ed. Svaglic (1967), 174; quoted OED *s.v.*; *Syllabus Errorum* (1864), no. 80.
2. Cf. *Syllabus* (1864), no. 60.
3. J. S. Mill, *On Liberty*, ed. H. B. Acton (1972), 13.
4. Ibid. 73.
5. J. S. Mill, *Autobiography* (World's Classics ed.), 89.
6. *On Liberty*, ed. cit. 79, 83.
7. M. Cowling, *Mill and Liberalism* (1963).
8. *On Liberty*, ed. cit. 124.
9. Hegel, *Über die wissenschaftlichen Behandlungsarten des Naturrechts, Werke*, 1 (1832), 400; F. H. Bradley, *Ethical Studies* (1927), 200, 173.
10. J. B. Bury, *History of Freedom of Thought*, end.
11. Fitzjames Stephen, *Liberty, Equality, Fraternity*, ed. R. J. White (1967), 94, 100–1.
12. David Hume, 'On the Liberty of the Press', in *Essays, Moral Political and Literary* (World's Classics ed.), 12, note.
13. *Church Congress Report* (1896), 460; (1893), 501.
14. *History of the Times*, 2, 269, 479; Claude Bellanger, *Histoire générale*

de la presse française (Paris, 1969–), 2, 281. The anonymous author of
Perversion was W. J. Conybeare. For its low view of the morality of
the press, see vol. II, 325ff. The *Times* review of it is in the issue of
14 October 1856 and runs to more than 2½ columns.

15. So Karl Marx, review in the *Rheinische Zeitung* on the press debate
    in the sixth Rhineland Landtag at Düsseldorf, *Werke*, 1 (1964), 60.
16. Bellanger, op. cit. 3, 240ff.
17. MacIntyre, *Secularization and Moral Change*, 54.
18. *Church Congress Report* (1893), 504.
19. *History of the Times*, 2, 468, 478–9, 491, 518 note. For the R.V., *The
    Times*, 12, 17, 25 May, 6 June 1881. Wace's review, 17 May 1881;
    Newman's *Grammar*, 21 April 1870, 10.
20. Wickham Steed, *Through Thirty Years* (1924), 1, 1–2.
21. 20 July 1920: Bellanger, op. cit. 3, 578.
22. *The Victorian Crisis of Faith*, ed. Anthony Symondson (1970), 102.
23. Stephen, *Liberty, Equality, Fraternity*, 119.
24. Ibid. 71; 78–9; 105; cf. J. N. Figgis, *Churches in the Modern
    State*, 2nd ed. (1914), 115, on the need of a society for 'directing
    ideas'.
25. Walter Lippmann, *Public Opinion* (1922), 15–16.
26. Lecky, *Democracy and Liberty* (1896), 2, 26–30.
27. E. Faguet, *Le Libéralisme* (Paris, 1902), 121.

NOTES TO CHAPTER THREE

1. D'Holbach, *Le Christianisme dévoilé* (1767), 226. For history of the
   notion, cf. Werner Post, *Kritik der Religion bei Karl Marx* (1971),
   166ff. H. Gollwitzer, *The Christian Faith and the Marxist Criticism of
   Religion*, Eng. trans. (1970), 15–16. For the *Einundzwanzig Bogen*
   (= twenty-one sheets) and Hess, see Edmund Silberner, *Moses Hess*
   (Leyden, 1966), 123ff.; Text in Moses Hess, *Sozialistische Aufsätze
   1841–7*, ed. Theodor Zlocisti (Berlin, 1921), 37ff.
2. D. McLellan, *Marx before Marxism* (1970), 43ff. H. Monz, *Karl
   Marx und Trier* (Trier, 1964, Schriftenreihe zur Trierischen Landes-
   geschichte und Volkskunde, 12), 134ff.
3. Letter in *Frühe Schriften*, eds H. J. Lieber and Peter Furth (Stuttgart,
   1962), I, 7. Eleanor Marx says that Karl Marx always carried with him a
   photograph of his father, McLellan, ibid. 32. But father died too
   early to have been photographed. If Karl carried a photograph, it
   must have been the photograph of a portrait.
4. Words of the school report (by J. A. Küpper) in Monz, op. cit. 151.
5. English translation in *Marx–Engels Collected Works*, 1 (1975).
6. E. Barnikol, *Bruno Bauer: Studien und Materialien: aus dem Nachlass
   ausgewählt* (Assen, 1972).
7. *Frühe Schriften*, I, 107–9; McLellan, *Karl Marx: Early Texts*, 23ff:
   Luther as Judge between Strauss and Feuerbach. The article was not
   published till 1843.
8. H. R. Mackintosh, *Types of Modern Theology*, 130.
9. K. Marx to Arnold Ruge, 30 November 1842; *Marx–Engels Gesam-*

tausgabe, I, i (2), 286; Eng. trans. in McLellan, *Karl Marx: Early Texts*, 53.

10. *Deutsch-französische Jahrbücher*, 182-214; *Frühe Schriften*, I, 451-87; Eng. trans. in McLellan, *Karl Marx: Early Texts*, 85ff. The article was written in autumn 1843.

11. A term of Feuerbach; man is distinguished from animals in being conscious of himself as one of a species.

12. *Karl Marx: Early Texts*, 99.

13. E.g. E. H. Carr, *Marx*, 1; E. Kamenka, 'The Baptism of Karl Marx', in *Hibbert Journal* LVI (1958), 340-51; E. Kamenka, *The Ethical Foundations of Marxism*, 2nd ed. (1972), 28-31. For 'the criticism of religion' etc., *Frühe Schriften*, I, 497.

14. 'Der Kommunismus des *Rheinischen Beobachters*': *Marx-Engels, Gesamtausgabe*, I, 6, 278; Marx-Engels, *On Religion* (Moscow, 1957), 83.

15. *The German Ideology*, ed. R. Pascal (rev. ed. 1940), 14; *Werke* (Berlin, 1962), 3, 26-7.

16. *Economic and Philosophical Mss. of 1844*, in McClellan, *Karl Marx: Early Texts*, 149.

17. The address was given in English but published in German in the *Sozialdemokrat* of 22 March 1883: Marx-Engels, *Werke* (Berlin, 1962), 19, 335.

18. Cf. H. Desroche, *Marxisme et religions* (Paris, 1962), 61.

19. *Deutsche-Brüsseler Zeitung*, 12 September 1847, 'Der Kommunismus des *Rheinischen Beobachters*'; *Marx-Engels Gesamtausgabe*, I, 6, 278.

20. *Marx-Engels Gesamtausgabe*, I, 5, 227.

21. H. Desroche, *Socialismes et sociologie religieuse* (Paris, 1966), 201 nn. 15-16.

22. *Marx-Engels Gesamtausgabe*, I, 2, 465ff.

23. Ibid. I, 2, 485ff.

24. Engels to F. Graeber, 27 July 1839; ibid. I, 2, 532: the other was Schleiermacher.

25. Ibid. I, 2, 426; *Die Lage Englands*, on Carlyle's *Past and Present*.

26. Marx-Engels, *On Religion*, 141; Marx-Engels, *Werke* (Berlin, 1964), 18, 531.

27. *Marx-Engels Gesamtausgabe*, I, 2, 435-49; originally in *New Moral World*, November 1843.

28. Engels, 'Continental Socialism', in *New Moral World*, October 1844; Marx-Engels, *Werke* (Berlin, 1962), 2, 507.

29. Engels, *Beschreibung der in neuerer Zeit entstandenen und noch bestehenden Kommunistischen Ansiedlungen*; commented by Desroche, *Socialismes et sociologie religieuse*, 90ff.; Marx-Engels *Werke*, 2, 521.

30. See above, n. 28.

31. Saint-Simon, *Oeuvres* (1966), III, 109, 113, 115, 117 etc.

32. Cabet, *Vrai Christianisme*, 628-9; quoted Desroche, *Socialismes*, 134 n. 53.

33. Wilhelm Weitling, 1808-71: tailor; liberal views took him to Paris where he formed 'The League of the Proscribed'. He owed something to Lamennais and translated his *The Book of the People* into German:

in Switzerland, 1841–3, when he was arrested and expelled; founded the first German Communist newspaper; visited Britain; met Marx in Brussels 1846 and quarrelled with him; went to New York; took part in the German revolution of 1848 but was expelled after its failure and returned to New York. *The Gospel of the Poor Sinner* has an Eng. trans., 1969.

34. Post, *Kritik der Religion bei Karl Marx*, 118.
35. E.g. *Neuer Social-Demokrat*, 1872, 38: among press illustrations in R. Schuster, *Die Social-Demokratie im Spiegel ihrer eigenen Presse* (Stuttgart, 1875), 174–5.
36. *Volkstaat*, 1873, 32: Schuster, 177; *Volkstaat*, 1872, 103: Schuster, 186; *Volkstaat*, 1872, 56: Schuster, 189.
37. Bebel's speech *Stenographische Berichte über die Verhandlungen des Deutschen Reichstages*, xxv, 1082; cf. Bebel, *Aus meinem Leben* (Stuttgart, 1920), ii, 256, 254. For occasional modifications by Bebel of his views, see Franz Klühs, *August Bebel* (Berlin, 1923), 112–25.
38. *Volkstaat*, 1874, 38; Schuster, 178.
39. *Volkstaat*, 1874, 25; Schuster 179; cf. ibid 181. The most intellectual of the socialist-materialist leader-writers was J. Dietzgen; for whom see H. Roland-Holst, *Josef Dietzgens Philosophie gemeinverständlich erläutert in ihrer Bedeutung für das Proletariat* (Munich, 1910)
40. J. Rae, *Contemporary Socialism* (1901), 42–3; F. S. Nitti, *Catholic Socialism* (1895), 383.
41. E. Milhaud, *La Democratie socialiste allemande* (Paris, 1903), 254ff.
42. W. O. Shanahan, *German Protestants Face the Social Question*, i (1954), 325 n. 37; Goehre, *Three Months in a Workshop* (Eng. trans., 1895), original German edition, 1891.
43. Goehre, *Wie ein Pfarrer Sozialdemokrat wurde*, 2nd ed. (Berlin, 1900); extracts in Milhaud, *La Démocratie socialiste allemande*, 256ff.; for Goehre's career, see *Neue Deutsche Biographie*, 6, 513. He did not combine Christianity and socialism long. By 1906 he urged everyone to leave the churches. Blumhardt's consistory expelled him from his parish when he joined the party. His Christianity remained powerful to the end of his life, and he was not without influence on Karl Barth; career in *Neue Deutsche Biographie*, 2, 334–5.
44. Józef Chmura [Rosa Luxemburg], *Kósciól a socjalizm;* it was provoked by the Russian revolution of 1905: Russian edition of 1920, French of 1937, Eng. trans. from French in *Rosa Luxemburg Speaks*, ed. M. A. Waters (New York, 1970), 132ff. The Trotskyists in modern Ceylon have almost canonized it as a text, cf. J. P. Nettl, *Rosa Luxemburg* (1966), i, 323. She disliked Trotsky.
45. Rae, *Contemporary Socialism*, 254.
46. Gollwitzer, *Christian Faith and Marxist Criticism of Religion*, 131, n. 8.
47. *Annales du Sénat et du Corps Législatif* (Paris, 1868), x, 14; J. McManners, *Church and State in France, 1870–1914* (1972), 18.

NOTES TO CHAPTER FOUR

1. E. Royle, *Victorian Infidels* (Manchester, 1974), 89, 92.
2. W. N. Molesworth, *History of England* (1874), II, 236; Royle, 233. I owe thanks to Dr Royle for allowing me to see his evidence and conclusions before they were published.
3. *Christianity and Secularism: report of the public discussion between the Reverend Brewin Grant and G. J. Holyoake*, (1854), 4; Royle, 151–2.
4. *Reasoner*, e.g. 25 June 1851, XI, 87–8; 14 January 1852, XII, 129–31; cf. Royle, 155. According to Holyoake himself, the word *secularist* was first used to signify a way of thinking in the *Reasoner* of 3 December 1851 (XII, 34), and the word *secularism* first appeared in the press a week later (*Reasoner*, XII, 62); cf. Holyoake, *The Origin and Nature of Secularism* (1896), 51–2.
5. Royle, 188.
6. W. L. Arnstein, *The Bradlaugh Case* (Oxford, 1965), 288–9; using British Museum Add. Mss. 44481, 38; for Bradlaugh's dress, D. H. Tribe, *President Charles Bradlaugh M.P.* (1971), 58.
7. Cf. D. M. Thompson, 'The Churches and Society in Leicestershire 1851–1881' (unpublished Cambridge thesis), 1969.
8. K. Schmaltz, *Kirchengeschichte Mecklenburgs*, III (1952), 391ff.
9. G. W. E. Russell, *Arthur Stanton* (1917), 72; J. H. S. Kent in *The Victorian City*, eds Dyos and Wolff (1973), 866.
10. E. R. Wickham, *Church and People in an Industrial City* (1957), 146–147.
11. McManners, *Church and State in France, 1870–1914*, 6–7.
12. de Broglie, *Le Présent et l'avenir du Catholicisme en France* (1892); McManners, 7–8.
13. Royle, *Victorian Infidels*, 184.
14. Owen Chadwick, *The Victorian Church*, II, 268; for the general theme see now especially Hugh MacLeod, *Religion and Class in the Victorian City* (1974).
15. Voltaire, *Œuvres complètes*, ed. L. Moland (Paris, 1877–85), XXVI, 511–12.
16. Geoffrey Rowell, *Hell and the Victorians* (1974), 119ff.; Pusey to Tait in Rowell, 120.
17. Ibid. 149, from the F. W. Farrar papers.
18. Ibid. 148–9, from the Farrar papers.
19. George Lansbury, *My Life* (1928), 28.
20. H. Pirenne, *Histoire de Belgique*, VII, 290.

NOTES TO CHAPTER FIVE

1. A. Debidour, *L'Eglise Catholique et l'État sous la troisième République (1870–1906)*, I (Paris, 1906), 42 n. 2.
2. Daniel Mornet, *Les origines intellectuelles de la Révolution française* (Paris, 1933), 154.
3. *Guardian* (1865), 96.
4. *Guardian* (1874), 438.

5. Liddon, *Passiontide Sermons* (1883), 274.
6. Georges Weill, *Histoire de l'idée laïque en France au XIXe siècle*, new ed. (1929), 75. But Guizot was so much moved by the Syllabus and its aftermath as to declare that Christianity and liberty are necessary to each other; cf. his *Christianity Viewed in Relation to the Present State of Society and Opinion*, Eng. trans., (1871).
7. *Acta Sanctae Sedis*, XI (1878), 370, 372.
8. *Annales du Sénat et de la Chambre des Députés*, IX (1879), 294; a much interrupted speech on an enquiry into his own election.
9. Carl Sarasin, in W. O. Shanahan, *German Protestants face the Social Question*, 1 (Notre Dame, 1954), 335.
10. Public Record Office, F. O. 912/84, 66, crown copyright.
11. Peyrat was said to have said this in 1864, the year of the Syllabus. But it has been doubted whether he actually said it. Gambetta may have misremembered a phrase in a letter from Peyrat of April 1863 to the newspaper *Temps*. Cf. Guy Chapman, *The Third Republic of France* (1962), 171; J. P. T. Bury, *Gambetta* (1973), 70 note.
12. *Guardian* (1874), 650.
13. E. M. Fraser, *Le renouveau religieux d'après le roman français de 1886 à 1914* (1934), 78.
14. *Summa*, II, 2, q. 101, art. 1.
15. E. Faguet, *Le Libéralisme* (Paris 1903), 114.
16. F. A. Isambert, *Christianisme et classe ouvrière* (Paris 1961), 154, 165, 171–2; and four essays in T. Zeldin (ed.), *Conflicts in French Society* (1970); R. R. Locke, *French Legitimists and the Politics of Moral Order* (Princeton, 1974); numerous helpful articles in the *Archives de sociologie religieuse*.
17. McManners, *Church and State in France, 1870–1914*, 6.
18. Debidour, *Eglise Catholique*, I, 175.
19. BM, Add. Mss. 44249/282.
20. Debidour, I, 158 note, 171.
21. E.g. Carlton Hayes, *A Generation of Materialism, 1871–1900* (New York 1941), 135.
22. E. Kedourie, *Nationalism*, 3rd ed. (1966), 106, 119, 133. Cf. Georges Weill, *L'Europe du XIXe siècle et l'idée de nationalité* (Paris, 1938), 4–6, 304.
23. McManners, *Church and State*, 41; cf. also Gladstone's controversy over the Vatican Decrees in 1874–5.
24. Treitschke, *Politics*, Eng. trans. (1916), I, 334–5.
25. H. W. C. Davis, *The Political Thought of Heinrich von Treitschke* (1914), 32, using Treitschke, *Briefe* (1912–13), 2, no. 407.
26. Fichte, *Werke*, XI (Bonn, 1835), 423; from *Über Machiavelli als Schriftsteller*; G. Ritter, *The Sword and the Sceptre*, Eng. trans. of 3rd revised ed. (1972), I, 208. See also F. Meinecke, *Cosmopolitanism and the National State*, Eng. trans. (Princeton, 1970), 71ff.
27. Hegel, *Grundlinien der Philosophie des Rechtes* (1821), paras 257–8, 270, 324; Ritter, I, 208–9.
28. Hermann Heller, *Hegel und der nationale Machtstaatsgedanke in Deutschland* (1921) (reprinted 1963), 199–201.

29. Hans Schleier, *Sybel und Treitschke* (Berlin, 1965), 107.
30. F. Meineke, *Machiavellism* (*Der Idee der Staatsräson*, 1924), Eng. trans. (1957), 395.
31. Lecky thought the conception very important and believed it also to be the 'central principle' of Buckle's *History of Civilization* and of his own early work *Leaders of Public Opinion*; cf. *Letters of Lecky*, 41–2, 44–5; *Influence of Rationalism*, 2, chapter 5.
32. F. Hayward, *Le dernier siècle de la Rome pontificale*, 2 (1928), 113; F. Hayward, *Pie IX*, 85.
33. Peter Berger, *The Social Reality of Religion* (Penguin, 1973); first published in America as *The Sacred Canopy* (1967): 116ff.; 126, 129, 159.
34. Berger appealed for this line of thought to origins in Max Weber, *The Protestant Ethic and the Spirit of Capitalism*, Troeltsch on the significance of Protestantism for the modern world, Karl Holl's *The Cultural Significance of the Reformation*, Eng. trans., 19.

NOTES TO CHAPTER SIX

1. Boswell, *Life of Johnson* (Oxford, 1946), I, 227, 339, 419; II, 199, 251, 269, 312, 419.
2. D.N.B., *s.v.* David Williams (1738–1816); Hugh Downman.
3. Byron, *Childe Harold's Pilgrimage*, III, 100, 106, etc. For the whole background, Harold Orel, 'English Romantic Poets and the Enlightenment', in *Studies on Voltaire and the Eighteenth Century*, ed. Theodore Besterman (1973).
4. Henry Brougham, *Men of Letters in the Time of George III* (1845), I, 132–3. The *Quarterly Review*, LXXVI (1845), 62ff., thought all this far too lenient.
5. R. W. Jelf, *Grounds for laying before the Council of King's College, London, certain statements...by the Rev. F. D. Maurice, M.A.*, 3rd ed. (1853), 11.
6. *Encyclopaedia Britannica* (1810), *s.v.* Europe.
7. Ibid. 8th ed., *s.v.* Voltaire, 665–70.
8. James Gillman, *Life of Coleridge* (1838), 23–4.
9. E. Abbott and L. Campbell, *Life and Letters of Jowett* (1897), II, 38, 293.
10. *Fraser's Magazine* (1872), v, 678.
11. V. Conzemius, *Döllingers Briefwechsel* (Munich, 1971), III, 308; cf. III, 259 and 316. The change already began in the 1860s: e.g. Lecky, *Influence of Rationalism* (1865), I, 106, 108; II, 352, 385, 407; Fitzjames Stephen, 'Voltaire as a theologian, moralist and metaphysician' in *Fraser's Magazine* (November 1867), 541ff. Charles Kingsley's *Three Lectures on the Ancien Regime* (1867) was the first book by an English professor of history to ask for a proper reconsideration of Voltaire.
12. J. Morley, *Diderot* (1878), I, 8.
13. Cf. the evidence in F. W. Hirst, *Early Life and Letters of John Morley* (1927), I, 305–7.

14. Morley, *Rousseau* (1873), II, 201–2, 211.
15. Morley, *Diderot*, I, 5.
16. J. H. Burton, *Life and Correspondence of David Hume* (1846), 2, 185–8.
17. Kogan, *The Great E.B.*, 83.
18. Morley, *Voltaire* (1872), 293–4. The subsequent change in tone of biographies is striking. E. B. Hamley (1877) wants to relieve Voltaire of the charge of responsibility for the Revolution – 'Yet it must not be supposed that he is here held up as a pattern man' – a very good man but 'without the crowning grace of reverence' (204). J. Parton (2 vols, 1881) is a panegyric.
    The same process is traceable in Germany. Cf. du Bois-Reymond's address to the Berlin Academy of January 1868, the neglect or contempt for Voltaire in the earlier part of the century, and now 'we are all Voltaireans more or less, Voltaireans without knowing it...', cf. Espinasse, *Voltaire* (1892), 200.
19. Lamartine, *History of the Girondists*, Eng. trans. (1847), I, 152.
20. de Maistre, *Soirées de S. Petersburg, IVe Soirée* (1862), I, 238. Cf. Madame de Staël, 'Voltaire's wretched and conceited irreligion'. But Chateaubriand liked him; Victor Cousin did him justice; Vigny thought him an authentic reformer in the line of Christian reformers like Luther, cf. Pomeau, *La Religion de Voltaire* (Paris, 1956), 7–9.
21. Jules Michelet, *Journal* (ed. Paul Viallaneix), 1 (1959), 657.
22. Ibid. 1, 658.
23. Cf. Quinet, *Ultramontanism* (1844), Eng. trans. (1845), 118, 46; cf. *Œuvres complètes* (1857), 2, 176; for Quinet generally, R. H. Powers, *Edgar Quinet, A study in French Patriotism* (Dallas, 1957).
24. Pomeau, *La Religion de Voltaire*, 455.
25. Ibid. 461.
26. Crouslé to Taine, March 1852: *Life and Letters of Taine*, Eng. trans. (1902), 1, 189 note; Advielle's editing, Pomeau, 9.
27. Parton, *Life of Voltaire* (1881), 2, 633.
28. Taine to de Witt, 1863; *Life and Letters of Taine*, 2, 201.
29. Extracts, Parton, *Voltaire*, 2, 634–5.
30. *Guardian* (1878), 778, cf. 702.
31. Cf. J. Hillairet, *Dictionnaire historique...de Paris*, 2 vols (1963). G. Pessard, *Nouveau dictionnaire historique de Paris* (1904); Edgar Quinet, *Le Panthéon* (1883).
32. E.g. Quinet (*Panthéon*, 156–7), Saintsbury, André Maurois and even the first edition of Noyes.
33. Pomeau, *La Religion de Voltaire*, 460.

NOTES TO CHAPTER SEVEN

1. Draper, *History of the Conflict between Religion and Science* (New York, 1874). I use the second edition (London, 1875). Preface, x: 'I have little to say respecting the two great Christian confessions, the Protestant and the Greek Churches. As to the latter, it has never, since the restoration of science, arranged itself in opposition to the advance-

ment of knowledge.' The context shows that he means 'As to the former'.

2. Ibid. 321ff. A good deal of the Conflict was taken from his earlier book *The Intellectual Development of Europe*, published at New York 1863, London 1864; a deterministic history but claimed to have been written before Buckle published; a kind of Lecky but an inferior Lecky, inferior in knowledge, grasp, style and subtlety of understanding. It was widely read, reprinted as late as 1918, and much translated. No less a man than Rudolf Virchow gave the book to a son when the boy left home to study. Fleming, *Draper*, 94.

3. It came from Vogt's *Physiologische Briefe* (1847); cf. F. Mauthner, *Der Atheismus und seine Geschichte im Abendland* (1923), IV, 223; F. Lange, *History of Materialism*, Eng. trans. (1877), II, 242; Johannes Jung, *Karl Vogts Weltanschauung* (Paderborn, 1915), 73–4. The idea was not quite original, being found in Cabanis.

4. Karl Vogt, *Lehrbuch der Geologie und Petrefactenkunde. Zum Gebrauche bei Vorlesungen und zum Selbstunterrichte*, 2 vols (Brunswick, 1846), II, 376; Jung, *Vogts Weltanschauung*, 21.

5. Wilhelm Vogt, *La Vie d'un homme*, 48.

6. Though Quatrefages gave a respectful portrait in *Les Émules de Darwin* (Paris, 1894), II, chap. 4.

7. Lange, *History of Materialism*, III, 118; cf. 88; far the best exposition of Vogt is to be found in Jung, *Vogts Weltanschauung*. For the Microcephali, see *Mémoire sur les Microcéphales ou Homme-Singes*, 1867 (Mémoires de l'Institut National Genevois, X, no. 2); using studies of 42 idiots. For the accusation of frivolity at its worst, see the attacks by zoologists on *Bilder aus dem Tierleben*, cited Jung, ibid. 120.

8. Jakob Moleschott, *Für Meine Freunde* (Giessen, 1894).

9. Moleschott, *Lehre der Nahrungsmittel. Für das Volk* (Erlangen, 1850), 116; Feuerbach's review in *Blätter für Litterarische Unterhaltung* (9 November 1850), 1082, quoted *Für Meine Freunde*, 208.

10. *N.D.B. s.v.* Büchner.

11. Büchner, *Last Words on Materialism*, Eng. trans. (1901), xxi–xxii.

12. Cf. Büchner, ibid. 9.

13. T. H. Huxley, *Essays* (1892), IX, 128–30, an essay of 1886.

14. P. Janet, *Materialism*, Eng. trans. (1866), ix; *La crise philosophique* (1865), 115; Littré and Robin's edition of the *Dictionnaire* of Nysten; a well-established medical dictionary of which the second edition was published in 1809, and the eleventh edition by Littré and Robin in 1858. The twelfth edition was rewritten in 1865.

15. Filippo de Filippi, *L'Uomi e le scimmie*, a famous lecture of 11 January 1864, the first important Darwinian utterance in Italy; and Quatrefages, *Les Émules de Darwin*, II, 46ff.

16. *Nature*, XXVII, (11 January 1883), 245–6.

17. Wilhelm Bölsche, *Haeckel*, Eng. trans. (1906), 131.

18. Charles Darwin, *The Descent of Man* (1901 ed.), 4. Haeckel visited Darwin at Down twice. They always remained friends by letter. Darwin occasionally tried to persuade Haeckel not to be so violent with his opponents, Bölsche, *Haeckel*, Eng. trans., 241–4. Haeckel

admired Draper and Büchner. He actually owed as much or more to D. F. Strauss than to Darwin, so far as his philosophy went, but this is less prominent in his confessed obligations.

19. Bölsche, 254; cf. 298.

20. The English pamphlet was by 'Saladin' (William Stewart Ross), *God and his Book*, 1887 (2nd ed. 1906); not published but privately circulated. It had a German translation also printed privately, and called to shock, *Jehovas gesammelte Werke* (Leipzig, 1896). For all this, cf. F. Loofs, *Anti-Haeckel*, Eng. trans. (1903), 6ff., especially 28–9; for Ross's career as a secularist, see DNB *s.v.*; R. B. Hithersay and G. Ernest, *Sketch of the Life of Saladin; Agnostic Journal*, 8 December 1906.

For the Social Darwinist aspect of Haeckel and monism, and its relation to Nazi philosophy (which can easily be overstated) see D. Gasman, *The Scientific Origins of National Socialism* (1971); H. G. Zmarzlik, 'Der Sozialdarwinismus in Deutschland als geschichtliches Problem', in *Vierteljahrshefte für Zeitgeschichte*, XI (1963), 246–73.

21. J. McCabe, *Haeckel's Critics Answered* (1906), 113.

22. *Volkstaat* (1873), 31; (1874), 24; Schuster, *Die Social-Demokratie im Spiegel ihrer eigenen Presse*, 192ff.

23. Bölsche, *Haeckel*, Eng. trans., 301, 303, 312; Nitti, *Catholic Socialism*, 23.

24. *The Possessed*, II, 6, 2.

25. Cf. Draper, *History of the Conflict* (1875), 173–5.

24. Disraeli, *Lothair* (new ed. 1870), 404.

27. Hallam Tennyson, *Alfred, Lord Tennyson* (1897), I, 314.

28. In July 1956 in Moscow a group of British academics were assailed in conversation by an eminent Russian theologian. He said, 'How is it that the British are such a logical race that they can produce John Stuart Mill and Charles Darwin, and yet such an illogical race that they can produce you, who are Christians and nevertheless admire John Stuart Mill and Charles Darwin?'

29. R. Vallery-Radot, *The Life of Pasteur*, Eng. trans. (1902), I, 115ff.

30. G. L. Prestige, *The Life of Charles Gore* (1935), 431–2.

31. Haeckel, *The Riddle of the Universe*, Eng. trans. (1900), 339; 'Most of the educated people of our time (as distinct from the uncultured masses) remain in the conviction that religion is a separate branch of our mental life, independent of science, and not less valuable and indispensable.'

32. Carlton Hayes, *A Generation of Materialism* (1941), 149.

33. Francis Darwin, *The Life and Letters of Charles Darwin*, 3rd ed. (1887), I, 307.

NOTES TO CHAPTER EIGHT

1. André Chevrillon, *Taine, formation de sa pensée* (Paris, 1932), 221.

2. In *Historische Vierteljahresschrift* (Leipzig, 1908), 11, 441–59; Hubert Jedin, 'Kirchengeschichte als Heilgeschichte', in *Kirche des Glaubens, Kirche der Geschichte* (Freiburg, 1966), I, 37ff. The idea was not so new as Fester seemed to think. In the Introduction to the *Essay on Development* of 1845 Newman wrote with melancholy that 'perhaps'

the only English writer with the claim to be considered an ecclesiastical historian is 'the infidel Gibbon'. For Fester, cf. also Hermann Lübbe, *Säkularisierung: Geschichte eines ideenpolitischen Begriffs* (Freiburg, 1965), 56–7.

3. Alan Richardson, *History, Sacred and Profane* (1964), 208.
4. Michelet, *History of the French Revolution*, Eng. trans. (1847), I, 10.
5. By Thibaudet, *Histoire de la littérature française* (1936), 273, quoted by O. A. Haac, *Les principes inspirateurs de Michelet* (1951), 31.
6. Mark Pattison, *Essays*, II, 414–15; Aulard, *Etudes et leçons sur la Révolution française* (1893), I, 36–7.
7. Michelet, *French Revolution*, Introduction, I, 1.
8. Ibid. preface, cf. M. E. Johnson, *Michelet et le christianisme* (Paris, 1955).
9. G. P. Gooch, *History and Historians in the Nineteenth Century* (1913), 184.
10. Renan, *Réponse au discours de M. de Lesseps*, 23 April 1885, in *Œuvres complètes*, I, 815; for the widow's pain, Renan to Madame Michelet, 26 April 1885, in *Correspondance*, no. 717, *Œuvres complètes*, x, 933.
11. The claim was first made in 1835 by the Belgian statistician Quetelet; and then used preeminently by Buckle, *History of Civilization* (1857), I, 16.
12. Taine is sometimes regarded as a direct heir of Comte. But his private papers as a young man show no sign of any study of Comte, cf. André Chevrillon, *Taine: Formation de sa pensée* (1932), 223 n. 2. The influence of Comte came later.
13. Taine, *History of English Literature*, Eng. trans. (1871), I, 14.
14. Ibid. I, 315.
15. Ibid. 317, 340.
16. Ibid. 293.
17. Ibid. 143.
18. Taine, *Life and Letters*, Eng. trans., III, 181; Taine to Gaston Paris, 2 July 1877; *Hist. Eng. Lit.*, Eng. trans., I, 461, on the morals of the English restoration, 463.
19. Taine, *Ancien Régime*, Eng. trans. (1876), 209–10.
20. Renan, *Souvenirs*, Eng. trans. as *Recollections of my youth* (1929), 228–9.
21. Ibid. xl.
22. Renan, *La chaire d'Hébreu au collège de France*, ap. *Questions contemporaines* (1868), *Œuvres complètes*, I, 169–70.
23. Gabriel Monod, *Les maîtres de l'histoire* (1894), 37.
24. Renan, *Souvenirs*, Eng. trans., 224.
25. Ibid. 260.
26. Renan to Cognat, Tréguier, 14 August 1845: printed in appendix to ibid. 335.
27. Ibid. 273.
28. H. W. Wardman, *Ernest Renan* (1964), 107.
29. Renan, *Life of Jesus*, Eng. trans. (1898), Introd. ad. fin.
30. Ibid. 143, 139.

31. Ibid. 223.
32. Ibid. 221.
33. Renan to Berthelot, Naples, 7 January 1850; *Renan–Berthelot Correspondance* (1898), 75–6.
34. Wardman, *Ernest Renan*, 206.
35. Renan, *Discours prononcé à Tréguier* (1881), *Discours et Conférences* in *Œuvres complètes*, I, 850.
36. *Souvenirs*, Eng. trans., 171.
37. *Life of Jesus*, Eng. trans., 107, cf. 141.
38. Ibid. 218.
39. Ibid. 222.

NOTES TO CHAPTER NINE

1. *Nineteenth Century* (1877), 356; and Chadwick, *Victorian Church*, II, 121–2.
2. Nietzsche, *Genealogy of Morals*, Preface, vi.
3. Lévy-Bruhl, *The Philosophy of Auguste Comte*, Eng. trans. (1903), 311.
4. W. M. Simon, *European Positivism in the Nineteenth Century* (1963), 119.
5. Littré, *Paroles de philosophie positive*, 1859, 2nd ed. (1863), 49.
6. At the end of vol. IV of *Politique positive*, Eng. trans. (1877).
7. Cf. Lévy-Bruhl, *Philosophy of Comte*, Eng. trans., 334–6.
8. E. M. Fraser, *Le renouveau religieux d'après le roman français de 1886 à 1914* (1934), 48.
9. Anatole France, *La Vie littéraire*, ser. 3 (1895), 56, 306.
10. Brunetière, *Revue des deux Mondes* (1892), IV, 614–55.
11. *Revue* (1895), I, 97–118.
12. F. J. Hemmings, *The Russian Novel in France* (Oxford, 1950), 1–2.
13. Vogüé, *The Russian Novel*, Eng. trans., 297, 311–12, 327.
14. Comte, *The Catechism of Positive Religion*, Eng. trans. by Richard Congreve (1858), 54.

NOTES TO CHAPTER TEN

1. Nietzsche, *Genealogy of Morals*, I, ix.
2. Renan, *Dialogues philosophiques*, in *Œuvres complètes*, I, 563, 570ff., 594.
3. *The Genealogy of Morals*, I, ix.
4. Renan, *Caliban* (1878), *Œuvres complètes*, III, 433; *L'eau de Jouvence*, *Œuvres complètes*, III, 478; René Ternois, *Zola et son temps* (Paris, 1961), 14–15.
5. Renan, *Œuvres complètes*, I, 852; *Discours prononcé à Tréguier*, 2 August 1884.
6. Renan on Amiel, *Œuvres complètes*, II, 1147–60.
7. *Nouvelle Revue*, 15 December 1882, an article on Taine; when he republished it he changed the text to make it clear that he ascribed this opinion to Taine, not necessarily to himself: René Ternois, *Zola et son temps*, 21, n. 2. Bourget, *Nouveaux essais de psychologie contemporaine*, in *Œuvres*, I, 185.

8. A. France, 'Pourquoi sommes-nous tristes?' in *La Vie littéraire*, 3rd ser. (1895), 7–9.
9. *Confessions and Testament of Auguste Comte*, Eng. trans. (1910), 305ff.
10. H. Gouhier, *La vie d'Auguste Comte*, 2nd ed. (1965), 227.
11. Wisdom 3, 1–6.
12. *Guardian* (1870), 1191, 1222.
13. H. P. Liddon, published posthumously (1892), in *Some Words of Christ*, sermon III.
14. *Tablet*, 18 December 1875.
15. *Church Times*, leader, 19 April 1912, 529.
16. *Church Times*, ibid.: cf. *Guardian* (1912), 481, 513; *The Times*, 22 April 1912, H. H. Henson's sermon on 'Vaunted Science'.
17. Liddon, *Some Words of Christ*, 38.
18. Cf. Lübbe, *Säkularisierung* (Freiburg, 1965), 86.

INDEX

Acton, Lord, 41, 112, 115, 128, 150, 192, 195, 226
Addison, Joseph, 145
alienation, 62ff., 102
Amberley, Viscount, 151, 250
Amiel, H. F., 278
anarchists, 85–6, 110, *see also* Bakunin
anthropomorphism, 188
anticlericalism, 39, 45–6, 95, 211, 214, and chapter 5 *passim*
antisemitism, 39
Antonelli, Cardinal, 112
Aquinas, St Thomas, 114, 154
Arius, 191
Arnold, Matthew, 123
Aron, Raymond, 16
Ashurst, W. H., 91
Athanasius, 191
atheism, 9, 88ff.
Augustine, St, of Hippo, 13, 252, 258
Aulard, F. A., 199, 277
authority, nature of, 27ff., 35ff., 85–6, 110–11
Aveling, E. B., 180

Babeuf, F. N., 85
Bakunin, Michael, 13, 74, 85–6
Balfour, Arthur, 14
Barcelona, 'tragic week', 119–20
Barnikol, Ernst, 53, 268
Barth, Karl, 270
Baudelaire, C. P., 255
Bauer, Bruno, 49, 52ff., 69, 268
Baur, F. C., 225
Bautz, Josef, 88
Bayle, Pierre, 10, 230
Bebel, August, 80–3, 85, 103, 270
Berger, P., 273
Bergson, Henri, 239
Berkeley, Bishop, 164–5, 169
biogenesis, 88
Bismarck, Prince, 45, 81, 127, 136–7, 139
Blumhardt, Christoph, 83, 270

Bois-Reymond, E. du, 274
Bonn University, 51, 53
Bossuet, J. B., 151, 157, 198, 206
Boswell, James, 146, 273
Bourget, P. C. J., 114, 278
Bovio, Giovanni, 178–80
Bradlaugh, C., 90–2, 103, 271
Bradley, F. H., 33–4, 267
Bridges, Robert, 261
British Association (meeting of 1860), 163
Broglie, Abbé de, 97
Broglie, Duc de, 124
Bronn, H. G., 88
Brougham, Henry, 146, 273
Brunetière, F., 240ff.
Bruno, Giordano, 178–80
Büchner, Ludwig, 80, 88, 165, 170ff., 181, 231, 242, 275–6
Buckle, H. T., 80, 227, 273, 275
Bunce, Thackray, 40
Bungener, F. L., 147
Burckhardt, Jakob, 192, 224
Burke, Edmund, 31, 33
Bury, J. B., 5–6, 15, 34, 195, 209–10, 267
Butler, Joseph, 230
Byron, Lord, 147, 273

Cabet, E., 76, 269
Caird, Edward, 151
Calvin, John, 193–4
Calvinism, 8, 68, 105
Campbell, W., 146
Captain, H.M.S., 259–60
Carlyle, Thomas, 34, 70, 144, 152, 202, 205, 269
census of 1851 (British religions), 90
Charlesworth, Martin, 227
Chartists, 78, 91
Chateaubriand, F. R., Vicomte de, 274
Chambers, Robert, 165
Christian socialists, 58, 103, 109
church extension, 97

INDEX

Hamley, E. B., 274
Hartmann, K. R. E., 254
harvest festivals, 96
Hazard, Paul, 9
Hébert, J. R., 86
Hegel, G. W. F., 31, 33, 49, 51ff.,
   61ff., 66ff., 70, 132–3, 151, 205,
   267, 272
Hegelians, Young, 51ff.
hell, 104ff.
Henson, H. H., 279
Herder, J. G. von, 205, 216
Hermelink, Heinrich, 11, 267
Hermes, Georg, 52
Hess, Moses, 49, 77, 268
history and secularization, chapter 8
Hohoff, Wilhelm, 81
Holbach, Baron d', 49, 164–5, 268
Holl, Karl, 273
Holyoake, G. J., 88ff., 103
Home and Foreign Review, 115
Hooker, J. D., 163
Hopkins, G. M., 261–2
Hugo, Victor, 106, 154, 157, 159,
   230
Hume, David, 5, 36, 153, 185, 189,
   205, 267, 274
Huxley, T. H., 161, 163ff., 275

Icarian Communism, 76
Ignatius Loyola, 193–4
illegitimate births, 3
Imitation of Christ, the, 239
imperialism, use of word, 134
industrialization, 93ff.
Irving, Edward, 22, 267

Jaurès, Jean, 201
Jelf, R. W., 147, 273
Jena, University of, 53, 88
Jesuits, 125
Jews, 39, 49–50, 55–9, 84, 102, 131
Joan of Arc, St, 252
Jodl, Friedrich, 229
Johnson, Samuel, 88, 146, 164, 169,
   273
Jowett, Benjamin, 150, 273

Kampschulte, F. W., 193–4
Kant, Immanuel, 10, 52, 143, 151,
   230, 235
Kingsley, Charles, 13, 41, 183, 190,
   195–6, 202, 273
Kliefoth, Theodore, 95
Krieger, L., 132

Kulturkampf, 45, 124, 127, 138–9,
   260

Lamarck, 165
Lamartine, 274
Lamennais, 76, 77, 78, 122, 154,
   269
Landseck, R., 88
Lansbury, George, 106, 271
La Salette, 123
Laski, H. J., 47
Lassalle, 79–80
Lasson, Adolf, 133
Le Bras, Gabriel, 120
Lecky, W. E. H., 5–6, 45, 134–7,
   148, 157, 195, 202, 209–10, 268,
   273, 275
Leibniz, G. W., 5
Lenin, 48–9, 65, 67
Leningrad, Church of the Virgin,
   16
Leo XIII, Pope, 41, 46, 81, 110,
   178–9, 242
Lewis, C. S., 13, 190
liberalism, 21ff.
Liddon, H. P., 109–10, 260, 263,
   272, 279
Liebknecht, Wilhelm, 80, 82
Lippmann, Walter, 44, 268
Littré, M. P. F., 115, 157, 173, 237–
   238, 275, 278
Locke, John, 5, 25
Lonsdale, J., Bishop of Lichfield, 105
Louis Napoleon, 118, 123, 146, 157,
   159, 198, 214
Lourdes, 123–4, 251
Luther, Martin, 23, 73, 126, 147–8,
   150, 203, 274
Luxemburg, Rosa, 84–5, 270

Macaulay, T. B., 209
McCabe, Joseph, 180, 276
Machiavelli, 87, 137
MacIntyre, Alasdair, 11–12, 267
Mackonochie, A. H., 96
MacMahon, Marshal, 124
Maistre, Joseph de, 154, 274
Manchester Guarlian, 40, 42
Mann, Horace, 90
Manning, H. E., 125, 134, 260
Marseilles, lawyers in, 109
Martin, David, 2, 267
Martin, Emma, 88
Marx, Eleanor, 268
Marx, Heinrich, 50

283